SUPER HOROSCOPE
CANCER

2007

JUNE 21 – JULY 20

BERKLEY BOOKS, NEW YORK

THE BERKLEY PUBLISHING GROUP
Published by the Penguin Group
Penguin Group (USA) Inc.
375 Hudson Street, New York, New York 10014, USA
Penguin Group (Canada), 90 Eglinton Avenue East, Suite 700, Toronto, Ontario M4P 2Y3, Canada
(a division of Pearson Penguin Canada Inc.)
Penguin Books Ltd., 80 Strand, London WC2R 0RL, England
Penguin Group Ireland, 25 St. Stephen's Green, Dublin 2, Ireland (a division of Penguin Books Ltd.)
Penguin Group (Australia), 250 Camberwell Road, Camberwell, Victoria 3124, Australia
(a division of Pearson Australia Group Pty. Ltd.)
Penguin Books India Pvt. Ltd., 11 Community Centre, Panchsheel Park, New Delhi—110 017, India
Penguin Group (NZ), Cnr. Airborne and Rosedale Roads, Albany, Auckland 1310, New Zealand
(a division of Pearson New Zealand Ltd.)
Penguin Books (South Africa) (Pty.) Ltd., 24 Sturdee Avenue, Rosebank, Johannesburg 2196,
South Africa

Penguin Books Ltd., Registered Offices: 80 Strand, London WC2R 0RL, England

2007 SUPER HOROSCOPE CANCER

The publishers regret that they cannot answer individual letters requesting personal horoscope information.

PRINTING HISTORY
Berkley trade paperback edition / July 2006

Berkley trade paperback ISBN: 0-425-20930-X

Library of Congress Cataloging-in-Publication Data

ISSN: 1535-8933

PRINTED IN THE UNITED STATES OF AMERICA

10 9 8 7 6 5 4 3 2 1

CONTENTS

THE CUSP-BORN CANCER

Are you *really* a Cancer? If your birthday falls during the fourth week of June, at the beginning of Cancer, will you still retain the traits of Gemini, the sign of the Zodiac before Cancer? And what if you were born late in July—are you more Leo than Cancer? Many people born at the edge, or cusp, of a sign have difficulty determining exactly what sign they are. If you are one of these people, here's how you can figure it out, once and for all.

Consult the cusp table on the facing page, then locate the year of your birth. The table will tell you the precise days on which the Sun entered and left your sign for the year of your birth. In that way you can determine if you are a true Cancer—or whether you are a Gemini or Leo—according to the variations in cusp dates from year to year (see also page 17).

If you were born at the beginning or end of Cancer, yours is a lifetime reflecting a process of subtle transformation. Your life on Earth will symbolize a significant change in consciousness, for you are either about to enter a whole new way of living or are leaving one behind.

If you were born during the fourth week of June, you may want to read the Gemini book as well as Cancer. Because Gemini holds the keys to the more hidden sides of your personality, many of your dilemmas and uncertainties about the world and people around you can be revealed. You can tune in to your secret wishes, and your potential for cosmic unfoldment.

Although you feel you have a lot to say, you will often withdraw and remain silent. Sometimes, the more you say the more confused a situation can get. Talking can drain you, and you are vulnerable to gossip. You feel secure surrounded by intimates you can trust, but sometimes the neighbors—even your own relatives—seem to be talking behind your back and you sense a vague plot in the air.

You symbolize the birth of feeling, the silent but rich condition of a fertilized seed growing full with life. The family is always an issue. At best you are a "feeling" type whose power of sensing things remains a force behind everything you think and do.

If you were born the fourth week of July, you may want to read the horoscope book for Leo as well as Cancer, for Leo could be your greatest asset. You need a warm embrace, the comfort and safety of being cared for, protected, fed. You need strong ties to the past, to the family. Attachments are natural for you. You want to be your own person, yet you often find ties and attachments prohibiting you from the rebirth you are anticipating. You may find it hard to separate yourself from dependencies without being drawn backward again and again.

You symbolize the fullness of growth, the condition of being nearly ripe, the new life about to emerge from the shadows into the sunshine.

THE CUSPS OF CANCER

DATES SUN ENTERS CANCER (LEAVES GEMINI)

June 21 every year from 1900 to 2010, except for the following:

June 20	June 22		
1988	1902	1915	1931
1992	03	18	35
1996	06	19	39
2000	07	22	43
2004	10	23	47
2008	11	26	51
	14	27	55

DATES SUN LEAVES CANCER (ENTERS LEO)

July 23 every year from 1900 to 2010, except for the following:

July 22						
1928	1953	1968	1981	1992	2001	2010
32	56	69	84	93	2002	
36	57	72	85	94	2004	
40	60	73	86	96	2005	
44	61	76	88	97	2006	
48	64	77	89	98	2008	
52	65	80	90	2000	2009	

THE ASCENDANT: CANCER RISING

Could you be a "double" Cancer? That is, could you have Cancer as your Rising sign as well as your Sun sign? The tables on pages 8–9 will tell you Cancer people what your Rising sign happens to be. Just find the hour of your birth, then find the day of your birth, and you will see which sign of the Zodiac is your Ascendant, as the Rising sign is called. The Ascendant is called that because it is the sign rising on the eastern horizon at the time of your birth. For a more detailed discussion of the Rising sign and the twelve houses of the Zodiac, see pages 17–20.

The Ascendant, or Rising sign, is placed on the 1st house in a horoscope, of which there are twelve houses. The 1st house represents your response to the environment—your unique response. Call it identity, personality, ego, self-image, facade, come-on, body-mind-spirit—whatever term best conveys to you the meaning of the you that acts and reacts in the world. It is a you that is always changing, discovering a new you. Your identity started with birth and early environment, over which you had little conscious control, and continues to experience, to adjust, to express itself. The 1st house also represents how others see you. Has anyone ever guessed your sign to be your Rising sign? People may respond to that personality, that facade, that body type governed by your Rising sign.

Your Ascendant, or Rising sign, modifies your basic Sun sign personality, and it affects the way you act out the daily predictions for your Sun sign. If your Rising sign indeed is Cancer, what follows is a description of its effect on your horoscope. If your Rising sign is not Cancer, but some other sign of the Zodiac, you may wish to read the horoscope book for that sign as well.

With Cancer on the Ascendant, that is, in the 1st house, the ruling planet of the 1st house is the Moon. The Moon here gives you an especially keen ability to sense patterns and changes in the environment. The Moon in this position makes you more than just receptive; it makes you reactive and adaptive. You can integrate the most fleeting, irrational impressions received from the environment. There is, however, the danger that such sensory overload, so to speak, could inhibit your ability to act appropriately in a given situation.

Cancer in the 1st house accentuates your ambitiousness. Tenacity, a strong Cancer trait, is translated here into a highly developed power of focus. You can focus your energy on several levels at once—social, emotional, even psychic—in order to realize your aims. But always the scene of struggle and realization is personal rather than public, concrete rather than abstract. Your three basic loves—food, home, money—are all personal ones. Power is not a burning issue for you, but on the other hand, concepts of right and wrong are. You may also hide behind your concepts, posing as a more intellectual person than you really feel, whenever you become too timid to express your strongly emotional nature.

Sympathy and sensitivity are basic personality traits for Cancer Rising. That combination may lead to a subjective view of the world, one which has little in common with the views of other people. For that reason, you may appear to be shy, when in fact you are merely retiring from a possible occasion of misunderstanding or conflict. You prefer to protect yourself and those you love from any pain or suffering. You want to provide a comfortable haven for all the hurt creatures of the world. You can, therefore, be labeled a homebody or a mothering type.

Although the concept of home is central in your life, you are not a stick-in-the-mud; indeed, you do not necessarily like to be rooted in one place. You would like a family, to nurture and protect it, to develop and instill pervasive attitudes of right conduct. If you don't have a natural family, you will be happy serving a community cause, even if that service takes you far and wide and results in reversals of fortune along the way. There may be many travels and voyages in the lifetimes of those of you with Cancer Rising. Home is where your heart is. Possessions, too, have little meaning for you unless they are connected with a special person or intimate situation.

Supportiveness to others continually wars with inner insecurity, making you doubt the value and extent of your attachment. You need to feel appreciated by everyone in your immediate environment. Emotional satisfaction may be more compelling than honor and success. You could enter secret love affairs or alliances just for the personal gratification they provide, and despite the dangers they pose. There may be an aura of mystery surrounding you, inspired partly by your fondness for secrets, partly by your hidden, inaccessible, unsteady emotionality, partly by your success in isolation; some of you may engender enemies and long-standing rivals as a result.

Intuition and imagination are the key words for Cancer Rising. You can put them to use in the service of a fruitful lifestyle, or you can squander them in complaints. You are at your best when you are building something.

RISING SIGNS FOR CANCER

Hour of Birth*	Day of Birth		
	June 20–25	June 26–30	July 1–5
Midnight	Pisces; Aries 6/22	Aries	Aries
1 AM	Aries	Taurus	Taurus
2 AM	Taurus	Taurus	Taurus
3 AM	Gemini	Gemini	Gemini
4 AM	Gemini	Gemini	Gemini; Cancer 7/3
5 AM	Cancer	Cancer	Cancer
6 AM	Cancer	Cancer	Cancer
7 AM	Cancer; Leo 6/23	Leo	Leo
8 AM	Leo	Leo	Leo
9 AM	Leo	Leo; Virgo 6/30	Virgo
10 AM	Virgo	Virgo	Virgo
11 AM	Virgo	Virgo	Virgo
Noon	Virgo; Libra 6/24	Libra	Libra
1 PM	Libra	Libra	Libra
2 PM	Libra	Libra; Scorpio 6/29	Scorpio
3 PM	Scorpio	Scorpio	Scorpio
4 PM	Scorpio	Scorpio	Scorpio
5 PM	Scorpio; Sagittarius 6/23	Sagittarius	Sagittarius
6 PM	Sagittarius	Sagittarius	Sagittarius
7 PM	Sagittarius	Sagittarius; Capricorn 6/27	Capricorn
8 PM	Capricorn	Capricorn	Capricorn
9 PM	Capricorn	Aquarius	Aquarius
10 PM	Aquarius	Aquarius	Aquarius

*Hour of birth given here is for Standard Time in any time zone. If your hour of birth was recorded in Daylight Saving Time, subtract one hour from it and consult that hour in the table above. For example, if you were born at 6 AM D.S.T., see 5 AM above.

Hour of Birth*	Day of Birth		
	July 6–10	July 11–17	July 18–23
Midnight	Aries	Taurus	Taurus
1 AM	Taurus	Taurus	Taurus; Gemini 7/19
2 AM	Gemini	Gemini	Gemini
3 AM	Gemini	Gemini	Gemini
4 AM	Cancer	Cancer	Cancer
5 AM	Cancer	Cancer	Cancer; Leo 7/23
6 AM	Leo	Leo	Leo
7 AM	Leo	Leo	Leo
8 AM	Leo	Leo; Virgo 7/15	Virgo
9 AM	Virgo	Virgo	Virgo
10 AM	Virgo	Virgo	Virgo; Libra 7/23
11 AM	Libra	Libra	Libra
Noon	Libra	Libra	Libra
1 PM	Libra	Libra; Scorpio 7/15	Scorpio
2 PM	Scorpio	Scorpio	Scorpio
3 PM	Scorpio	Scorpio	Scorpio; Sagittarius 7/23
4 PM	Scorpio; Sagittarius 7/7	Sagittarius	Sagittarius
5 PM	Sagittarius	Sagittarius	Sagittarius
6 PM	Sagittarius	Capricorn	Capricorn
7 PM	Capricorn	Capricorn	Capricorn
8 PM	Capricorn	Aquarius	Aquarius
9 PM	Aquarius	Aquarius	Pisces
10 PM	Pisces	Pisces	Pisces; Aries 7/22
11 PM	Pisces; Aries 7/7	Aries	Aries

*See note on facing page.

THE PLACE OF ASTROLOGY IN TODAY'S WORLD

Does astrology have a place in the fast-moving, ultra-scientific world we live in today? Can it be justified in a sophisticated society whose outriders are already preparing to step off the moon into the deep space of the planets themselves? Or is it just a hangover of ancient superstition, a psychological dummy for neurotics and dreamers of every historical age?

These are the kind of questions that any inquiring person can be expected to ask when they approach a subject like astrology which goes beyond, but never excludes, the materialistic side of life.

The simple, single answer is that astrology works. It works for many millions of people in the western world alone. In the United States there are 10 million followers and in Europe, an estimated 25 million. America has more than 4000 practicing astrologers, Europe nearly three times as many. Even down-under Australia has its hundreds of thousands of adherents. In the eastern countries, astrology has enormous followings, again, because it has been proved to work. In India, for example, brides and grooms for centuries have been chosen on the basis of their astrological compatibility.

Astrology today is more vital than ever before, more practicable because all over the world the media devotes much space and time to it, more valid because science itself is confirming the precepts of astrological knowledge with every new exciting step. The ordinary person who daily applies astrology intelligently does not have to wonder whether it is true nor believe in it blindly. He can see it working for himself. And, if he can use it—and this book is designed to help the reader to do just that—he can make living a far richer experience, and become a more developed personality and a better person.

Astrology and Relationships

Astrology is the science of relationships. It is not just a study of planetary influences on man and his environment. It is the study of man himself.

We are at the center of our personal universe, of all our relationships. And our happiness or sadness depends on how we act, how we relate to the people and things that surround us. The emotions that we generate have a distinct effect—for better or worse—on the world around us. Our friends and our enemies will confirm this. Just look in the mirror the next time you are angry. In other words, each of us is a kind of sun or planet or star radiating our feelings on the environment around us. Our influence on our personal universe, whether loving, helpful, or destructive, varies with our changing moods, expressed through our individual character.

Our personal "radiations" are potent in the way they affect our moods and our ability to control them. But we usually are able to throw off our emotion in some sort of action—we have a good cry, walk it off, or tell someone our troubles—before it can build up too far and make us physically ill. Astrology helps us to understand the universal forces working on us, and through this understanding, we can become more properly adjusted to our surroundings so that we find ourselves coping where others may flounder.

The Challenge of Love

The challenge of love lies in recognizing the difference between infatuation, emotion, sex, and, sometimes, the intentional deceit of the other person. Mankind, with its record of broken marriages, despair, and disillusionment, is obviously not very good at making these distinctions.

Can astrology help?

Yes. In the same way that advance knowledge can usually help in any human situation. And there is probably no situation as human, as poignant, as pathetic and universal, as the failure of man's love.

Love, of course, is not just between man and woman. It involves love of children, parents, home, and friends. But the big problems usually involve the choice of partner.

Astrology has established degrees of compatibility that exist between people born under the various signs of the Zodiac. Because people are individuals, there are numerous variations and modifications. So the astrologer, when approached on mate and marriage matters, makes allowances for them. But the fact remains that some groups of people are suited for each other and some are not, and astrology has expressed this in terms of characteristics we all can study and use as a personal guide.

No matter how much enjoyment and pleasure we find in the different aspects of each other's character, if it is not an overall compatibility, the chances of our finding fulfillment or enduring happiness in each other are pretty hopeless. And astrology can help us to find someone compatible.

Astrology and Science

Closely related to our emotions is the "other side" of our personal universe, our physical welfare. Our body, of course, is largely influenced by things around us over which we have very little control. The phone rings, we hear it. The train runs late. We snag our stocking or cut our face shaving. Our body is under a constant bombardment of events that influence our daily lives to varying degrees.

The question that arises from all this is, what makes each of us act so that we have to involve other people and keep the ball of activity and evolution rolling? This is the question that both science and astrology are involved with. The scientists have attacked it from different angles: anthropology, the study of human evolution as body, mind and response to environment; anatomy, the study of bodily structure; psychology, the science of the human mind; and so on. These studies have produced very impressive classifications and valuable information, but because the approach to the problem is fragmented, so is the result. They remain "branches" of science. Science generally studies effects. It keeps turning up wonderful answers but no lasting solutions. Astrology, on the other hand, approaches the question from the broader viewpoint. Astrology began its inquiry with the totality of human experience and saw it as an effect. It then looked to find the cause, or at least the prime movers, and during thousands of years of observation of man and his *universal* environment came up with the extraordinary principle of planetary influence—or astrology, which, from the Greek, means the science of the stars.

Modern science, as we shall see, has confirmed much of astrology's foundations—most of it unintentionally, some of it reluctantly, but still, indisputably.

It is not difficult to imagine that there must be a connection between outer space and Earth. Even today, scientists are not too sure how our Earth was created, but it is generally agreed that it is only a tiny part of the universe. And as a part of the universe, people on Earth see and feel the influence of heavenly bodies in almost every aspect of our existence. There is no doubt that the Sun has the greatest influence on life on this planet. Without it there would be no life, for without it there would be no warmth, no division into day and night, no cycles of time or season at all. This is clear and easy to see. The influence of the Moon, on the other hand, is more subtle, though no less definite.

There are many ways in which the influence of the Moon manifests itself here on Earth, both on human and animal life. It is a well-known fact, for instance, that the large movements of water on our planet—that is the ebb and flow of the tides—are caused by the Moon's gravitational pull. Since this is so, it follows that these water movements do not occur only in the oceans, but that all bodies of water are affected, even down to the tiniest puddle.

The human body, too, which consists of about 70 percent water, falls within the scope of this lunar influence. For example the menstrual cycle of most women corresponds to the 28-day lunar month; the period of pregnancy in humans is 273 days, or equal to nine lunar months. Similarly, many illnesses reach a crisis at the change of the Moon, and statistics in many countries have shown that the crime rate is highest at the time of the Full Moon. Even human sexual desire has been associated with the phases of the Moon. But it is in the movement of the tides that we get the clearest demonstration of planetary influence, which leads to the irresistible correspondence between the so-called metaphysical and the physical.

Tide tables are prepared years in advance by calculating the future positions of the Moon. Science has known for a long time that the Moon is the main cause of tidal action. But only in the last few years has it begun to realize the possible extent of this influence on mankind. To begin with, the ocean tides do not rise and fall as we might imagine from our personal observations of them. The Moon as it orbits around Earth sets up a circular wave of attraction which pulls the oceans of the world after it, broadly in an east to west direction. This influence is like a phantom wave crest, a loop of power stretching from pole to pole which passes over and around the Earth like an invisible shadow. It travels with equal effect across the land masses and, as scientists were recently amazed to observe, caused oysters placed in the dark in the middle of the United States where there is no sea to open their shells to receive the nonexistent tide. If the land-locked oysters react to this invisible signal, what effect does it have on us who not so long ago in evolutionary time came out of the sea and still have its salt in our blood and sweat?

Less well known is the fact that the Moon is also the primary force behind the circulation of blood in human beings and animals, and the movement of sap in trees and plants. Agriculturists have established that the Moon has a distinct influence on crops, which explains why for centuries people have planted according to Moon cycles. The habits of many animals, too, are directed by the movement of the Moon. Migratory birds, for instance, depart only at or near the time of the Full Moon. And certain sea creatures, eels in particular, move only in accordance with certain phases of the Moon.

Know Thyself—Why?

In today's fast-changing world, everyone still longs to know what the future holds. It is the one thing that everyone has in common: rich and poor, famous and infamous, all are deeply concerned about tomorrow.

But the key to the future, as every historian knows, lies in the past. This is as true of individual people as it is of nations. You cannot understand your future without first understanding your past, which is simply another way of saying that you must first of all know yourself.

The motto "know thyself" seems obvious enough nowadays, but it was originally put forward as the foundation of wisdom by the ancient Greek philosophers. It was then adopted by the "mystery religions" of the ancient Middle East, Greece, Rome, and is still used in all genuine schools of mind training or mystical discipline, both in those of the East, based on yoga, and those of the West. So it is universally accepted now, and has been through the ages.

But how do you go about discovering what sort of person you are? The first step is usually classification into some sort of system of types. Astrology did this long before the birth of Christ. Psychology has also done it. So has modern medicine, in its way.

One system classifies people according to the source of the impulses they respond to most readily: the muscles, leading to direct bodily action; the digestive organs, resulting in emotion; or the brain and nerves, giving rise to thinking. Another such system says that character is determined by the endocrine glands, and gives us such labels as "pituitary," "thyroid," and "hyperthyroid" types. These different systems are neither contradictory nor mutually exclusive. In fact, they are very often different ways of saying the same thing.

Very popular, useful classifications were devised by Carl Jung, the eminent disciple of Freud. Jung observed among the different faculties of the mind, four which have a predominant influence on character. These four faculties exist in all of us without exception, but not in perfect balance. So when we say, for instance, that someone is a "thinking type," it means that in any situation he or she tries to be rational. Emotion, which may be the opposite of thinking, will be his or her weakest function. This thinking type can be sensible and reasonable, or calculating and unsympathetic. The emotional type, on the other hand, can often be recognized by exaggerated language—everything is either marvelous or terrible—and in extreme cases they even invent dramas and quarrels out of nothing just to make life more interesting.

The other two faculties are intuition and physical sensation. The sensation type does not only care for food and drink, nice clothes and furniture; he or she is also interested in all forms of physical experience. Many scientists are sensation types as are athletes and nature-lovers. Like sensation, intuition is a form of perception and we all possess it. But it works through that part of the mind which is not under conscious control—consequently it sees meanings and connections which are not obvious to thought or emotion. Inventors and original thinkers are always intuitive, but so, too, are superstitious people who see meanings where none exist.

Thus, sensation tells us what is going on in the world, feeling (that is, emotion) tells us how important it is to ourselves, thinking enables us to interpret it and work out what we should do about it, and intuition tells us what it means to ourselves and others. All four faculties are essential, and all are present in every one of us. But some people are guided chiefly by one, others by another. In addition, Jung also observed a division of the human personality into the extrovert and the introvert, which cuts across these four types.

A disadvantage of all these systems of classification is that one cannot tell very easily where to place oneself. Some people are reluctant to admit that they act to please their emotions. So they deceive themselves for years by trying to belong to whichever type they think is the "best." Of course, there is no best; each has its faults and each has its good points.

The advantage of the signs of the Zodiac is that they simplify classification. Not only that, but your date of birth is personal—

it is unarguably yours. What better way to know yourself than by going back as far as possible to the very moment of your birth? And this is precisely what your horoscope is all about, as we shall see in the next section.

WHAT IS A HOROSCOPE?

If you had been able to take a picture of the skies at the moment of your birth, that photograph would be your horoscope. Lacking such a snapshot, it is still possible to recreate the picture—and this is at the basis of the astrologer's art. In other words, your horoscope is a representation of the skies with the planets in the exact positions they occupied at the time you were born.

The year of birth tells an astrologer the positions of the distant, slow-moving planets Jupiter, Saturn, Uranus, Neptune, and Pluto. The month of birth indicates the Sun sign, or birth sign as it is commonly called, as well as indicating the positions of the rapidly moving planets Venus, Mercury, and Mars. The day and time of birth will locate the position of our Moon. And the moment—the exact hour and minute—of birth determines the houses through what is called the Ascendant, or Rising sign.

With this information the astrologer consults various tables to calculate the specific positions of the Sun, Moon, and other planets relative to your birthplace at the moment you were born. Then he or she locates them by means of the Zodiac.

The Zodiac

The Zodiac is a band of stars (constellations) in the skies, centered on the Sun's apparent path around the Earth, and is divided into twelve equal segments, or signs. What we are actually dividing up is the Earth's path around the Sun. But from our point of view here on Earth, it seems as if the Sun is making a great circle around our planet in the sky, so we say it is the Sun's apparent path. This twelvefold division, the Zodiac, is a reference system for the astrologer. At any given moment the planets—and in astrology both the Sun and Moon are considered to be planets—can all be located at a specific point along this path.

Now where in all this are you, the subject of the horoscope? Your character is largely determined by the sign the Sun is in. So that is where the astrologer looks first in your horoscope, at your Sun sign.

The Sun Sign and the Cusp

There are twelve signs in the Zodiac, and the Sun spends approximately one month in each sign. But because of the motion of the Earth around the Sun—the Sun's apparent motion—the dates when the Sun enters and leaves each sign may change from year to year. Some people born near the cusp, or edge, of a sign have difficulty determining which is their Sun sign. But in this book a Table of Cusps is provided for the years 1900 to 2010 (page 5) so you can find out what your true Sun sign is.

Here are the twelve signs of the Zodiac, their ancient zodiacal symbol, and the dates when the Sun enters and leaves each sign for the year 2007. Remember, these dates may change from year to year.

ARIES	Ram	March 20–April 20
TAURUS	Bull	April 20–May 21
GEMINI	Twins	May 21–June 21
CANCER	Crab	June 21–July 23
LEO	Lion	July 23–August 23
VIRGO	Virgin	August 23–September 23
LIBRA	Scales	September 23–October 23
SCORPIO	Scorpion	October 23–November 22
SAGITTARIUS	Archer	November 22–December 22
CAPRICORN	Sea Goat	December 22–January 20
AQUARIUS	Water Bearer	January 20–February 18
PISCES	Fish	February 18–March 20

It is possible to draw significant conclusions and make meaningful predictions based simply on the Sun sign of a person. There are many people who have been amazed at the accuracy of the description of their own character based only on the Sun sign. But an astrologer needs more information than just your Sun sign to interpret the photograph that is your horoscope.

The Rising Sign and the Zodiacal Houses

An astrologer needs the exact time and place of your birth in order to construct and interpret your horoscope. The illustration on the next page shows the flat chart, or natural wheel, an astrologer uses. Note the inner circle of the wheel labeled 1 through 12. These 12 divisions are known as the houses of the Zodiac.

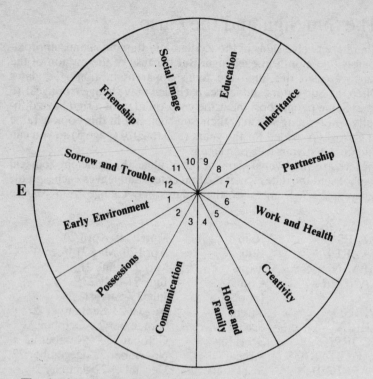

The 1st house always starts from the position marked E, which corresponds to the eastern horizon. The rest of the houses 2 through 12 follow around in a "counterclockwise" direction. The point where each house starts is known as a cusp, or edge.

The cusp, or edge, of the 1st house (point E) is where an astrologer would place your Rising sign, the Ascendant. And, as already noted, the exact time of your birth determines your Rising sign. Let's see how this works.

As the Earth rotates on its axis once every 24 hours, each one of the twelve signs of the Zodiac appears to be "rising" on the horizon, with a new one appearing about every 2 hours. Actually it is the turning of the Earth that exposes each sign to view, but in our astrological work we are discussing apparent motion. This Rising sign marks the Ascendant, and it colors the whole orientation of a horoscope. It indicates the sign governing the 1st house of the chart, and will thus determine which signs will govern all the other houses.

To visualize this idea, imagine two color wheels with twelve divisions superimposed upon each other. For just as the Zodiac is divided into twelve constellations that we identify as the signs, another twelvefold division is used to denote the houses. Now imagine one wheel (the signs) moving slowly while the other wheel (the houses) remains still. This analogy may help you see how the signs keep shifting the "color" of the houses as the Rising sign continues to change every two hours. To simplify things, a Table of Rising Signs has been provided (pages 8–9) for your specific Sun sign.

Once your Rising sign has been placed on the cusp of the 1st house, the signs that govern the rest of the 11 houses can be placed on the chart. In any individual's horoscope the signs do not necessarily correspond with the houses. For example, it could be that a sign covers part of two adjacent houses. It is the interpretation of such variations in an individual's horoscope that marks the professional astrologer.

But to gain a workable understanding of astrology, it is not necessary to go into great detail. In fact, we just need a description of the houses and their meanings, as is shown in the illustration above and in the table below.

THE 12 HOUSES OF THE ZODIAC

1st	Individuality, body appearance, general outlook on life	Personality house
2nd	Finance, possessions, ethical principles, gain or loss	Money house
3rd	Relatives, communication, short journeys, writing, education	Relatives house
4th	Family and home, parental ties, land and property, security	Home house
5th	Pleasure, children, creativity, entertainment, risk	Pleasure house
6th	Health, harvest, hygiene, work and service, employees	Health house
7th	Marriage and divorce, the law, partnerships and alliances	Marriage house
8th	Inheritance, secret deals, sex, death, regeneration	Inheritance house
9th	Travel, sports, study, philosophy Ω house	Travel house
10th	Career, social standing, success and honor	Business house
11th	Friendship, social life, hopes and wishes	Friends house
12th	Troubles, illness, secret enemies, hidden agendas	Trouble house

The Planets in the Houses

An astrologer, knowing the exact time and place of your birth, will use tables of planetary motion in order to locate the planets in your horoscope chart. He or she will determine which planet or planets are in which sign and in which house. It is not uncommon, in an individual's horoscope, for there to be two or more planets in the same sign and in the same house.

The characteristics of the planets modify the influence of the Sun according to their natures and strengths.

Sun: Source of life. Basic temperament according to the Sun sign. The conscious will. Human potential.

Moon: Emotions. Moods. Customs. Habits. Changeable. Adaptive. Nurturing.

Mercury: Communication. Intellect. Reasoning power. Curiosity. Short travels.

Venus: Love. Delight. Charm. Harmony. Balance. Art. Beautiful possessions.

Mars: Energy. Initiative. War. Anger. Adventure. Courage. Daring. Impulse.

Jupiter: Luck. Optimism. Generous. Expansive. Opportunities. Protection.

Saturn: Pessimism. Privation. Obstacles. Delay. Hard work. Research. Lasting rewards after long struggle.

Uranus: Fashion. Electricity. Revolution. Independence. Freedom. Sudden changes. Modern science.

Neptune: Sensationalism. Theater. Dreams. Inspiration. Illusion. Deception.

Pluto: Creation and destruction. Total transformation. Lust for power. Strong obsessions.

Superimpose the characteristics of the planets on the functions of the house in which they appear. Express the result through the character of the Sun sign, and you will get the basic idea.

Of course, many other considerations have been taken into account in producing the carefully worked out predictions in this book: the aspects of the planets to each other; their strength according to position and sign; whether they are in a house of exaltation or decline; whether they are natural enemies or not; whether a planet occupies its own sign; the position of a planet in relation to its own house or sign; whether the sign is male or female; whether the sign is a fire, earth, water, or air sign. These are only a few of the colors on the astrologer's pallet which he or she must mix with the inspiration of the artist and the accuracy of the mathematician.

How To Use These Predictions

A person reading the predictions in this book should understand that they are produced from the daily position of the planets for a group of people and are not, of course, individually specialized. To get the full benefit of them our readers should relate the predictions to their own character and circumstances, coordinate them, and draw their own conclusions from them.

If you are a serious observer of your own life, you should find a definite pattern emerging that will be a helpful and reliable guide.

The point is that we always retain our free will. The stars indicate certain directional tendencies but we are not compelled to follow. We can do or not do, and wisdom must make the choice.

We all have our good and bad days. Sometimes they extend into cycles of weeks. It is therefore advisable to study daily predictions in a span ranging from the day before to several days ahead.

Daily predictions should be taken very generally. The word "difficult" does not necessarily indicate a whole day of obstruction or inconvenience. It is a warning to you to be cautious. Your caution will often see you around the difficulty before you are involved. This is the correct use of astrology.

In another section (pages 78–84), detailed information is given about the influence of the Moon as it passes through each of the twelve signs of the Zodiac. There are instructions on how to use the Moon Tables (pages 85–92), which provide Moon Sign Dates throughout the year as well as the Moon's role in health and daily affairs. This information should be used in conjunction with the daily forecasts to give a fuller picture of the astrological trends.

HISTORY OF ASTROLOGY

The origins of astrology have been lost far back in history, but we do know that reference is made to it as far back as the first written records of the human race. It is not hard to see why. Even in primitive times, people must have looked for an explanation for the various happenings in their lives. They must have wanted to know why people were different from one another. And in their search they turned to the regular movements of the Sun, Moon, and stars to see if they could provide an answer.

It is interesting to note that as soon as man learned to use his tools in any type of design, or his mind in any kind of calculation, he turned his attention to the heavens. Ancient cave dwellings reveal dim crescents and circles representative of the Sun and Moon, rulers of day and night. Mesopotamia and the civilization of Chaldea, in itself the foundation of those of Babylonia and Assyria, show a complete picture of astronomical observation and well-developed astrological interpretation.

Humanity has a natural instinct for order. The study of anthropology reveals that primitive people—even as far back as prehistoric times—were striving to achieve a certain order in their lives. They tried to organize the apparent chaos of the universe. They had the desire to attach meaning to things. This demand for order has persisted throughout the history of man. So that observing the regularity of the heavenly bodies made it logical that primitive peoples should turn heavenward in their search for an understanding of the world in which they found themselves so random and alone.

And they did find a significance in the movements of the stars. Shepherds tending their flocks, for instance, observed that when the cluster of stars now known as the constellation Aries was in sight, it was the time of fertility and they associated it with the Ram. And they noticed that the growth of plants and plant life corresponded with different phases of the Moon, so that certain times were favorable for the planting of crops, and other times were not. In this way, there grew up a tradition of seasons and causes connected with the passage of the Sun through the twelve signs of the Zodiac.

Astrology was valued so highly that the king was kept informed of the daily and monthly changes in the heavenly bodies, and the results of astrological studies regarding events of the future. Head astrologers were clearly men of great rank and position, and the office was said to be a hereditary one.

Omens were taken, not only from eclipses and conjunctions of the Moon or Sun with one of the planets, but also from storms and earthquakes. In the eastern civilizations, particularly, the reverence inspired by astrology appears to have remained unbroken since the very earliest days. In ancient China, astrology, astronomy, and religion went hand in hand. The astrologer, who was also an astronomer, was part of the official government service and had his own corner in the Imperial Palace. The duties of the Imperial astrologer, whose office was one of the most important in the land, were clearly defined, as this extract from early records shows:

This exalted gentleman must concern himself with the stars in the heavens, keeping a record of the changes and movements of the Planets, the Sun and the Moon, in order to examine the movements of the terrestrial world with the object of prognosticating good and bad fortune. He divides the territories of the nine regions of the empire in accordance with their dependence on particular celestial bodies. All the fiefs and principalities are connected with the stars and from this their prosperity or misfortune should be ascertained. He makes prognostications according to the twelve years of the Jupiter cycle of good and evil of the terrestrial world. From the colors of the five kinds of clouds, he determines the coming of floods or droughts, abundance or famine. From the twelve winds, he draws conclusions about the state of harmony of heaven and earth, and takes note of good and bad signs that result from their accord or disaccord. In general, he concerns himself with five kinds of phenomena so as to warn the Emperor to come to the aid of the government and to allow for variations in the ceremonies according to their circumstances.

The Chinese were also keen observers of the fixed stars, giving them such unusual names as Ghost Vehicle, Sun of Imperial Concubine, Imperial Prince, Pivot of Heaven, Twinkling Brilliance, Weaving Girl. But, great astrologers though they may have been, the Chinese lacked one aspect of mathematics that the Greeks applied to astrology—deductive geometry. Deductive geometry was the basis of much classical astrology in and after the time of the Greeks, and this explains the different methods of prognostication used in the East and West.

Down through the ages the astrologer's art has depended, not so much on the uncovering of new facts, though this is important, as on the interpretation of the facts already known. This is the essence of the astrologer's skill.

But why should the signs of the Zodiac have any effect at all on the formation of human character? It is easy to see why people thought they did, and even now we constantly use astrological expressions in our everyday speech. The thoughts of "lucky star," "ill-fated," "star-crossed," "mooning around," are interwoven into the very structure of our language.

Wherever the concept of the Zodiac is understood and used, it could well appear to have an influence on the human character. Does this mean, then, that the human race, in whose civilization the idea of the twelve signs of the Zodiac has long been embedded, is divided into only twelve types? Can we honestly believe that it is really as simple as that? If so, there must be pretty wide ranges of variation within each type. And if, to explain the variation, we call in heredity and environment, experiences in early childhood, the thyroid and other glands, and also the four functions of the mind together with extroversion and introversion, then one begins to wonder if the original classification was worth making at all. No sensible person believes that his favorite system explains everything. But even so, he will not find the system much use at all if it does not even save him the trouble of bothering with the others.

In the same way, if we were to put every person under only one sign of the Zodiac, the system becomes too rigid and unlike life. Besides, it was never intended to be used like that. It may be convenient to have only twelve types, but we know that in practice there is every possible gradation between aggressiveness and timidity, or between conscientiousness and laziness. How, then, do we account for this?

A person born under any given Sun sign can be mainly influenced by one or two of the other signs that appear in their individual horoscope. For instance, famous persons born under the sign of Gemini include Henry VIII, whom nothing and no one could have induced to abdicate, and Edward VIII, who did just that. Obviously, then, the sign Gemini does not fully explain the complete character of either of them.

Again, under the opposite sign, Sagittarius, were both Stalin, who was totally consumed with the notion of power, and Charles V, who freely gave up an empire because he preferred to go into a monastery. And we find under Scorpio many uncompromising characters such as Luther, de Gaulle, Indira Gandhi, and Montgomery, but also Petain, a successful commander whose name later became synonymous with collaboration.

A single sign is therefore obviously inadequate to explain the differences between people; it can only explain resemblances, such as the combativeness of the Scorpio group, or the far-reaching devotion of Charles V and Stalin to their respective ideals—the Christian heaven and the Communist utopia.

But very few people have only one sign in their horoscope chart.

In addition to the month of birth, the day and, even more, the hour to the nearest minute if possible, ought to be considered. Without this, it is impossible to have an actual horoscope, for the word horoscope literally means "a consideration of the hour."

The month of birth tells you only which sign of the Zodiac was occupied by the Sun. The day and hour tell you what sign was occupied by the Moon. And the minute tells you which sign was rising on the eastern horizon. This is called the Ascendant, and, as some astrologers believe, it is supposed to be the most important thing in the whole horoscope.

The Sun is said to signify one's heart, that is to say, one's deepest desires and inmost nature. This is quite different from the Moon, which signifies one's superficial way of behaving. When the ancient Romans referred to the Emperor Augustus as a Capricorn, they meant that he had the Moon in Capricorn. Or, to take another example, a modern astrologer would call Disraeli a Scorpion because he had Scorpio Rising, but most people would call him Sagittarius because he had the Sun there. The Romans would have called him Leo because his Moon was in Leo.

So if one does not seem to fit one's birth month, it is always worthwhile reading the other signs, for one may have been born at a time when any of them were rising or occupied by the Moon. It also seems to be the case that the influence of the Sun develops as life goes on, so that the month of birth is easier to guess in people over the age of forty. The young are supposed to be influenced mainly by their Ascendant, the Rising sign, which characterizes the body and physical personality as a whole.

It is nonsense to assume that all people born at a certain time will exhibit the same characteristics, or that they will even behave in the same manner. It is quite obvious that, from the very moment of its birth, a child is subject to the effects of its environment, and that this in turn will influence its character and heritage to a decisive extent. Also to be taken into account are education and economic conditions, which play a very important part in the formation of one's character as well.

People have, in general, certain character traits and qualities which, according to their environment, develop in either a positive or a negative manner. Therefore, selfishness (inherent selfishness, that is) might emerge as unselfishness; kindness and consideration as cruelty and lack of consideration toward others. In the same way, a naturally constructive person may, through frustration, become destructive, and so on. The latent characteristics with which people are born can, therefore, through environment and good or bad training, become something that would appear to be its opposite, and so give the lie to the astrologer's description of their character.

But this is not the case. The true character is still there, but it is buried deep beneath these external superficialities.

Careful study of the character traits of various signs of the Zodiac are of immeasurable help, and can render beneficial service to the intelligent person. Undoubtedly, the reader will already have discovered that, while he is able to get on very well with some people, he just "cannot stand" others. The causes sometimes seem inexplicable. At times there is intense dislike, at other times immediate sympathy. And there is, too, the phenomenon of love at first sight, which is also apparently inexplicable. People appear to be either sympathetic or unsympathetic toward each other for no apparent reason.

Now if we look at this in the light of the Zodiac, we find that people born under different signs are either compatible or incompatible with each other. In other words, there are good and bad interrelating factors among the various signs. This does not, of course, mean that humanity can be divided into groups of hostile camps. It would be quite wrong to be hostile or indifferent toward people who happen to be born under an incompatible sign. There is no reason why everybody should not, or cannot, learn to control and adjust their feelings and actions, especially after they are aware of the positive qualities of other people by studying their character analyses, among other things.

Every person born under a certain sign has both positive and negative qualities, which are developed more or less according to our free will. Nobody is entirely good or entirely bad, and it is up to each of us to learn to control ourselves on the one hand and at the same time to endeavor to learn about ourselves and others.

It cannot be emphasized often enough that it is free will that determines whether we will make really good use of our talents and abilities. Using our free will, we can either overcome our failings or allow them to rule us. Our free will enables us to exert sufficient willpower to control our failings so that they do not harm ourselves or others.

Astrology can reveal our inclinations and tendencies. Astrology can tell us about ourselves so that we are able to use our free will to overcome our shortcomings. In this way astrology helps us do our best to become needed and valuable members of society as well as helpmates to our family and our friends. Astrology also can save us a great deal of unhappiness and remorse.

Yet it may seem absurd that an ancient philosophy could be a prop to modern men and women. But below the materialistic surface of modern life, there are hidden streams of feeling and thought. Symbology is reappearing as a study worthy of the scholar; the psychosomatic factor in illness has passed from the writings of the crank to those of the specialist; spiritual healing in all its forms is no longer a pious hope but an accepted phenomenon. And it is into this context that we consider astrology, in the sense that it is an analysis of human types.

Astrology and medicine had a long journey together, and only parted company a couple of centuries ago. There still remain in medical language such astrological terms as "saturnine," "choleric," and "mercurial," used in the diagnosis of physical tendencies. The herbalist, for long the handyman of the medical profession, has been dominated by astrology since the days of the Greeks. Certain herbs traditionally respond to certain planetary influences, and diseases must therefore be treated to ensure harmony between the medicine and the disease.

But the stars are expected to foretell and not only to diagnose.

Astrological forecasting has been remarkably accurate, but often it is wide of the mark. The brave person who cares to predict world events takes dangerous chances. Individual forecasting is less clear cut; it can be a help or a disillusionment. Then we come to the nagging question: if it is possible to foreknow, is it right to foretell? This is a point of ethics on which it is hard to pronounce judgment. The doctor faces the same dilemma if he finds that symptoms of a mortal disease are present in his patient and that he can only prognosticate a steady decline. How much to tell an individual in a crisis is a problem that has perplexed many distinguished scholars. Honest and conscientious astrologers in this modern world, where so many people are seeking guidance, face the same problem.

Five hundred years ago it was customary to call in a learned man who was an astrologer who was probably also a doctor and a philosopher. By his knowledge of astrology, his study of planetary influences, he felt himself qualified to guide those in distress. The world has moved forward at a fantastic rate since then, and yet people are still uncertain of themselves. At first sight it seems fantastic in the light of modern thinking that they turn to the most ancient of all studies, and get someone to calculate a horoscope for them. But is it really so fantastic if you take a second look? For astrology is concerned with tomorrow, with survival. And in a world such as ours, tomorrow and survival are the keywords for the twenty-first century.

ASTROLOGICAL BRIDGE TO THE 21st CENTURY

Themes connecting past, present, and future are in play as the first decade reveals hidden paths and personal hints for achieving your potential. Make the most of the messages from the planets.

With the dawning of the twenty-first century look first to Jupiter, the planet of good fortune. Each new yearly Jupiter cycle follows the natural progression of the Zodiac. First is Jupiter in Aries and in Taurus through spring 2000, next Jupiter is in Gemini to summer 2001, then in Cancer to midsummer 2002, in Leo to late summer 2003, in Virgo to early autumn 2004, in Libra to midautumn 2005, and so on through Jupiter in Pisces through June 2010. The beneficent planet Jupiter promotes your professional and educational goals while urging informed choice and deliberation, providing a rich medium for creativity. Planet Jupiter's influence is protective, the generous helper that comes to the rescue just in the nick of time. And while safeguarding good luck, Jupiter can turn unusual risks into achievable aims.

In order to take advantage of luck and opportunity, to gain wisdom from experience, to persevere against adversity, look to beautiful planet Saturn. Saturn, planet of reason and responsibility, began a new cycle in earthy Taurus at the turn of the century. Saturn in Taurus until spring 2001 inspires industry and affection, blends practicality and imagination, all the while inviting caution and care. Saturn in Taurus lends beauty, order, and structure to your life. Then Saturn is in Gemini, the sign of mind and communication, until June 2003. Saturn in Gemini gives a lively intellectual capacity, so the limits of creativity can be stretched and boundaries broken. Saturn in Gemini holds the promise of fruitful endeavor through sustained study, learning, and application. Saturn in Cancer from early June 2003 to mid-July 2005 poses issues of long-term security versus immediate gratification. Rely on deliberation and choice to make sense out of diversity and change. Saturn in Cancer can be a revealing cycle, leading to the desired outcomes of growth and maturity. Saturn in Leo from mid-July 2005 to early September 2007 can be a test of boldness versus caution. Here every challenge must be met with benevolent authority, matched by a caring and generous outlook. Saturn in Virgo early September 2007 into October 2009 sharpens and deepens the mind, conferring precise writing and teaching skills. Saturn in Virgo presents chances to excel, to accomplish a great deal, and to gain prominence through good words and good works.

Uranus, planet of innovation and surprise, started an important new cycle in January of 1996. At that time Uranus entered its natural home in airy Aquarius. Uranus in Aquarius into the year 2003 has a profound effect on your personality and the lens through which you see the world. A basic change in the way you project yourself is just one impact of Uranus in Aquarius. More significantly, a whole new consciousness is evolving. Winds of change blowing your way emphasize movement and freedom. Uranus in Aquarius poses involvement in the larger community beyond self, family, friends, lovers, associates. Radical ideas and progressive thought signal a journey of liberation. As the new century begins, follow Uranus on the path of humanitarianism. A new Uranus cycle begins March 2003 when Uranus visits Pisces, briefly revisits Aquarius, then returns late in 2003 to Pisces where it will stay into May 2010. Uranus in Pisces, a strongly intuitive force, urges work and service for the good of humankind to make the world a better place for all people.

Neptune, planet of vision and mystery, is enjoying a long cycle that excites creativity and imaginative thinking. Neptune is in airy Aquarius from November 1998 to February of 2012. Neptune in Aquarius, the sign of the Water Bearer, represents two sides of the coin of wisdom: inspiration and reason. Here Neptune stirs powerful currents bearing a rich and varied harvest, the fertile breeding ground for idealistic aims and practical considerations. Neptune's fine intuition tunes in to your dreams, your imagination, your spirituality. You can never turn your back on the mysteries of life. Uranus and Neptune, the planets of enlightenment and idealism, give you glimpses into the future, letting you peek through secret doorways into the twenty-first century.

Pluto, planet of beginnings and endings, began a new cycle of growth and learning late in 1995. Pluto entered fiery Sagittarius and remains there into the year 2008. Pluto in Sagittarius during its long stay over twelve years can create significant change. The great power of Pluto in Sagittarius is already starting its transformation of your character and lifestyle. Pluto in Sagittarius takes you on a new journey of exploration and learning. The awakening you experience on intellectual and artistic levels heralds a new cycle of growth. Uncompromising Pluto, seeker of truth, challenges your identity, persona, and self-expression. Uncovering the real you, Pluto holds the key to understanding and meaningful communication. Pluto in Sagittarius can be the guiding light illuminating the first decade of the twenty-first century. Good luck is riding on the waves of change.

THE SIGNS OF THE ZODIAC

Dominant Characteristics

Aries: March 21–April 20

The Positive Side of Aries

The Aries has many positive points to his character. People born under this first sign of the Zodiac are often quite strong and enthusiastic. On the whole, they are forward-looking people who are not easily discouraged by temporary setbacks. They know what they want out of life and they go out after it. Their personalities are strong. Others are usually quite impressed by the Ram's way of doing things. Quite often they are sources of inspiration for others traveling the same route. Aries men and women have a special zest for life that can be contagious; for others, they are a fine example of how life should be lived.

The Aries person usually has a quick and active mind. He is imaginative and inventive. He enjoys keeping busy and active. He generally gets along well with all kinds of people. He is interested in mankind, as a whole. He likes to be challenged. Some would say he thrives on opposition, for it is when he is set against that he often does his best. Getting over or around obstacles is a challenge he generally enjoys. All in all, Aries is quite positive and young-thinking. He likes to keep abreast of new things that are happening in the world. Aries are often fond of speed. They like things to be done quickly, and this sometimes aggravates their slower colleagues and associates.

The Aries man or woman always seems to remain young. Their whole approach to life is youthful and optimistic. They never say die, no matter what the odds. They may have an occasional setback, but it is not long before they are back on their feet again.

The Negative Side of Aries

Everybody has his less positive qualities—and Aries is no exception. Sometimes the Aries man or woman is not very tactful in communicating with others; in his hurry to get things done he is apt to be a little callous or inconsiderate. Sensitive people are likely to find him somewhat sharp-tongued in some situations. Often in his eagerness to get the show on the road, he misses the mark altogether and cannot achieve his aims.

At times Aries can be too impulsive. He can occasionally be stubborn and refuse to listen to reason. If things do not move quickly enough to suit the Aries man or woman, he or she is apt to become rather nervous or irritable. The uncultivated Aries is not unfamiliar with moments of doubt and fear. He is capable of being destructive if he does not get his way. He can overcome some of his emotional problems by steadily trying to express himself as he really is, but this requires effort.

Taurus: April 21–May 20

The Positive Side of Taurus

The Taurus person is known for his ability to concentrate and for his tenacity. These are perhaps his strongest qualities. The Taurus man or woman generally has very little trouble in getting along with others; it's his nature to be helpful toward people in need. He can always be depended on by his friends, especially those in trouble.

Taurus generally achieves what he wants through his ability to persevere. He never leaves anything unfinished but works on something until it has been completed. People can usually take him at his word; he is honest and forthright in most of his dealings. The Taurus person has a good chance to make a success of his life because of his many positive qualities. The Taurus who aims high seldom falls short of his mark. He learns well by experience. He is thorough and does not believe in shortcuts of any kind. The Bull's thoroughness pays off in the end, for through his deliberateness he learns how to rely on himself and what he has learned. The Taurus person tries to get along with others, as a rule. He is not overly critical and likes people to be themselves. He is a tolerant person and enjoys peace and harmony—especially in his home life.

Taurus is usually cautious in all that he does. He is not a person

who believes in taking unnecessary risks. Before adopting any one line of action, he will weigh all of the pros and cons. The Taurus person is steadfast. Once his mind is made up it seldom changes. The person born under this sign usually is a good family person—reliable and loving.

The Negative Side of Taurus

Sometimes the Taurus man or woman is a bit too stubborn. He won't listen to other points of view if his mind is set on something. To others, this can be quite annoying. Taurus also does not like to be told what to do. He becomes rather angry if others think him not too bright. He does not like to be told he is wrong, even when he is. He dislikes being contradicted.

Some people who are born under this sign are very suspicious of others—even of those persons close to them. They find it difficult to trust people fully. They are often afraid of being deceived or taken advantage of. The Bull often finds it difficult to forget or forgive. His love of material things sometimes makes him rather avaricious and petty.

Gemini: May 21–June 20

The Positive Side of Gemini

The person born under this sign of the Heavenly Twins is usually quite bright and quick-witted. Some of them are capable of doing many different things. The Gemini person very often has many different interests. He keeps an open mind and is always anxious to learn new things.

Gemini is often an analytical person. He is a person who enjoys making use of his intellect. He is governed more by his mind than by his emotions. He is a person who is not confined to one view; he can often understand both sides to a problem or question. He knows how to reason, how to make rapid decisions if need be.

He is an adaptable person and can make himself at home almost anywhere. There are all kinds of situations he can adapt to. He is a person who seldom doubts himself; he is sure of his talents and his ability to think and reason. Gemini is generally most satisfied when he is in a situation where he can make use of his intellect. Never

short of imagination, he often has strong talents for invention. He is rather a modern person when it comes to life; Gemini almost always moves along with the times—perhaps that is why he remains so youthful throughout most of his life.

Literature and art appeal to the person born under this sign. Creativity in almost any form will interest and intrigue the Gemini man or woman.

The Gemini is often quite charming. A good talker, he often is the center of attraction at any gathering. People find it easy to like a person born under this sign because he can appear easygoing and usually has a good sense of humor.

The Negative Side of Gemini

Sometimes the Gemini person tries to do too many things at one time—and as a result, winds up finishing nothing. Some Twins are easily distracted and find it rather difficult to concentrate on one thing for too long a time. Sometimes they give in to trifling fancies and find it rather boring to become too serious about any one thing. Some of them are never dependable, no matter what they promise.

Although the Gemini man or woman often appears to be well-versed on many subjects, this is sometimes just a veneer. His knowledge may be only superficial, but because he speaks so well he gives people the impression of erudition. Some Geminis are sharp-tongued and inconsiderate; they think only of themselves and their own pleasure.

Cancer: June 21–July 20

The Positive Side of Cancer

The Moon Child's most positive point is his understanding nature. On the whole, he is a loving and sympathetic person. He would never go out of his way to hurt anyone. The Cancer man or woman is often very kind and tender; they give what they can to others. They hate to see others suffering and will do what they can to help someone in less fortunate circumstances than themselves. They are often very concerned about the world. Their interest in people generally goes beyond that of just their own families and close friends; they have a deep sense of community and respect humanitarian values. The Moon Child means what he says, as a rule; he is honest about his feelings.

The Cancer man or woman is a person who knows the art of patience. When something seems difficult, he is willing to wait until the situation becomes manageable again. He is a person who knows how to bide his time. Cancer knows how to concentrate on one thing at a time. When he has made his mind up he generally sticks with what he does, seeing it through to the end.

Cancer is a person who loves his home. He enjoys being surrounded by familiar things and the people he loves. Of all the signs, Cancer is the most maternal. Even the men born under this sign often have a motherly or protective quality about them. They like to take care of people in their family—to see that they are well loved and well provided for. They are usually loyal and faithful. Family ties mean a lot to the Cancer man or woman. Parents and in-laws are respected and loved. Young Cancer responds very well to adults who show faith in him. The Moon Child has a strong sense of tradition. He is very sensitive to the moods of others.

The Negative Side of Cancer

Sometimes Cancer finds it rather hard to face life. It becomes too much for him. He can be a little timid and retiring, when things don't go too well. When unfortunate things happen, he is apt to just shrug and say, "Whatever will be will be." He can be fatalistic to a fault. The uncultivated Cancer is a bit lazy. He doesn't have very much ambition. Anything that seems a bit difficult he'll gladly leave to others. He may be lacking in initiative. Too sensitive, when he feels he's been injured, he'll crawl back into his shell and nurse his imaginary wounds. The immature Moon Child often is given to crying when the smallest thing goes wrong.

Some Cancers find it difficult to enjoy themselves in environments outside their homes. They make heavy demands on others, and need to be constantly reassured that they are loved. Lacking such reassurance, they may resort to sulking in silence.

Leo: July 21–August 21

The Positive Side of Leo

Often Leos make good leaders. They seem to be good organizers and administrators. Usually they are quite popular with others. Whatever group it is that they belong to, the Leo man or woman is almost sure to be or become the leader. Loyalty, one of the Lion's noblest traits, enables him or her to maintain this leadership position.

Leo is generous most of the time. It is his best characteristic. He or she likes to give gifts and presents. In making others happy, the Leo person becomes happy himself. He likes to splurge when spending money on others. In some instances it may seem that the Lion's generosity knows no boundaries. A hospitable person, the Leo man or woman is very fond of welcoming people to his house and entertaining them. He is never short of company.

Leo has plenty of energy and drive. He enjoys working toward some specific goal. When he applies himself correctly, he gets what he wants most often. The Leo person is almost never unsure of himself. He has plenty of confidence and aplomb. He is a person who is direct in almost everything he does. He has a quick mind and can make a decision in a very short time.

He usually sets a good example for others because of his ambitious manner and positive ways. He knows how to stick to something once he's started. Although Leo may be good at making a joke, he is not superficial or glib. He is a loving person, kind and thoughtful.

There is generally nothing small or petty about the Leo man or woman. He does what he can for those who are deserving. He is a person others can rely upon at all times. He means what he says. An honest person, generally speaking, he is a friend who is valued and sought out.

The Negative Side of Leo

Leo, however, does have his faults. At times, he can be just a bit too arrogant. He thinks that no one deserves a leadership position except him. Only he is capable of doing things well. His opinion of himself is often much too high. Because of his conceit, he is

sometimes rather unpopular with a good many people. Some Leos are too materialistic; they can only think in terms of money and profit.

Some Leos enjoy lording it over others—at home or at their place of business. What is more, they feel they have the right to. Egocentric to an impossible degree, this sort of Leo cares little about how others think or feel. He can be rude and cutting.

Virgo: August 22–September 22

The Positive Side of Virgo

The person born under the sign of Virgo is generally a busy person. He knows how to arrange and organize things. He is a good planner. Above all, he is practical and is not afraid of hard work.

Often called the sign of the Harvester, Virgo knows how to attain what he desires. He sticks with something until it is finished. He never shirks his duties, and can always be depended upon. The Virgo person can be thoroughly trusted at all times.

The man or woman born under this sign tries to do everything to perfection. He doesn't believe in doing anything halfway. He always aims for the top. He is the sort of a person who is always learning and constantly striving to better himself—not because he wants more money or glory, but because it gives him a feeling of accomplishment.

The Virgo man or woman is a very observant person. He is sensitive to how others feel, and can see things below the surface of a situation. He usually puts this talent to constructive use.

It is not difficult for the Virgo to be open and earnest. He believes in putting his cards on the table. He is never secretive or underhanded. He's as good as his word. The Virgo person is generally plainspoken and down to earth. He has no trouble in expressing himself.

The Virgo person likes to keep up to date on new developments in his particular field. Well-informed, generally, he sometimes has a keen interest in the arts or literature. What he knows, he knows well. His ability to use his critical faculties is well-developed and sometimes startles others because of its accuracy.

Virgos adhere to a moderate way of life; they avoid excesses. Virgo is a responsible person and enjoys being of service.

The Negative Side of Virgo

Sometimes a Virgo person is too critical. He thinks that only he can do something the way it should be done. Whatever anyone else does is inferior. He can be rather annoying in the way he quibbles over insignificant details. In telling others how things should be done, he can be rather tactless and mean.

Some Virgos seem rather emotionless and cool. They feel emotional involvement is beneath them. They are sometimes too tidy, too neat. With money they can be rather miserly. Some Virgos try to force their opinions and ideas on others.

Libra: September 23–October 22

The Positive Side of Libra

Libras love harmony. It is one of their most outstanding character traits. They are interested in achieving balance; they admire beauty and grace in things as well as in people. Generally speaking, they are kind and considerate people. Libras are usually very sympathetic. They go out of their way not to hurt another person's feelings. They are outgoing and do what they can to help those in need.

People born under the sign of Libra almost always make good friends. They are loyal and amiable. They enjoy the company of others. Many of them are rather moderate in their views; they believe in keeping an open mind, however, and weighing both sides of an issue fairly before making a decision.

Alert and intelligent, Libra, often known as the Lawgiver, is always fair-minded and tries to put himself in the position of the other person. They are against injustice; quite often they take up for the underdog. In most of their social dealings, they try to be tactful and kind. They dislike discord and bickering, and most Libras strive for peace and harmony in all their relationships.

The Libra man or woman has a keen sense of beauty. They appreciate handsome furnishings and clothes. Many of them are artistically inclined. Their taste is usually impeccable. They know how to use color. Their homes are almost always attractively arranged and inviting. They enjoy entertaining people and see to it that their guests always feel at home and welcome.

Libra gets along with almost everyone. He is well-liked and socially much in demand.

The Negative Side of Libra

Some people born under this sign tend to be rather insincere. So eager are they to achieve harmony in all relationships that they will even go so far as to lie. Many of them are escapists. They find facing the truth an ordeal and prefer living in a world of make-believe.

In a serious argument, some Libras give in rather easily even when they know they are right. Arguing, even about something they believe in, is too unsettling for some of them.

Libras sometimes care too much for material things. They enjoy possessions and luxuries. Some are vain and tend to be jealous.

Scorpio: October 23–November 22

The Positive Side of Scorpio

The Scorpio man or woman generally knows what he or she wants out of life. He is a determined person. He sees something through to the end. Scorpio is quite sincere, and seldom says anything he doesn't mean. When he sets a goal for himself he tries to go about achieving it in a very direct way.

The Scorpion is brave and courageous. They are not afraid of hard work. Obstacles do not frighten them. They forge ahead until they achieve what they set out for. The Scorpio man or woman has a strong will.

Although Scorpio may seem rather fixed and determined, inside he is often quite tender and loving. He can care very much for others. He believes in sincerity in all relationships. His feelings about someone tend to last; they are profound and not superficial.

The Scorpio person is someone who adheres to his principles no matter what happens. He will not be deterred from a path he believes to be right.

Because of his many positive strengths, the Scorpion can often achieve happiness for himself and for those that he loves.

He is a constructive person by nature. He often has a deep understanding of people and of life, in general. He is perceptive and unafraid. Obstacles often seem to spur him on. He is a positive person who enjoys winning. He has many strengths and resources; challenge of any sort often brings out the best in him.

The Negative Side of Scorpio

The Scorpio person is sometimes hypersensitive. Often he imagines injury when there is none. He feels that others do not bother to recognize him for his true worth. Sometimes he is given to excessive boasting in order to compensate for what he feels is neglect.

Scorpio can be proud, arrogant, and competitive. They can be sly when they put their minds to it and they enjoy outwitting persons or institutions noted for their cleverness.

Their tactics for getting what they want are sometimes devious and ruthless. They don't care too much about what others may think. If they feel others have done them an injustice, they will do their best to seek revenge. The Scorpion often has a sudden, violent temper; and this person's interest in sex is sometimes quite unbalanced or excessive.

Sagittarius: November 23–December 20

The Positive Side of Sagittarius

People born under this sign are honest and forthright. Their approach to life is earnest and open. Sagittarius is often quite adult in his way of seeing things. They are broad-minded and tolerant people. When dealing with others the person born under the sign of the Archer is almost always open and forthright. He doesn't believe in deceit or pretension. His standards are high. People who associate with Sagittarius generally admire and respect his tolerant viewpoint.

The Archer trusts others easily and expects them to trust him. He is never suspicious or envious and almost always thinks well of others. People always enjoy his company because he is so friendly and easygoing. The Sagittarius man or woman is often good-humored. He can always be depended upon by his friends, family, and co-workers.

The person born under this sign of the Zodiac likes a good joke every now and then. Sagittarius is eager for fun and laughs, which makes him very popular with others.

A lively person, he enjoys sports and outdoor life. The Archer is fond of animals. Intelligent and interesting, he can begin an ani-

mated conversation with ease. He likes exchanging ideas and discussing various views.

He is not selfish or proud. If someone proposes an idea or plan that is better than his, he will immediately adopt it. Imaginative yet practical, he knows how to put ideas into practice.

The Archer enjoys sport and games, and it doesn't matter if he wins or loses. He is a forgiving person, and never sulks over something that has not worked out in his favor.

He is seldom critical, and is almost always generous.

The Negative Side of Sagittarius

Some Sagittarius are restless. They take foolish risks and seldom learn from the mistakes they make. They don't have heads for money and are often mismanaging their finances. Some of them devote much of their time to gambling.

Some are too outspoken and tactless, always putting their feet in their mouths. They hurt others carelessly by being honest at the wrong time. Sometimes they make promises which they don't keep. They don't stick close enough to their plans and go from one failure to another. They are undisciplined and waste a lot of energy.

Capricorn: December 21–January 19

The Positive Side of Capricorn

The person born under the sign of Capricorn, known variously as the Mountain Goat or Sea Goat, is usually very stable and patient. He sticks to whatever tasks he has and sees them through. He can always be relied upon and he is not averse to work.

An honest person, Capricorn is generally serious about whatever he does. He does not take his duties lightly. He is a practical person and believes in keeping his feet on the ground.

Quite often the person born under this sign is ambitious and knows how to get what he wants out of life. The Goat forges ahead and never gives up his goal. When he is determined about something, he almost always wins. He is a good worker—a hard worker. Although things may not come easy to him, he will not complain, but continue working until his chores are finished.

He is usually good at business matters and knows the value of money. He is not a spendthrift and knows how to put something away for a rainy day; he dislikes waste and unnecessary loss.

Capricorn knows how to make use of his self-control. He can apply himself to almost anything once he puts his mind to it. His ability to concentrate sometimes astounds others. He is diligent and does well when involved in detail work.

The Capricorn man or woman is charitable, generally speaking, and will do what is possible to help others less fortunate. As a friend, he is loyal and trustworthy. He never shirks his duties or responsibilities. He is self-reliant and never expects too much of the other fellow. He does what he can on his own. If someone does him a good turn, then he will do his best to return the favor.

The Negative Side of Capricorn

Like everyone, Capricorn, too, has faults. At times, the Goat can be overcritical of others. He expects others to live up to his own high standards. He thinks highly of himself and tends to look down on others.

His interest in material things may be exaggerated. The Capricorn man or woman thinks too much about getting on in the world and having something to show for it. He may even be a little greedy.

He sometimes thinks he knows what's best for everyone. He is too bossy. He is always trying to organize and correct others. He may be a little narrow in his thinking.

Aquarius: January 20–February 18

The Positive Side of Aquarius

The Aquarius man or woman is usually very honest and forthright. These are his two greatest qualities. His standards for himself are generally very high. He can always be relied upon by others. His word is his bond.

Aquarius is perhaps the most tolerant of all the Zodiac personalities. He respects other people's beliefs and feels that everyone is entitled to his own approach to life.

He would never do anything to injure another's feelings. He is never unkind or cruel. Always considerate of others, the Water

Bearer is always willing to help a person in need. He feels a very strong tie between himself and all the other members of mankind.

The person born under this sign, called the Water Bearer, is almost always an individualist. He does not believe in teaming up with the masses, but prefers going his own way. His ideas about life and mankind are often quite advanced. There is a saying to the effect that the average Aquarius is fifty years ahead of his time.

Aquarius is community-minded. The problems of the world concern him greatly. He is interested in helping others no matter what part of the globe they live in. He is truly a humanitarian sort. He likes to be of service to others.

Giving, considerate, and without prejudice, Aquarius have no trouble getting along with others.

The Negative Side of Aquarius

Aquarius may be too much of a dreamer. He makes plans but seldom carries them out. He is rather unrealistic. His imagination has a tendency to run away with him. Because many of his plans are impractical, he is always in some sort of a dither.

Others may not approve of him at all times because of his unconventional behavior. He may be a bit eccentric. Sometimes he is so busy with his own thoughts that he loses touch with the realities of existence.

Some Aquarius feel they are more clever and intelligent than others. They seldom admit to their own faults, even when they are quite apparent. Some become rather fanatic in their views. Their criticism of others is sometimes destructive and negative.

Pisces: February 19–March 20

The Positive Side of Pisces

Known as the sign of the Fishes, Pisces has a sympathetic nature. Kindly, he is often dedicated in the way he goes about helping others. The sick and the troubled often turn to him for advice and assistance. Possessing keen intuition, Pisces can easily understand people's deepest problems.

He is very broad-minded and does not criticize others for their faults. He knows how to accept people for what they are. On the whole, he is a trustworthy and earnest person. He is loyal to his friends and will do what he can to help them in time of need. Generous and good-natured, he is a lover of peace; he is often willing to help others solve their differences. People who have taken a wrong turn in life often interest him and he will do what he can to persuade them to rehabilitate themselves.

He has a strong intuitive sense and most of the time he knows how to make it work for him. Pisces is unusually perceptive and often knows what is bothering someone before that person, himself, is aware of it. The Pisces man or woman is an idealistic person, basically, and is interested in making the world a better place in which to live. Pisces believes that everyone should help each other. He is willing to do more than his share in order to achieve cooperation with others.

The person born under this sign often is talented in music or art. He is a receptive person; he is able to take the ups and downs of life with philosophic calm.

The Negative Side of Pisces

Some Pisces are often depressed; their outlook on life is rather glum. They may feel that they have been given a bad deal in life and that others are always taking unfair advantage of them. Pisces sometimes feel that the world is a cold and cruel place. The Fishes can be easily discouraged. The Pisces man or woman may even withdraw from the harshness of reality into a secret shell of his own where he dreams and idles away a good deal of his time.

Pisces can be lazy. He lets things happen without giving the least bit of resistance. He drifts along, whether on the high road or on the low. He can be lacking in willpower.

Some Pisces people seek escape through drugs or alcohol. When temptation comes along they find it hard to resist. In matters of sex, they can be rather permissive.

Sun Sign Personalities

ARIES: Hans Christian Andersen, Pearl Bailey, Marlon Brando, Wernher Von Braun, Charlie Chaplin, Joan Crawford, Da Vinci, Bette Davis, Doris Day, W.C. Fields, Alec Guinness, Adolf Hitler, William Holden, Thomas Jefferson, Nikita Khrushchev, Elton John, Arturo Toscanini, J.P. Morgan, Paul Robeson, Gloria Steinem, Sarah Vaughn, Vincent van Gogh, Tennessee Williams

TAURUS: Fred Astaire, Charlotte Brontë, Carol Burnett, Irving Berlin, Bing Crosby, Salvador Dali, Tchaikovsky, Queen Elizabeth II, Duke Ellington, Ella Fitzgerald, Henry Fonda, Sigmund Freud, Orson Welles, Joe Louis, Lenin, Karl Marx, Golda Meir, Eva Peron, Bertrand Russell, Shakespeare, Kate Smith, Benjamin Spock, Barbra Streisand, Shirley Temple, Harry Truman

GEMINI: Ruth Benedict, Josephine Baker, Rachel Carson, Carlos Chavez, Walt Whitman, Bob Dylan, Ralph Waldo Emerson, Judy Garland, Paul Gauguin, Allen Ginsberg, Benny Goodman, Bob Hope, Burl Ives, John F. Kennedy, Peggy Lee, Marilyn Monroe, Joe Namath, Cole Porter, Laurence Olivier, Harriet Beecher Stowe, Queen Victoria, John Wayne, Frank Lloyd Wright

CANCER: "Dear Abby," Lizzie Borden, David Brinkley, Yul Brynner, Pearl Buck, Marc Chagall, Princess Diana, Babe Didrikson, Mary Baker Eddy, Henry VIII, John Glenn, Ernest Hemingway, Lena Horne, Oscar Hammerstein, Helen Keller, Ann Landers, George Orwell, Nancy Reagan, Rembrandt, Richard Rodgers, Ginger Rogers, Rubens, Jean-Paul Sartre, O.J. Simpson

LEO: Neil Armstrong, James Baldwin, Lucille Ball, Emily Brontë, Wilt Chamberlain, Julia Child, William J. Clinton, Cecil B. De Mille, Ogden Nash, Amelia Earhart, Edna Ferber, Arthur Goldberg, Alfred Hitchcock, Mick Jagger, George Meany, Annie Oakley, George Bernard Shaw, Napoleon, Jacqueline Onassis, Henry Ford, Francis Scott Key, Andy Warhol, Mae West, Orville Wright

VIRGO: Ingrid Bergman, Warren Burger, Maurice Chevalier, Agatha Christie, Sean Connery, Lafayette, Peter Falk, Greta Garbo, Althea Gibson, Arthur Godfrey, Goethe, Buddy Hackett, Michael Jackson, Lyndon Johnson, D.H. Lawrence, Sophia Loren, Grandma Moses, Arnold Palmer, Queen Elizabeth I, Walter Reuther, Peter Sellers, Lily Tomlin, George Wallace

LIBRA: Brigitte Bardot, Art Buchwald, Truman Capote, Dwight D. Eisenhower, William Faulkner, F. Scott Fitzgerald, Gandhi, George Gershwin, Micky Mantle, Helen Hayes, Vladimir Horowitz, Doris Lessing, Martina Navratalova, Eugene O'Neill, Luciano Pavarotti, Emily Post, Eleanor Roosevelt, Bruce Springsteen, Margaret Thatcher, Gore Vidal, Barbara Walters, Oscar Wilde

SCORPIO: Vivien Leigh, Richard Burton, Art Carney, Johnny Carson, Billy Graham, Grace Kelly, Walter Cronkite, Marie Curie, Charles de Gaulle, Linda Evans, Indira Gandhi, Theodore Roosevelt, Rock Hudson, Katherine Hepburn, Robert F. Kennedy, Billie Jean King, Martin Luther, Georgia O'Keeffe, Pablo Picasso, Jonas Salk, Alan Shepard, Robert Louis Stevenson

SAGITTARIUS: Jane Austen, Louisa May Alcott, Woody Allen, Beethoven, Willy Brandt, Mary Martin, William F. Buckley, Maria Callas, Winston Churchill, Noel Coward, Emily Dickinson, Walt Disney, Benjamin Disraeli, James Doolittle, Kirk Douglas, Chet Huntley, Jane Fonda, Chris Evert Lloyd, Margaret Mead, Charles Schulz, John Milton, Frank Sinatra, Steven Spielberg

CAPRICORN: Muhammad Ali, Isaac Asimov, Pablo Casals, Dizzy Dean, Marlene Dietrich, James Farmer, Ava Gardner, Barry Goldwater, Cary Grant, J. Edgar Hoover, Howard Hughes, Joan of Arc, Gypsy Rose Lee, Martin Luther King, Jr., Rudyard Kipling, Mao Tse-tung, Richard Nixon, Gamal Nasser, Louis Pasteur, Albert Schweitzer, Stalin, Benjamin Franklin, Elvis Presley

AQUARIUS: Marian Anderson, Susan B. Anthony, Jack Benny, John Barrymore, Mikhail Baryshnikov, Charles Darwin, Charles Dickens, Thomas Edison, Clark Gable, Jascha Heifetz, Abraham Lincoln, Yehudi Menuhin, Mozart, Jack Nicklaus, Ronald Reagan, Jackie Robinson, Norman Rockwell, Franklin D. Roosevelt, Gertrude Stein, Charles Lindbergh, Margaret Truman

PISCES: Edward Albee, Harry Belafonte, Alexander Graham Bell, Chopin, Adelle Davis, Albert Einstein, Golda Meir, Jackie Gleason, Winslow Homer, Edward M. Kennedy, Victor Hugo, Mike Mansfield, Michelangelo, Edna St. Vincent Millay, Liza Minelli, John Steinbeck, Linus Pauling, Ravel, Renoir, Diana Ross, William Shirer, Elizabeth Taylor, George Washington

The Signs and Their Key Words

		POSITIVE	NEGATIVE
ARIES	self	courage, initiative, pioneer instinct	brash rudeness, selfish impetuosity
TAURUS	money	endurance, loyalty, wealth	obstinacy, gluttony
GEMINI	mind	versatility	capriciousness, unreliability
CANCER	family	sympathy, homing instinct	clannishness, childishness
LEO	children	love, authority, integrity	egotism, force
VIRGO	work	purity, industry, analysis	faultfinding, cynicism
LIBRA	marriage	harmony, justice	vacillation, superficiality
SCORPIO	sex	survival, regeneration	vengeance, discord
SAGITTARIUS	travel	optimism, higher learning	lawlessness
CAPRICORN	career	depth	narrowness, gloom
AQUARIUS	friends	human fellowship, genius	perverse unpredictability
PISCES	confinement	spiritual love, universality	diffusion, escapism

The Elements and Qualities of The Signs

Every sign has both an *element* and a *quality* associated with it. The element indicates the basic makeup of the sign, and the quality describes the kind of activity associated with each.

Element	Sign	Quality	Sign
FIRE	ARIES LEO SAGITTARIUS	CARDINAL	ARIES LIBRA CANCER CAPRICORN
EARTH	TAURUS VIRGO CAPRICORN	FIXED	TAURUS LEO SCORPIO AQUARIUS
AIR	GEMINI LIBRA AQUARIUS	MUTABLE	GEMINI VIRGO SAGITTARIUS PISCES
WATER	CANCER SCORPIO PISCES		

Signs can be grouped together according to their element and quality. Signs of the same element share many basic traits in common. They tend to form stable configurations and ultimately harmonious relationships. Signs of the same quality are often less harmonious, but they share many dynamic potentials for growth as well as profound fulfillment.

Further discussion of each of these sign groupings is provided on the following pages.

The Fire Signs

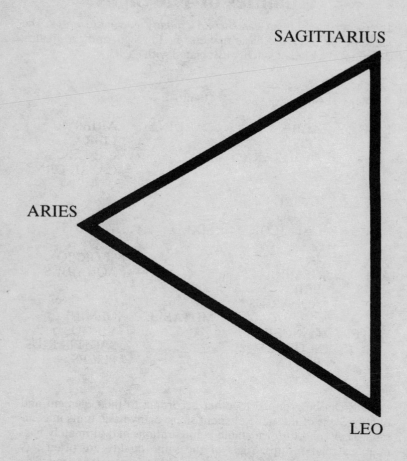

SAGITTARIUS

ARIES

LEO

This is the fire group. On the whole these are emotional, volatile types, quick to anger, quick to forgive. They are adventurous, powerful people and act as a source of inspiration for everyone. They spark into action with immediate exuberant impulses. They are intelligent, self-involved, creative, and idealistic. They all share a certain vibrancy and glow that outwardly reflects an inner flame and passion for living.

The Earth Signs

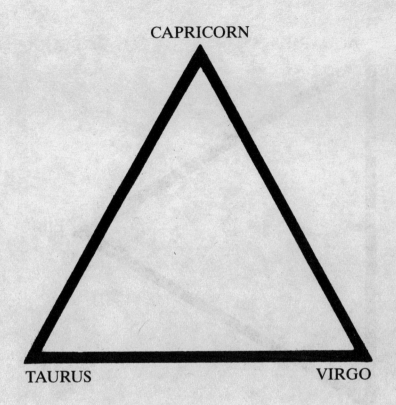

CAPRICORN

TAURUS   **VIRGO**

This is the earth group. They are in constant touch with the material world and tend to be conservative. Although they are all capable of spartan self-discipline, they are earthy, sensual people who are stimulated by the tangible, elegant, and luxurious. The thread of their lives is always practical, but they do fantasize and are often attracted to dark, mysterious, emotional people. They are like great cliffs overhanging the sea, forever married to the ocean but always resisting erosion from the dark, emotional forces that thunder at their feet.

The Air Signs

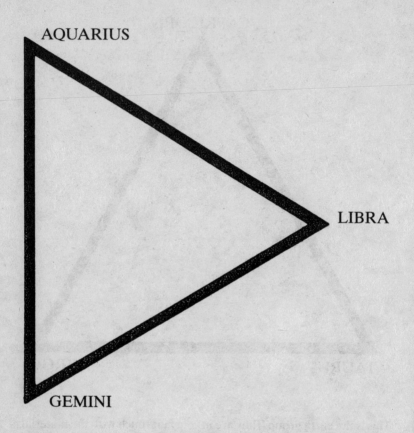

AQUARIUS

LIBRA

GEMINI

This is the air group. They are light, mental creatures desirous of contact, communication, and relationship. They are involved with people and the forming of ties on many levels. Original thinkers, they are the bearers of human news. Their language is their sense of word, color, style, and beauty. They provide an atmosphere suitable and pleasant for living. They add change and versatility to the scene, and it is through them that we can explore new territory of human intelligence and experience.

The Water Signs

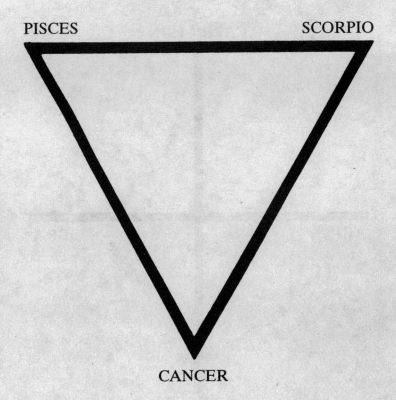

PISCES   SCORPIO

CANCER

This is the water group. Through the water people, we are all joined together on emotional, nonverbal levels. They are silent, mysterious types whose magic hypnotizes even the most determined realist. They have uncanny perceptions about people and are as rich as the oceans when it comes to feeling, emotion, or imagination. They are sensitive, mystical creatures with memories that go back beyond time. Through water, life is sustained. These people have the potential for the depths of darkness or the heights of mysticism and art.

The Cardinal Signs

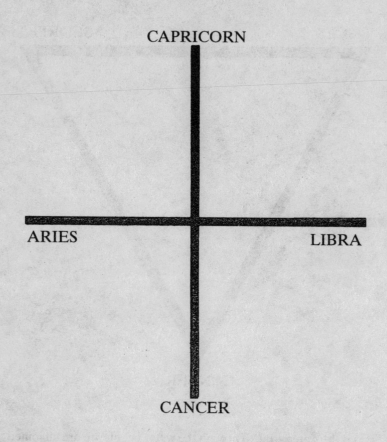

CAPRICORN

ARIES

LIBRA

CANCER

Put together, this is a clear-cut picture of dynamism, activity, tremendous stress, and remarkable achievement. These people know the meaning of great change since their lives are often characterized by significant crises and major successes. This combination is like a simultaneous storm of summer, fall, winter, and spring. The danger is chaotic diffusion of energy; the potential is irrepressible growth and victory.

The Fixed Signs

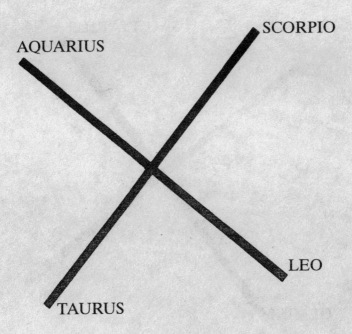

Fixed signs are always establishing themselves in a given place or area of experience. Like explorers who arrive and plant a flag, these people claim a position from which they do not enjoy being deposed. They are staunch, stalwart, upright, trusty, honorable people, although their obstinacy is well-known. Their contribution is fixity, and they are the angels who support our visible world.

The Mutable Signs

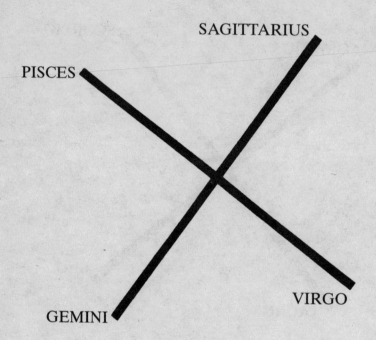

Mutable people are versatile, sensitive, intelligent, nervous, and deeply curious about life. They are the translators of all energy. They often carry out or complete tasks initiated by others. Combinations of these signs have highly developed minds; they are imaginative and jumpy and think and talk a lot. At worst their lives are a Tower of Babel. At best they are adaptable and ready creatures who can assimilate one kind of experience and enjoy it while anticipating coming changes.

THE PLANETS
OF THE SOLAR SYSTEM

This section describes the planets of the solar system. In astrology, both the Sun and the Moon are considered to be planets. Because of the Moon's influence in our day-to-day lives, the Moon is described in a separate section following this one.

The Planets and the Signs They Rule

The signs of the Zodiac are linked to the planets in the following way. Each sign is governed or ruled by one or more planets. No matter where the planets are located in the sky at any given moment, they still rule their respective signs, and when they travel through the signs they rule, they have special dignity and their effects are stronger.

Following is a list of the planets and the signs they rule. After looking at the list, read the definitions of the planets and see if you can determine how the planet ruling *your* Sun sign has affected your life.

SIGNS	RULING PLANETS
Aries	Mars, Pluto
Taurus	Venus
Gemini	Mercury
Cancer	Moon
Leo	Sun
Virgo	Mercury
Libra	Venus
Scorpio	Mars, Pluto
Sagittarius	Jupiter
Capricorn	Saturn
Aquarius	Saturn, Uranus
Pisces	Jupiter, Neptune

Characteristics of the Planets

The following pages give the meaning and characteristics of the planets of the solar system. They all travel around the Sun at different speeds and different distances. Taken with the Sun, they all distribute individual intelligence and ability throughout the entire chart.

The planets modify the influence of the Sun in a chart according to their own particular natures, strengths, and positions. Their positions must be calculated for each year and day, and their function and expression in a horoscope will change as they move from one area of the Zodiac to another.

We start with a description of the sun.

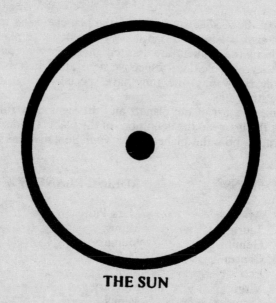

THE SUN

SUN

This is the center of existence. Around this flaming sphere all the planets revolve in endless orbits. Our star is constantly sending out its beams of light and energy without which no life on Earth would be possible. In astrology it symbolizes everything we are trying to become, the center around which all of our activity in life will always revolve. It is the symbol of our basic nature and describes the natural and constant thread that runs through everything that we do from birth to death on this planet.

To early astrologers, the Sun seemed to be another planet because it crossed the heavens every day, just like the rest of the bodies in the sky.

It is the only star near enough to be seen well—it is, in fact, a dwarf star. Approximately 860,000 miles in diameter, it is about ten times as wide as the giant planet Jupiter. The next nearest star is nearly 300,000 times as far away, and if the Sun were located as far away as most of the bright stars, it would be too faint to be seen without a telescope.

Everything in the horoscope ultimately revolves around this singular body. Although other forces may be prominent in the charts of some individuals, still the Sun is the total nucleus of being and symbolizes the complete potential of every human being alive. It is vitality and the life force. Your whole essence comes from the position of the Sun.

You are always trying to express the Sun according to its position by house and sign. Possibility for all development is found in the Sun, and it marks the fundamental character of your personal radiations all around you.

It is the symbol of strength, vigor, wisdom, dignity, ardor, and generosity, and the ability for a person to function as a mature individual. It is also a creative force in society. It is consciousness of the gift of life.

The underdeveloped solar nature is arrogant, pushy, undependable, and proud, and is constantly using force.

MERCURY

Mercury is the planet closest to the Sun. It races around our star, gathering information and translating it to the rest of the system. Mercury represents your capacity to understand the desires of your own will and to translate those desires into action.

In other words it is the planet of mind and the power of communication. Through Mercury we develop an ability to think, write, speak, and observe—to become aware of the world around us. It colors our attitudes and vision of the world, as well as our capacity to communicate our inner responses to the outside world. Some people who have serious disabilities in their power of verbal communication have often wrongly been described as people lacking intelligence.

Although this planet (and its position in the horoscope) indicates your power to communicate your thoughts and perceptions to the world, intelligence is something deeper. Intelligence is distributed throughout all the planets. It is the relationship of the planets to each other that truly describes what we call intelligence. Mercury rules speaking, language, mathematics, draft and design, students, messengers, young people, offices, teachers, and any pursuits where the mind of man has wings.

VENUS

Venus is beauty. It symbolizes the harmony and radiance of a rare and elusive quality: beauty itself. It is refinement and delicacy, softness and charm. In astrology it indicates grace, balance, and the aesthetic sense. Where Venus is we see beauty, a gentle drawing in of energy and the need for satisfaction and completion. It is a special touch that finishes off rough edges. It is sensitivity, and affection, and it is always the place for that other elusive phenomenon: love. Venus describes our sense of what is beautiful and loving. Poorly developed, it is vulgar, tasteless, and self-indulgent. But its ideal is the flame of spiritual love—Aphrodite, goddess of love, and the sweetness and power of personal beauty.

MARS

Mars is raw, crude energy. The planet next to Earth but outward from the Sun is a fiery red sphere that charges through the horoscope with force and fury. It represents the way you reach out for new adventure and new experience. It is energy and drive, initiative, courage, and daring. It is the power to start something and see it through. It can be thoughtless, cruel and wild, angry and hostile, causing cuts, burns, scalds, and wounds. It can stab its way through a chart, or it can be the symbol of healthy spirited adventure, well-channeled constructive power to begin and keep up the drive. If you have trouble starting things, if you lack the get-up-and-go to start the ball rolling, if you lack aggressiveness and self-confidence, chances are there's another planet influencing your Mars. Mars rules soldiers, butchers, surgeons, salesmen—any field that requires daring, bold skill, operational technique, or self-promotion.

JUPITER

This is the largest planet of the solar system. Scientists have recently learned that Jupiter reflects more light than it receives from the Sun. In a sense it is like a star itself. In astrology it rules good luck and good cheer, health, wealth, optimism, happiness, success, and joy. It is the symbol of opportunity and always opens the way for new possibilities in your life. It rules exuberance, enthusiasm, wisdom, knowledge, generosity, and all forms of expansion in general. It rules actors, statesmen, clerics, professional people, religion, publishing, and the distribution of many people over large areas.

Sometimes Jupiter makes you think you deserve everything, and you become sloppy, wasteful, careless and rude, prodigal and lawless, in the illusion that nothing can ever go wrong. Then there is the danger of overconfidence, exaggeration, undependability, and overindulgence.

Jupiter is the minimization of limitation and the emphasis on spirituality and potential. It is the thirst for knowledge and higher learning.

SATURN

Saturn circles our system in dark splendor with its mysterious rings, forcing us to be awakened to whatever we have neglected in the past. It will present real puzzles and problems to be solved, causing delays, obstacles, and hindrances. By doing so, Saturn stirs our own sensitivity to those areas where we are laziest.

Here we must patiently develop *method*, and only through painstaking effort can our ends be achieved. It brings order to a horoscope and imposes reason just where we are feeling least reasonable. By creating limitations and boundary, Saturn shows the consequences of being human and demands that we accept the changing cycles inevitable in human life. Saturn rules time, old age, and sobriety. It can bring depression, gloom, jealousy, and greed, or serious acceptance of responsibilities out of which success will develop. With Saturn there is nothing to do but face facts. It rules laborers, stones, granite, rocks, and crystals of all kinds.

THE OUTER PLANETS:
URANUS, NEPTUNE, PLUTO

Uranus, Neptune, Pluto are the outer planets. They liberate human beings from cultural conditioning, and in that sense are the law-breakers. In early times it was thought that Saturn was the last planet of the system—the outer limit beyond which we could never go. The discovery of the next three planets ushered in new phases of human history, revolution, and technology.

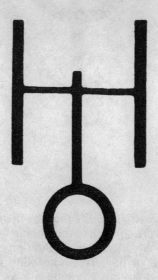

URANUS

Uranus rules unexpected change, upheaval, revolution. It is the symbol of total independence and asserts the freedom of an individual from all restriction and restraint. It is a breakthrough planet and indicates talent, originality, and genius in a horoscope. It usually causes last-minute reversals and changes of plan, unwanted separations, accidents, catastrophes, and eccentric behavior. It can add irrational rebelliousness and perverse bohemianism to a personality or a streak of unaffected brilliance in science and art. It rules technology, aviation, and all forms of electrical and electronic advancement. It governs great leaps forward and topsy-turvy situations, and *always* turns things around at the last minute. Its effects are difficult to predict, since it rules sudden last-minute decisions and events that come like lightning out of the blue.

NEPTUNE

Neptune dissolves existing reality the way the sea erodes the cliffs beside it. Its effects are subtle like the ringing of a buoy's bell in the fog. It suggests a reality higher than definition can usually describe. It awakens a sense of higher responsibility often causing guilt, worry, anxieties, or delusions. Neptune is associated with all forms of escape and can make things seem a certain way so convincingly that you are absolutely sure of something that eventually turns out to be quite different.

It is the planet of illusion and therefore governs the invisible realms that lie beyond our ordinary minds, beyond our simple factual ability to prove what is "real." Treachery, deceit, disillusionment, and disappointment are linked to Neptune. It describes a vague reality that promises eternity and the divine, yet in a manner so complex that we cannot really fathom it at all. At its worst Neptune is a cheap intoxicant; at its best it is the poetry, music, and inspiration of the higher planes of spiritual love. It has dominion over movies, photographs, and much of the arts.

PLUTO

Pluto lies at the outpost of our system and therefore rules finality in a horoscope—the final closing of chapters in your life, the passing of major milestones and points of development from which there is no return. It is a final wipeout, a closeout, an evacuation. It is a distant, subtle but powerful catalyst in all transformations that occur. It creates, destroys, then recreates. Sometimes Pluto starts its influence with a minor event or insignificant incident that might even go unnoticed. Slowly but surely, little by little, everything changes, until at last there has been a total transformation in the area of your life where Pluto has been operating. It rules mass thinking and the trends that society first rejects, then adopts, and finally outgrows.

Pluto rules the dead and the underworld—all the powerful forces of creation and destruction that go on all the time beneath, around, and above us. It can bring a lust for power with strong obsessions.

It is the planet that rules the metamorphosis of the caterpillar into a butterfly, for it symbolizes the capacity to change totally and forever a person's lifestyle, way of thought, and behavior.

THE MOON IN EACH SIGN

The Moon is the nearest planet to the Earth. It exerts more observable influence on us from day to day than any other planet. The effect is very personal, very intimate, and if we are not aware of how it works it can make us quite unstable in our ideas. And the annoying thing is that at these times we often see our own instability but can do nothing about it. A knowledge of what can be expected may help considerably. We can then be prepared to stand strong against the Moon's negative influences and use its positive ones to help us to get ahead. Who has not heard of going with the tide?

The Moon reflects, has no light of its own. It reflects the Sun—the life giver—in the form of vital movement. The Moon controls the tides, the blood rhythm, the movement of sap in trees and plants. Its nature is inconstancy and change so it signifies our moods, our superficial behavior—walking, talking, and especially thinking. Being a true reflector of other forces, the Moon is cold, watery like the surface of a still lake, brilliant and scintillating at times, but easily ruffled and disturbed by the winds of change.

The Moon takes about 27⅓ days to make a complete transit of the Zodiac. It spends just over 2¼ days in each sign. During that time it reflects the qualities, energies, and characteristics of the sign and, to a degree, the planet which rules the sign. When the Moon in its transit occupies a sign incompatible with our own birth sign, we can expect to feel a vague uneasiness, perhaps a touch of irritableness. We should not be discouraged nor let the feeling get us down, or, worse still, allow ourselves to take the discomfort out on others. Try to remember that the Moon has to change signs within 55 hours and, provided you are not physically ill, your mood will probably change with it. It is amazing how frequently depression lifts with the shift in the Moon's position. And, of course, when the Moon is transiting a sign compatible or sympathetic to yours, you will probably feel some sort of stimulation or just be plain happy to be alive.

In the horoscope, the Moon is such a powerful indicator that competent astrologers often use the sign it occupied at birth as the birth sign of the person. This is done particularly when the Sun is on the cusp, or edge, of two signs. Most experienced astrologers, however, coordinate both Sun and Moon signs by reading and confirming from one to the other and secure a far more accurate and personalized analysis.

For these reasons, the Moon tables which follow this section (see pages 86–92) are of great importance to the individual. They show the days and the exact times the Moon will enter each sign of the Zodiac for the year. Remember, you have to adjust the indicated times to local time. The corrections, already calculated for most of the main cities, are at the beginning of the tables. What follows now is a guide to the influences that will be reflected to the Earth by the Moon while it transits each of the twelve signs. The influence is at its peak about 26 hours after the Moon enters a sign. As you read the daily forecast, check the Moon sign for any given day and glance back at this guide.

MOON IN ARIES
This is a time for action, for reaching out beyond the usual self-imposed limitations and faint-hearted cautions. If you have plans in your head or on your desk, put them into practice. New ventures, applications, new jobs, new starts of any kind—all have a good chance of success. This is the period when original and dynamic impulses are being reflected onto Earth. Such energies are extremely vital and favor the pursuit of pleasure and adventure in practically every form. Sick people should feel an improvement. Those who are well will probably find themselves exuding confidence and optimism. People fond of physical exercise should find their bodies growing with tone and well-being. Boldness, strength, determination should characterize most of your activities with a readiness to face up to old challenges. Yesterday's problems may seem petty and exaggerated—so deal with them. Strike out alone. Self-reliance will attract others to you. This is a good time for making friends. Business and marriage partners are more likely to be impressed with the man and woman of action. Opposition will be overcome or thrown aside with much less effort than usual. CAUTION: Be dominant but not domineering.

MOON IN TAURUS
The spontaneous, action-packed person of yesterday gives way to the cautious, diligent, hardworking "thinker." In this period ideas will probably be concentrated on ways of improving finances. A great deal of time may be spent figuring out and going over

schemes and plans. It is the right time to be careful with detail. People will find themselves working longer than usual at their desks. Or devoting more time to serious thought about the future. A strong desire to put order into business and financial arrangements may cause extra work. Loved ones may complain of being neglected and may fail to appreciate that your efforts are for their ultimate benefit. Your desire for system may extend to criticism of arrangements in the home and lead to minor upsets. Health may be affected through overwork. Try to secure a reasonable amount of rest and relaxation, although the tendency will be to "keep going" despite good advice. Work done conscientiously in this period should result in a solid contribution to your future security. CAUTION: Try not to be as serious with people as the work you are engaged in.

MOON IN GEMINI

The humdrum of routine and too much work should suddenly end. You are likely to find yourself in an expansive, quicksilver world of change and self-expression. Urges to write, to paint, to experience the freedom of some sort of artistic outpouring, may be very strong. Take full advantage of them. You may find yourself finishing something you began and put aside long ago. Or embarking on something new which could easily be prompted by a chance meeting, a new acquaintance, or even an advertisement. There may be a yearning for a change of scenery, the feeling to visit another country (not too far away), or at least to get away for a few days. This may result in short, quick journeys. Or, if you are planning a single visit, there may be some unexpected changes or detours on the way. Familiar activities will seem to give little satisfaction unless they contain a fresh element of excitement or expectation. The inclination will be toward untried pursuits, particularly those that allow you to express your inner nature. The accent is on new faces, new places. CAUTION: Do not be too quick to commit yourself emotionally.

MOON IN CANCER

Feelings of uncertainty and vague insecurity are likely to cause problems while the Moon is in Cancer. Thoughts may turn frequently to the warmth of the home and the comfort of loved ones. Nostalgic impulses could cause you to bring out old photographs and letters and reflect on the days when your life seemed to be much more rewarding and less demanding. The love and understanding of parents and family may be important, and, if it is not forthcoming, you may have to fight against bouts of self-pity. The cordiality of friends and the thought of good times with them that are sure to be repeated will help to restore you to a happier frame of mind. The desire to be alone may follow minor setbacks or rebuffs at this time, but solitude is unlikely to help. Better to get on the telephone or visit someone. This period often causes peculiar dreams and upsurges of imaginative thinking which can be helpful to authors of occult and mystical works. Preoccupation with the personal world of simple human needs can overshadow any material strivings. CAUTION: Do not spend too much time thinking—seek the company of loved ones or close friends.

MOON IN LEO
New horizons of exciting and rather extravagant activity open up. This is the time for exhilarating entertainment, glamorous and lavish parties, and expensive shopping sprees. Any merrymaking that relies upon your generosity as a host has every chance of being a spectacular success. You should find yourself right in the center of the fun, either as the life of the party or simply as a person whom happy people like to be with. Romance thrives in this heady atmosphere and friendships are likely to explode unexpectedly into serious attachments. Children and younger people should be attracted to you and you may find yourself organizing a picnic or a visit to a fun-fair, the movies, or the beach. The sunny company and vitality of youthful companions should help you to find some unsuspected energy. In career, you could find an opening for promotion or advancement. This should be the time to make a direct approach. The period favors those engaged in original research. CAUTION: Bask in popularity, not in flattery.

MOON IN VIRGO
Off comes the party cap and out steps the busy, practical worker. He wants to get his personal affairs straight, to rearrange them, if necessary, for more efficiency, so he will have more time for more work. He clears up his correspondence, pays outstanding bills, makes numerous phone calls. He is likely to make inquiries, or sign up for some new insurance and put money into gilt-edged investment. Thoughts probably revolve around the need for future security—to tie up loose ends and clear the decks. There may be a tendency to be "finicky," to interfere in the routine of others, particularly friends and family members. The motive may be a genuine desire to help with suggestions for updating or streamlining their affairs, but these will probably not be welcomed. Sympathy may be felt for less fortunate sections of the community and a flurry of some sort of voluntary service is likely. This may be accompanied by strong feelings of responsibility on several fronts and health may suffer from extra efforts made. CAUTION: Everyone may not want your help or advice.

MOON IN LIBRA

These are days of harmony and agreement and you should find yourself at peace with most others. Relationships tend to be smooth and sweet-flowing. Friends may become closer and bonds deepen in mutual understanding. Hopes will be shared. Progress by cooperation could be the secret of success in every sphere. In business, established partnerships may flourish and new ones get off to a good start. Acquaintances could discover similar interests that lead to congenial discussions and rewarding exchanges of some sort. Love, as a unifying force, reaches its optimum. Marriage partners should find accord. Those who wed at this time face the prospect of a happy union. Cooperation and tolerance are felt to be stronger than dissension and impatience. The argumentative are not quite so loud in their bellowings, nor as inflexible in their attitudes. In the home, there should be a greater recognition of the other point of view and a readiness to put the wishes of the group before selfish insistence. This is a favorable time to join an art group. CAUTION: Do not be too independent—let others help you if they want to.

MOON IN SCORPIO

Driving impulses to make money and to economize are likely to cause upsets all around. No area of expenditure is likely to be spared the ax, including the household budget. This is a time when the desire to cut down on extravagance can become near fanatical. Care must be exercised to try to keep the aim in reasonable perspective. Others may not feel the same urgent need to save and may retaliate. There is a danger that possessions of sentimental value will be sold to realize cash for investment. Buying and selling of stock for quick profit is also likely. The attention turns to organizing, reorganizing, tidying up at home and at work. Neglected jobs could suddenly be done with great bursts of energy. The desire for solitude may intervene. Self-searching thoughts could disturb. The sense of invisible and mysterious energies in play could cause some excitability. The reassurance of loves ones may help. CAUTION: Be kind to the people you love.

MOON IN SAGITTARIUS

These are days when you are likely to be stirred and elevated by discussions and reflections of a religious and philosophical nature. Ideas of faraway places may cause unusual response and excitement. A decision may be made to visit someone overseas, perhaps a person whose influence was important to your earlier character development. There could be a strong resolution to get away from present intellectual patterns, to learn new subjects, and to meet more interesting people. The superficial may be rejected in all its forms. An impatience with old ideas and unimaginative contacts could lead to a change of companions and interests. There may be an upsurge of religious feeling and metaphysical inquiry. Even a new insight into the significance of astrology and other occult studies is likely under the curious stimulus of the Moon in Sagittarius. Physically, you may express this need for fundamental change by spending more time outdoors: sports, gardening, long walks appeal. CAUTION: Try to channel any restlessness into worthwhile study.

MOON IN CAPRICORN
Life in these hours may seem to pivot around the importance of gaining prestige and honor in the career, as well as maintaining a spotless reputation. Ambitious urges may be excessive and could be accompanied by quite acquisitive drives for money. Effort should be directed along strictly ethical lines where there is no possibility of reproach or scandal. All endeavors are likely to be characterized by great earnestness, and an air of authority and purpose which should impress those who are looking for leadership or reliability. The desire to conform to accepted standards may extend to sharp criticism of family members. Frivolity and unconventional actions are unlikely to amuse while the Moon is in Capricorn. Moderation and seriousness are the orders of the day. Achievement and recognition in this period could come through community work or organizing for the benefit of some amateur group. CAUTION: Dignity and esteem are not always self-awarded.

MOON IN AQUARIUS
Moon in Aquarius is in the second last sign of the Zodiac where ideas can become disturbingly fine and subtle. The result is often a mental "no-man's land" where imagination cannot be trusted with the same certitude as other times. The dangers for the individual are the extremes of optimism and pessimism. Unless the imagination is held in check, situations are likely to be misread, and rosy conclusions drawn where they do not exist. Consequences for the unwary can be costly in career and business. Best to think twice and not speak or act until you think again. Pessimism can be a cruel self-inflicted penalty for delusion at this time. Between the two extremes are strange areas of self-deception which, for example, can make the selfish person think he is actually being generous. Eerie dreams which resemble the reality and even seem to continue into the waking state are also possible. CAUTION: Look for the fact and not just for the image in your mind.

MOON IN PISCES

Everything seems to come to the surface now. Memory may be crystal clear, throwing up long-forgotten information which could be valuable in the career or business. Flashes of clairvoyance and intuition are possible along with sudden realizations of one's own nature, which may be used for self-improvement. A talent, never before suspected, may be discovered. Qualities not evident before in friends and marriage partners are likely to be noticed. As this is a period in which the truth seems to emerge, the discovery of false characteristics is likely to lead to disenchantment or a shift in attachments. However, when qualities are accepted, it should lead to happiness and deeper feeling. Surprise solutions could bob up for old problems. There may be a public announcement of the solving of a crime or mystery. People with secrets may find someone has "guessed" correctly. The secrets of the soul or the inner self also tend to reveal themselves. Religious and philosophical groups may make some interesting discoveries. CAUTION: Not a time for activities that depend on secrecy.

NOTE: When you read your daily forecasts, use the Moon Sign Dates that are provided in the following section of Moon Tables. Then you may want to glance back here for the Moon's influence in a given sign.

MOON TABLES

CORRECTION FOR NEW YORK TIME, FIVE HOURS WEST OF GREENWICH

Atlanta, Boston, Detroit, Miami, Washington, Montreal,
Ottawa, Quebec, Bogota,
Havana, Lima, Santiago .... Same time
Chicago, New Orleans, Houston, Winnipeg, Churchill,
Mexico City .... Deduct 1 hour
Albuquerque, Denver, Phoenix, El Paso, Edmonton,
Helena .... Deduct 2 hours
Los Angeles, San Francisco, Reno, Portland,
Seattle, Vancouver .... Deduct 3 hours
Honolulu, Anchorage, Fairbanks, Kodiak .... Deduct 5 hours
Nome, Samoa, Tonga, Midway .... Deduct 6 hours
Halifax, Bermuda, San Juan, Caracas, La Paz,
Barbados .... Add 1 hour
St. John's, Brasilia, Rio de Janeiro, Sao Paulo,
Buenos Aires, Montevideo .... Add 2 hours
Azores, Cape Verde Islands .... Add 3 hours
Canary Islands, Madeira, Reykjavik .... Add 4 hours
London, Paris, Amsterdam, Madrid, Lisbon,
Gibraltar, Belfast, Raba .... Add 5 hours
Frankfurt, Rome, Oslo, Stockholm, Prague,
Belgrade .... Add 6 hours
Bucharest, Beirut, Tel Aviv, Athens, Istanbul, Cairo,
Alexandria, Cape Town, Johannesburg .... Add 7 hours
Moscow, Leningrad, Baghdad, Dhahran,
Addis Ababa, Nairobi, Teheran, Zanzibar .... Add 8 hours
Bombay, Calcutta, Sri Lanka .... Add 10½
Hong Kong, Shanghai, Manila, Peking, Perth ...... Add 13 hours
Tokyo, Okinawa, Darwin, Pusan .... Add 14 hours
Sydney, Melbourne, Port Moresby, Guam .... Add 15 hours
Auckland, Wellington, Suva, Wake .... Add 17 hours

2007 MOON SIGN DATES—
NEW YORK TIME

JANUARY Day Moon Enters		FEBRUARY Day Moon Enters		MARCH Day Moon Enters	
1. Gemini		1. Leo	12:16 am	1. Leo	
2. Cancer	10:15 am	2. Leo		2. Virgo	4:33 pm
3. Cancer		3. Virgo	9:35 am	3. Virgo	
4. Leo	5:15 pm	4. Virgo		4. Virgo	
5. Leo		5. Libra	9:16 pm	5. Libra	4:26 am
6. Leo		6. Libra		6. Libra	
7. Virgo	1:19 am	7. Libra		7. Scorp.	5:18 pm
8. Virgo		8. Scorp.	10:11 am	8. Scorp.	
9. Libra	1:16 pm	9. Scorp.		9. Scorp.	
10. Libra		10. Sagitt.	10:02 pm	10. Sagitt.	5:36 am
11. Libra		11. Sagitt.		11. Sagitt.	
12. Scorp.	2:09 am	12. Sagitt.		12. Capric.	3:36 pm
13. Scorp.		13. Capric.	6:43 am	13. Capric.	
14. Sagitt.	1:12 pm	14. Capric.		14. Aquar.	9:53 am
15. Sagitt.		15. Aquar.	11:36 am	15. Aquar.	
16. Capric.	8:50 pm	16. Aquar.		16. Aquar.	
17. Capric.		17. Pisces	1:31 pm	17. Pisces	12:31 am
18. Capric.		18. Pisces		18. Pisces	
19. Aquar.	1:17 am	19. Aries	2:07 pm	19. Aries	12:43 am
20. Aquar.		20. Aries		20. Aries	
21. Pisces	3:49 am	21. Taurus	3:04 pm	21. Taurus	12:16 am
22. Pisces		22. Taurus		22. Taurus	
23. Aries	5:53 am	23. Gemini	5:43 pm	23. Gemini	1:07 am
24. Aries		24. Gemini		24. Gemini	
25. Taurus	8:30 am	25. Cancer	10:49 pm	25. Cancer	4:50 am
26. Taurus		26. Cancer		26. Cancer	
27. Gemini	12:11 pm	27. Cancer		27. Leo	12:05 pm
28. Gemini		28. Leo	6:31 am	28. Leo	
29. Cancer	5:17 pm			29. Virgo	10:28 pm
30. Cancer				30. Virgo	
31. Cancer				31. Virgo	

Daylight saving time to be considered where applicable.

2007 MOON SIGN DATES— NEW YORK TIME

APRIL Day Moon Enters		MAY Day Moon Enters		JUNE Day Moon Enters	
1. Libra	10:44 am	1. Scorp.	5:42 am	1. Sagitt.	
2. Libra		2. Scorp.		2. Capric.	10:10 am
3. Scorp.	11:37 pm	3. Sagitt.	5:49 pm	3. Capric.	
4. Scorp.		4. Sagitt.		4. Aquar.	6:16 pm
5. Scorp.		5. Sagitt.		5. Aquar.	
6. Sagitt.	11:58 am	6. Capric.	4:22 am	6. Aquar.	
7. Sagitt.		7. Capric.		7. Pisces	12:25 am
8. Capric.	10:37 pm	8. Aquar.	12:49 pm	8. Pisces	
9. Capric.		9. Aquar.		9. Aries	4:27 am
10. Capric.		10. Pisces	6:33 pm	10. Aries	
11. Aquar.	6:24 am	11. Pisces		11. Taurus	6:30 am
12. Aquar.		12. Aries	9:20 pm	12. Taurus	
13. Pisces	10:40 am	13. Aries		13. Gemini	7:25 am
14. Pisces		14. Taurus	9:49 pm	14. Gemini	
15. Aries	11:48 am	15. Taurus		15. Cancer	8:46 am
16. Aries		16. Gemini	9:35 pm	16. Cancer	
17. Taurus	11:12 am	17. Gemini		17. Leo	12:26 pm
18. Taurus		18. Cancer	10:39 pm	18. Leo	
19. Gemini	10:52 am	19. Cancer		19. Virgo	7:47 pm
20. Gemini		20. Cancer		20. Virgo	
21. Cancer	12:51 pm	21. Leo	2:58 am	21. Virgo	
22. Cancer		22. Leo		22. Libra	5:45 am
23. Leo	6:39 pm	23. Virgo	11:27 am	23. Libra	
24. Leo		24. Virgo		24. Scorp.	7:26 pm
25. Leo		25. Libra	11:17 pm	25. Scorp.	
26. Virgo	4:25 am	26. Libra		26. Scorp.	
27. Virgo		27. Libra		27. Sagitt.	7:25 am
28. Libra	4:46 pm	28. Scorp.	12:12 pm	28. Sagitt.	
29. Libra		29. Scorp.		29. Capric.	5:06 pm
30. Libra		30. Scorp.		30. Capric.	
		31. Sagitt.	12:06 am		

Daylight saving time to be considered where applicable.

2007 MOON SIGN DATES—
NEW YORK TIME

JULY Day Moon Enters		AUGUST Day Moon Enters		SEPTEMBER Day Moon Enters	
1. Capric.		1. Pisces		1. Taurus	12:36 am
2. Aquar.	12:25 am	2. Aries	3:44 pm	2. Taurus	
3. Aquar.		3. Aries		3. Gemini	2:31 am
4. Pisces	5:53 am	4. Taurus	6:17 pm	4. Gemini	
5. Pisces		5. Taurus		5. Cancer	6:09 am
6. Aries	9:58 am	6. Gemini	9:02 pm	6. Cancer	
7. Aries		7. Gemini		7. Leo	12:00 pm
8. Taurus	12:55 pm	8. Gemini		8. Leo	
9. Taurus		9. Cancer	12:37 am	9. Virgo	8:11 pm
10. Gemini	3:11 pm	10. Cancer		10. Virgo	
11. Gemini		11. Leo	5:43 am	11. Virgo	
12. Cancer	5:40 pm	12. Leo		12. Libra	6:32 am
13. Cancer		13. Virgo	1:04 pm	13. Libra	
14. Leo	9:44 pm	14. Virgo		14. Scorp.	6:38 pm
15. Leo		15. Libra	11:05 pm	15. Scorp.	
16. Leo		16. Libra		16. Scorp.	
17. Virgo	4:40 am	17. Libra		17. Sagitt.	7:22 am
18. Virgo		18. Scorp.	11:14 am	18. Sagitt.	
19. Libra	2:54 pm	19. Scorp.		19. Capric.	6:53 pm
20. Libra		20. Sagitt.	11:45 pm	20. Capric.	
21. Libra		21. Sagitt.		21. Capric.	
22. Scorp.	3:19 am	22. Sagitt.		22. Aquar.	3:19 am
23. Scorp.		23. Carpic.	10:21 am	23. Aquar.	
24. Sagitt.	3:31 pm	24. Capric.		24. Pisces	7:56 am
25. Sagitt.		25. Aquar.	5:36 pm	25. Pisces	
26. Sagitt.		26. Aquar.		26. Aries	9:24 am
27. Capric.	1:22 am	27. Pisces	9:35 pm	27. Aries	
28. Capric.		28. Pisces		28. Taurus	9:18 am
29. Aquar.	8:15 am	29. Aries	11:26 pm	29. Taurus	
30. Aquar.		30. Aries		30. Gemini	9:35 am
31. Pisces	12:42 pm	31. Aries			

Daylight saving time to be considered where applicable.

2007 MOON SIGN DATES
NEW YORK TIME

OCTOBER Day Moon Enters		NOVEMBER Day Moon Enters		DECEMBER Day Moon Enters	
1. Gemini		1. Leo		1. Virgo	
2. Cancer	11:58 am	2. Leo		2. Virgo	
3. Cancer		3. Virgo	7:46 am	3. Libra	1:02 am
4. Leo	5:26 pm	4. Virgo		4. Libra	
5. Leo		5. Libra	6:48 pm	5. Scorp.	1:32 pm
6. Leo		6. Libra		6. Scorp.	
7. Virgo	2:04 am	7. Libra		7. Scorp.	
8. Virgo		8. Scorp.	7:19 am	8. Sagitt.	2:12 am
9. Libra	12:59 pm	9. Scorp.		9. Sagitt.	
10. Libra		10. Sagitt.	8:00 pm	10. Capric.	1:52 pm
11. Libra		11. Sagitt.		11. Capric.	
12. Scorp.	1:14 am	12. Sagitt.		12. Capric.	
13. Scorp.		13. Capric.	8:02 am	13. Aquar.	12:02 am
14. Sagitt.	1:59 pm	14. Capric.		14. Aquar.	
15. Sagitt.		15. Aquar.	6:31 pm	15. Pisces	8:16 am
16. Sagitt.		16. Aqaur.		16. Pisces	
17. Capric.	2:04 am	17. Aquar.		17. Aries	1:54 pm
18. Capric.		18. Pisces	2:16 am	18. Aries	
19. Aquar.	11:52 am	19. Pisces		19. Taurus	4:39 pm
20. Aquar.		20. Aries	6:25 am	20. Taurus	
21. Pisces	6:03 pm	21. Aries		21. Gemini	5:15 pm
22. Pisces		22. Taurus	7:20 am	22. Gemini	
23. Aries	8:25 pm	23. Taurus		23. Cancer	5:19 pm
24. Aries		24. Gemini	6:30 am	24. Cancer	
25. Taurus	8:06 pm	25. Gemini		25. Leo	6:53 pm
26. Taurus		26. Cancer	6:08 am	26. Leo	
27. Gemini	7:12 pm	27. Cancer		27. Virgo	11:45 pm
28. Gemini		28. Leo	8:24 am	28. Virgo	
29. Cancer	7:51 pm	29. Leo		29. Virgo	
30. Cancer		30. Virgo	2:45 pm	30. Libra	8:38 am
31. Leo	11:49 pm			31. Libra	

Daylight saving time to be considered where applicable.

2007 PHASES OF THE MOON— NEW YORK TIME

New Moon	First Quarter	Full Moon	Last Quarter
Dec. 20 ('06)	Dec. 27 ('06)	Jan. 3	Jan. 11
Jan. 18	Jan. 25	Feb. 2	Feb. 10
Feb. 17	Feb. 24	March 3	March 11
March 18	March 25	April 2	April 10
April 17	April 24	May 2	May 9
May 16	May 23	May 31	June 8
June 14	June 22	June 30	July 7
July 14	July 22	July 29	August 5
August 12	August 20	August 28	Sept. 3
Sept. 11	Sept. 19	Sept. 26	Oct. 3
Oct. 11	Oct. 19	Oct. 26	Nov. 1
Nov. 9	Nov. 17	Nov. 24	Dec. 1
Dec. 9	Dec. 17	Dec. 23	Dec. 31

Each phase of the Moon lasts approximately seven to eight days, during which the Moon's shape gradually changes as it comes out of one phase and goes into the next.

There will be a solar eclipse during the New Moon phase on March 18 and September 11.

There will be a lunar eclipse during the Full Moon phase on March 3 and August 28.

2007 FISHING GUIDE

	Good	Best
January	1-5-6-19-25	2-3-4-11-30-31
February	1-2-3-4-17-24-28	16-26-27
March	1-2-3-4-11-18-30-31	5-6-25-26
April	17-24-29	2-3-4-5-9-29-30
May	4-5-10-24-31	1-2-15-29-30
June	1-2-14-28-29	3-4-8-23-26-30
July	2-3-7-27-29-30-31	13-23-28
August	2-12-20-26-27-30-31	1-5-24-28-29
September	4-11-22-23-26-27-28	20-24-25-29
October	18-24-25-28-29	3-10-22-26-27
November	2-17-21-22-24-25	9-23-26-27
December	1-10-17-21-22-23-26-27	24-25-31

2007 PLANTING GUIDE

	Aboveground Crops	Root Crops
January	3-21-22-26-30-31	3-10-11-12-13-17-18
February	18-22-23-26-27	6-7-8-9-14
March	21-22-25-26	5-6-7-8-9-13-14-18
April	1-18-22-23-29-30	2-3-4-5-9-10-14
May	1-19-20-26-27-28-29-30	1-2-11-12-15-16
June	15-16-22-23-24-25-26	3-4-7-8-11-12-30
July	20-21-22-23-28	3-4-9-13-14
August	16-17-18-19-24-25	1-5-6-10-28-29
September	12-13-14-15-16-20-21-25	2-5-6-29
October	12-13-18-22-23	3-10-26-27-30-31
November	14-15-18-19-22-23	7-8-9-26-27
December	11-12-16-20	4-5-6-7-24-25-30

	Pruning	Weeds and Pests
January	3-12-13	6-7-8-15-16
February	9-10	2-3-4-11-16
March	8-17-18	4-10-11-15-16
April	4-5-14	7-8-12-16
May	2-11-12	4-5-9-13-14
June	7-8	5-6-9-10-14
July	4-5-13-14	2-3-7-11-12-30
August	10-29	3-7-8-12-30-31
September	5-6	3-4-8-9-10-11-27
October	2-3-30-31	1-5-6-7-8-28-29
November	9-26-27	1-2-3-4-25-29-30
December	6-7-24-25	1-2-9-26-27-28-29

MOON'S INFLUENCE OVER PLANTS

Centuries ago it was established that seeds planted when the Moon is in signs and phases called Fruitful will produce more growth than seeds planted when the Moon is in a Barren sign.

Fruitful Signs: Taurus, Cancer, Libra, Scorpio, Capricorn, Pisces
Barren Signs: Aries, Gemini, Leo, Virgo, Sagittarius, Aquarius
Dry Signs: Aries, Gemini, Sagittarius, Aquarius

Activity	Moon In
Mow lawn, trim plants	**Fruitful sign:** 1st & 2nd quarter
Plant flowers	**Fruitful sign:** 2nd quarter; best in Cancer and Libra
Prune	**Fruitful sign:** 3rd & 4th quarter
Destroy pests; spray	**Barren sign:** 4th quarter
Harvest potatoes, root crops	**Dry sign:** 3rd & 4th quarter; Taurus, Leo, and Aquarius

MOON'S INFLUENCE OVER YOUR HEALTH

ARIES	Head, brain, face, upper jaw
TAURUS	Throat, neck, lower jaw
GEMINI	Hands, arms, lungs, shoulders, nervous system
CANCER	Esophagus, stomach, breasts, womb, liver
LEO	Heart, spine
VIRGO	Intestines, liver
LIBRA	Kidneys, lower back
SCORPIO	Sex and eliminative organs
SAGITTARIUS	Hips, thighs, liver
CAPRICORN	Skin, bones, teeth, knees
AQUARIUS	Circulatory system, lower legs
PISCES	Feet, tone of being

Try to avoid work being done on that part of the body when the Moon is in the sign governing that part.

MOON'S INFLUENCE OVER DAILY AFFAIRS

The Moon makes a complete transit of the Zodiac every 27 days 7 hours and 43 minutes. In making this transit the Moon forms different aspects with the planets and consequently has favorable or unfavorable bearings on affairs and events for persons according to the sign of the Zodiac under which they were born.

When the Moon is in conjunction with the Sun it is called a New Moon; when the Moon and Sun are in opposition it is called a Full Moon. From New Moon to Full Moon, first and second quarter—which takes about two weeks—the Moon is increasing or waxing. From Full Moon to New Moon, third and fourth quarter, the Moon is decreasing or waning.

Activity	Moon In
Business: buying and selling new, requiring public support	Sagittarius, Aries, Gemini, Virgo 1st and 2nd quarter
meant to be kept quiet	3rd and 4th quarter
Investigation	3rd and 4th quarter
Signing documents	1st & 2nd quarter, Cancer, Scorpio, Pisces
Advertising	2nd quarter, Sagittarius
Journeys and trips	1st & 2nd quarter, Gemini, Virgo
Renting offices, etc.	Taurus, Leo, Scorpio, Aquarius
Painting of house/apartment	3rd & 4th quarter, Taurus, Scorpio, Aquarius
Decorating	Gemini, Libra, Aquarius
Buying clothes and accessories	Taurus, Virgo
Beauty salon or barber shop visit	1st & 2nd quarter, Taurus, Leo, Libra, Scorpio, Aquarius
Weddings	1st & 2nd quarter

Cancer

CANCER

Character Analysis

Cancer is generally rather sensitive. He or she is quite often a generous person by nature, and is willing to help almost anyone in need. He is emotional and often feels sorry for people less fortunate than he. He could never refuse to answer someone's call for help. It is because of his sympathetic nature that others take advantage of him now and again.

In spite of his willingness to help others, the Cancer man or woman may seem difficult to approach by anyone not well acquainted with their character. On the whole, he seems subdued and reserved. Others may feel there is a wall between them and Cancer, although this may not be the case at all. The person born under this sign, which is ruled by the Moon, is careful not to let others hurt him. He has learned through hard experience that protection of some sort is necessary in order to get along in life. The person who wins his confidence and is able to get beyond this barrier will find the Moon Child a warm and loving person.

With his family and close friends, he is a very faithful and dependable person. In his quiet way, he can be affectionate and loving. He is generally not one given to demonstrative behavior. He can be fond of someone without telling them so a dozen times a day. With people he is close to, Cancer is more open about his own need for affection, and he enjoys being pampered by his loved ones. He likes to feel wanted and protected.

When he has made up his mind about something, he sticks to it, and is generally a very constant person. He knows how to hold his ground. He never wavers. People who don't know him may think him weak and easily managed, because he is so quiet and modest, but this is far from true. He can take a lot of punishment for an idea or a cause he believes in. For Cancer, right is right. In order to protect himself, the person born under this sign will sometimes put up a pose as someone bossy and domineering. Sometimes he is successful in fooling others with his brash front. People who have known him for a while, however, are seldom taken in.

Many people born under this sign of the Crab are shy and seemingly lacking in confidence. They know their own minds, though, even if they do not seem to. He responds to kindness and encouragement. He will be himself with people he trusts. A good person can bring out the best in the Crab. Disagreeable or unfeeling people can send him scurrying back into his shell. He is a person who does not appreciate sharp criticism. Some Crabs are worriers. They are very concerned about what others may think of them. This may bother them so much that they develop a deep feeling of inferiority. Sometimes this reaches the point where he is so unsure of himself in some matters that he allows himself to be influenced by someone who has a stronger personality. Also, some Crabs may be afraid that people will talk behind his back if he doesn't comply with their wishes. However, this does not stop him from doing what he feels is right. The cultivated Cancer learns to think for himself and has no fear of disapproval.

The Cancer man or woman is most himself at home. The person born under this sign is a real lover of domesticity. He likes a place where he can relax and feel properly sheltered. Cancers like things to stay as they are; they are not fond of changes of any sort. They are not very adaptable people. When visiting others or going to unfamiliar places, they are not likely to feel very comfortable. They are not the most talkative people at a party. In the comfort of their own homes, however, they blossom and bloom.

The Cancer man or woman sticks by the rules, whatever the game. He is not a person who would ever think of going against an established grain. He is conventional and moderate in almost all things. In a way he likes the old-fashioned things. However, in spite of this, he is interested in new things and does what he can to keep up with the times. In a way, he has two sides to his character. He is seldom forgetful. He has a memory like an elephant and can pick out any detail from the past with no trouble at all. He often reflects on things that have happened. He prefers the past to the future, which sometimes fills him with a feeling of apprehension.

This fourth sign of the Zodiac is a motherly one. Even the Cancer man has something maternal about him. He is usually kind and considerate, ready to help and protect. Others are drawn to Cancer because of these gentle qualities. People in trouble often turn to him for advice and sympathy. People find him easy to confide in.

The Cancer person in general is very forgiving. He almost never holds a grudge. Still, it would not be wise to anger him. Treat him fairly and he will treat you the same. He does not appreciate people who lose patience with him. Cancer is usually proud of his mind and does not like to be considered unintelligent. Even if others feel that he is somewhat slow in some areas, he would rather not have this opinion expressed in his presence. He's not a person to be played with; he can tell when someone is treating him like a fool.

Quite often people born under this sign are musically inclined. Some of them have a deep interest in religious matters. They are apt to be interested in mystical matters, as well. Although they are fascinated by these things, they may be somewhat afraid of being overwhelmed if they go into them too deeply. In spite of this feeling of apprehension, Moon Children try to satisfy their curiosity in these matters.

Health

For the person born under the sign of Cancer, the stomach is the weak point. Chances are that Cancer is easily susceptible to infection. Sometimes his health is affected by nervousness. He can be quite a worrier. Even little things eat at him from time to time, which is apt to lower his resistance to infectious illnesses. He is often upset by small matters.

A Cancer as a child is sometimes sickly and weak. His physique during this period of growth can be described in most cases as fragile. Some develop into physically strong adults, others may have the remnants of childhood ailments with them for a good part of their adult lives. They are frightened of being sick. Illness is a word they would rather not mention. Pain is also a thing they fear.

They are given to quick-changing moods at times, which often has an effect on their overall health. Worry or depression can have a subliminal effect on their general health. Usually their illnesses are not as serious as they imagine them to be. They sometimes find it easy to feel sorry for themselves.

On the whole, the Cancer man or woman is a quiet person. He is not one to brag or push his weight around. However, let it not be thought that he lacks the force that others have. He can be quite purposeful and energetic when the situation calls for it. However, when it comes to tooting their own horn, they can be somewhat shy and reticent. They may lack the get-up-and-go that others have when it comes to pushing their personal interests ahead.

Some Cancers are quite aware of the fact that they are not what one would call sturdy in physique or temperament. Some may go through life rather painfully trying to cover up the weak side of their nature.

Sons and daughters of the Moon may not be very vigorous or active. As a rule, they are not too fond of physical exercise, and they have a weakness for rich and heavy foods. As a result, in later life they could end up overweight. Some Cancers have trouble with their kidneys and intestines. Others digest their food poorly. The wise Cancer man or woman, however, adheres to a strict and well-balanced diet with plenty of fresh fruit and vegetables. Moreover, they see to it that they properly exercise daily. The Cancer man or woman who learns to cut down on rich foods and worry often lives to a ripe old age.

Occupation

Cancer generally has no trouble at all establishing himself in the business world. He has all those qualities that make one a success professionally. He is careful with his equipment as well as his money. He is patient and he knows how to persevere. Any job where he has a chance to use his mind instead of his body is usually a job in which he has no trouble succeeding. He can work well with people—especially people situated in dire straits. Welfare work is the kind of occupation in which he usually excels. He can really be quite a driving person if his job calls for it. Cancer is surprisingly resourceful. In spite of his retiring disposition, he is capable of accomplishing some very difficult tasks.

Cancer can put on an aggressive front, and in some cases it can carry him far. Quite often he is able to develop leadership qualities and make good use of them. He knows how to direct his energy so that he never becomes immediately exhausted. He'll work away at a difficult chore gradually, seldom approaching anything head-on. By working at something obliquely he often finds advantages along the way that are not apparent to others. In spite of his cautious approach, Cancer is often taxed by work that is too demanding of his energy. He may put up a good front of being strong and courageous while actually he is at the end of his emotional rope. Risks sometimes frighten the Crab. It is often fear that exhausts him. The possible dangers in the world of business set him to worrying.

Cancer does not boast about what he is going to do. He or she just quietly goes ahead and does it. Quite often he accomplishes more than others in this quiet way.

The person born under this sign enjoys helping others. By nature, he is quite a sympathetic individual. He does not like to see others suffer or do without. He is willing to make sacrifices for someone he trusts and cares for. Cancer's maternal streak works wonders with children. People born under the fourth sign of the Zodiac often make excellent teachers. They understand young people well and do what they can to help them grow up properly.

Cancers also are fairly intuitive. In business or financial matters, they often make an important strike by playing a strong hunch. In some cases they are able to rely almost entirely on their feelings rather than on reason.

Water attracts the Cancer person. Often they have connections with the oceans through their professions. Cancer homemakers experimenting in the kitchen often are very successful creating new drinks and blending liquid recipes. Overseas trade and commerce also appeal.

The average Cancer has many choices as far as a career is concerned. There are many things that he can do well once he puts his mind to it. In the arts he is quite likely to do well. The Cancer man or woman has a way with beauty, harmony, and creativity. Basically, he is a very capable person in many things; it depends on which of his talents he wants to develop to a professional point. He has a rich imagination and sometimes can make use of it in the area of painting, music, or sculpture.

When working for someone else, Cancer can always be depended upon. He makes a loyal and conscientious employee.

It is important for Cancer to select a job that is well suited to his talents and temperament. Although he may feel that earning money is important, Cancer eventually comes to the point where he realizes that it is even more important to enjoy the work he is doing. He should have a position that allows him to explore the recesses of his personality and to develop. When placed in the wrong job, the Cancer man or woman might wish they were somewhere else.

Cancers know the value of money. They are not the sort of people who go throwing money around recklessly. Cancer is honest and expects others to be the same. He is quite modest in most things and deplores unnecessary display. Cancers have a genius for making money and for investing or saving it.

Security is important to the person born under this sign. He'll always see to it that he has something put away for that inevitable rainy day. He is also a hard worker and is willing to put in long hours for the money it brings him. Financial success is usually the result of his own perseverance and industry. Through his own need for security, it is often easy for Cancer to sympathize with those of like dispositions. He is a helpful person. If he sees someone trying to do his best to get ahead—and still not succeeding—he is quite apt to put aside his own interests temporarily to help another.

Sometimes Cancer worries about money even when he has it. Even the wealthy Cancer can never be too secure. It would be better for him to learn how to relax and not to let his worries undermine his health. Financial matters often cause him considerable concern—even when it is not necessary.

Home and Family

Cancers are usually great home lovers. They are very domestic by nature; home for them spells security. Cancer is a family person. He respects those who are related to him. He feels a great responsibility toward all the members of his family. There is usually a very strong tie between Cancer and his mother that lasts through his whole life. Something a Cancer will not tolerate is for someone to speak ill of a member of his family. This for him is a painful and deep insult. He has a great respect for his family and family traditions. Quite often Cancer is well-acquainted with his family tree. If he happens to have a relative who has been quite successful in life, he is proud of the fact. Once he is home for the weekend, he generally stays there.

Cancer is sentimental about old things and habits. He is apt to have many things stored away from years ago. Something that was dear to his parents will probably be dear to him as well.

Many Cancers travel near and far from time to time. But no matter what their destination, they are always glad to be back where they feel they belong.

The home of a Cancer is usually quite comfortable and tastefully furnished. Cancer men and women are romantic, which is usually reflected in the way their house is arranged.

The Cancer child is always attached to his home and family. He may not care to go out and play with other children very much but enjoys it when his friends come to his house.

The maternal nature of the Cancer person comes out when he gives a party. He is a very attentive host and worries over a guest like a mother hen—anxious to see that they are comfortable and lack nothing. He does his best to make others happy and at home, and he is admired and loved for that. People who visit are usually deeply impressed by their outgoing ways. The Cancer host prepares unusual and delicious snacks for visitors. Cancer is very concerned about them and sees to it that they are well-fed while visiting.

Homebodies that they are, Cancers generally do what they can to make their home a comfortable and interesting place for themselves as well as for others. They feel very flattered when a visitor pays them a compliment on their home.

Children play a very important part in the lives of people born under this sign. Cancers fuss over their youngsters and give them the things they feel that they need. They generally like to have large families. They see to it that their children are well provided for and that they have the chances in life that their parents never had. The best mother of the Zodiac is usually someone born under the sign of Cancer. They have a strong protective nature. They usually have a strong sense of duty, and when their children are in difficulty they do everything they can to set matters right. Children, needless to say, are fond of their Cancer parent, and respond lovingly to make the parent-child relationship a harmonious one.

Social Relationships

Cancer may seem rather retiring and quiet, and this gives people the impression that he is not too warm or sympathetic. However, most Moon Children are very sensitive and loving. Their ability to understand and sympathize with others is great. Cancer likes to have close friends—people who love and understand him as well as he tries to love and understand them. He wants to be well-liked—to be noticed by people who he feels should like him. If he does not get the attention and affection he feels he is entitled to, he is apt to become sullen and difficult to deal with.

The Cancer man or woman has strong powers of intuition and can generally sense when he has met a person who is likely to turn into a good friend. Cancer suffers greatly if ever he should lose a friend. To him friendships are sacred. Sometimes Cancer sets friends on too high a pedestal. He or she is apt to feel crestfallen when he discovers that they have feet of clay. He is often romantic in his approach to friendship and is likely to seek people out for sentimental reasons rather than for practical ones.

Cancer is a very sensitive person and sometimes this contributes to making a friendship unsatisfactory. He sometimes makes the wrong interpretation of a remark that is made by a friend or acquaintance. He imagines something injurious behind a very innocent remark. He sometimes feels that people who profess to be his friends laugh at him cruelly behind his back. He has to be constantly reassured of a friend's sincerity, especially in the beginning of a relationship. If he wants to have the wide circle of friends he desires, Cancer must learn to curb these persecution fantasies.

Love and Marriage

The Cancer man or woman has to have love in their life, otherwise their existence is a dull and humdrum affair. When they love someone, Cancer will do everything in their power to make a lover happy. They are not afraid to sacrifice in order to make an important relationship work. To his loved one he is likely to seem uncertain and moody. Cancer is usually very influenced by the impression he has of his lover. They may even be content to let their romance partner have his or her own way in the relationship. He may not make many demands but be willing to follow those of his loved one. At times he may feel that he is not really loved, and draw away somewhat from the relationship. Sometimes it takes a lot of coaxing before he can be won over to the fact that he is indeed loved for himself alone.

Cancer is often possessive about people as well as material objects. This often makes the relationship difficult to accept for his partner.

His standards are sometimes impossibly high and because of this he is difficult to please. The Cancer man or woman is interested in finding someone with whom he can spend the rest of his life. He or she is not interested in any fly-by-night romance.

Romance and the Cancer Woman

The Cancer woman is sincere in her approach to love. Her feelings run deep. Still, she's moody, tempestuous, and changeable. She is so sensitive in romance that her lover may find her difficult to understand at times. The Moon Child knows exactly the sort of man she is looking for. If she can find him, she'll never let him go.

The trouble is she frequently goes through a lot of men in her search for the perfect lover. She surrenders completely to her emotions. She can experience the whole melodrama of falling in love, longing to be with her man, then being desolate when parted from him. If she does find her ideal mate, she will take to marriage for the rest of her life without looking back or even at another man. If she can't marry the man of her dreams, or even live with him, she might carry a torch for the rest of her days. That is the tenacity of the Cancer woman's pure devotion to the man she loves.

Marriage is a union suited to the Crab's temperament, which needs a safe haven in which her feelings can be nurtured. She longs for permanence in a relationship, and usually is not fond of flings or meaningless romantic adventures. Because her emotions are so deep, she can easily feel wronged by a minor slight. Once she imagines she has been hurt, she can retreat rapidly and withdraw deep within herself to brood. It may be quite a while before she comes out of her shell. She desires a man who is protective and affectionate, someone who can understand and cope with her moods so that she does not feel threatened.

As a Moon Child, Cancer is very temperamental. She'll soar to the heights of ecstasy, then plunge into the depths of despondency all with dazzling speed. She'll sparkle like champagne, then fizzle out before the high wears off. Such marked changes of personality can be bewildering to a lover who may have done nothing to provoke them. Reason and logic will not coax her out of a bad mood. Only patient love will work. And if do you not have staying power or refined sensibilities, then you don't stand the ghost of a chance with the Cancer woman.

Cancer's intuition is usually right on. She can size up a situation instinctively, and more times than not she is right. What her gut feelings tell her can be the cause of many a quarrel and the occasion for nagging her mate about a myriad of things. Because she is possessive, there can be discord. And she more she loves, the more possessive and jealous she can become. The demands she is likely to make can be overbearing at times. But as long as she is reassured and appreciated, all will be well.

The Cancer woman makes a devoted wife and mother who will do everything to keep her family together. The only danger is that she may transfer all her love to the children, making her man feel useless and left out. As long as her man participates fully in family life, there will be harmony and affection.

Romance and the Cancer Man

The Cancer man may come on as the reserved type. It can be difficult for some women to understand him. Generally, he is a very loving person, but sometimes he will not let his sensitive side show. He is afraid of being rejected or hurt, so he tries to keep his true feelings hidden until he knows that the intended object of his affections is capable of taking him seriously.

For him, love is a serious business. And he is so serious about love that you might say he lives for love—to give it and to receive it. True to the symbol of the sign of Cancer, which is the Crab, he feels his way very carefully in any romantic alliance. He is not going to make any rash mistakes. But even if it's only a brief affair, the Cancer man will treat his lover as the only woman in the world.

When he is convinced that you, too, are serious, then this sensuous idealist is all yours.

You must never play around with his feelings. Like the Crab, the Cancer man pretends to be tough and invulnerable on the outside, but on the inside he is so soft it hurts. He is perhaps the most sensitive person you have ever met. Your Moon Child is highly emotive and moody, reflecting the Moon's quick changeability and shifts of temperament. And, like his ruler the Moon, he is terribly responsive to the vibes coming from his lover. It's all or nothing with him, so jealousy and possessiveness can become a problem. He needs to be constantly reassured that you love him.

If you love him, tell him so often. And show him that you love him, not only with physical love but also with thoughtfully chosen fine gifts no matter how small. He is sentimental. He will treasure everything you give him. He will keep mementos of your happy moments together, especially souvenirs of the occasion when he became sure you would be the love his life.

When deeply in love, the Cancer man does everything in his power to hold the woman of his choice. He is very affectionate and may be extravagant from time to time with the woman he loves. He will lavish gifts upon you and will see that you never lack anything you desire to make your home life together warm and cozy.

Marriage is something the Cancer man sets as a goal early in his life. He wants to settle down with someone who will mother him to some extent. Often he looks for a woman who has the same qualities as his mother, especially if his early childhood revolved around his mother's central role in the family. The remembrance of things maternal makes him feel truly loved and secure.

The Cancer man is an attentive father. He is fond of large families. Sometimes his love for the children may be too possessive, and he can stifle their independence with smothering ways.

Woman—Man

CANCER WOMAN
ARIES MAN
Although it's possible that you could find happiness with a man born under the sign of the Ram, it's uncertain as to how long that happiness would last.

An Aries who has made his mark in the world and is somewhat steadfast in his outlooks and attitudes could be quite a catch for you. On the other hand, men under this sign are often swift-footed and quick-minded. Their industrious mannerisms may fail to impress you, especially if you feel that much of their get-up-and-go often leads nowhere.

When it comes to a fine romance, you want someone with a nice, broad shoulder to lean on. You are likely to find a relationship with someone who doesn't like to stay put for too long somewhat upsetting.

Aries may have a little trouble in understanding you, too, at least in the beginning of the relationship. He may find you too shy and moody. Aries speak their minds and can criticize at the drop of a hat.

You may find a Ram too demanding. He may give you the impression that he expects you to be at his beck and call. You have a barrelful of patience at your disposal and he may try every last bit of it. He is apt not to be as thorough as you are in everything that he does. In order to achieve success or a goal quickly, he will overlook small but important details—and regret it when it is far too late.

Being married to an Aries does not mean that you'll have a secure and safe life as far as finances are concerned. Not all Aries are rash with cash, but they lack that sound head you have for putting away something for that inevitable rainy day. He'll do his best, however, to see that you're adequately provided for, even though his efforts may leave something to be desired as far as you're concerned.

With an Aries mate, you'll find yourself constantly among people. Aries generally have many friends—and you may not heartily approve of them all. Rams are more interested in interesting people than they are in influential ones. Although there can be a family squabble from time to time, you are stable enough to take it all in your stride. Your love of permanence and a harmonious home life will help you to take the bitter with the sweet.

Aries men love children. They make wonderful fathers. Kids take to them like ducks to water. Their quick minds and behavior appeal to the young.

CANCER WOMAN
TAURUS MAN

Some Taurus men are strong and silent. They do all they can to protect and provide for the women they love. The Taurus man will never let you down. He's steady, sturdy, and reliable. He's pretty honest and practical, too. He says what he means and means what he says. He never indulges in deceit and will always put his cards on the table.

Taurus is very affectionate. Being loved, appreciated, and understood is very important for his well-being. Like you, he is also looking for peace, harmony, and security in his life. If you both work toward these goals together, they are easily attained.

If you should marry a Taurus, you can be sure that the wolf will never darken your door. They are notoriously good providers and do everything they can to make their families comfortable and happy.

He'll appreciate the way you have of making a home warm and inviting. Good meals and the evening papers are essential ingredients in making your Taurus husband happy at the end of the workday. Although he may be a big lug of a guy, he's fond of gentleness and soft things. If you puff up his pillow and tuck him in at night, he won't complain.

You probably won't complain about his friends. Taurus tends to seek out friends who are successful or prominent. You admire people, too, who work hard and achieve what they set out for. It helps to reassure your way of life and the way you look at things.

The Taurus man doesn't care too much for change. He's a stay-at-home of the first degree. Chances are that the house you move into after you're married will be the house you'll live in for the rest of your life.

You'll find that the man born under the sign of the Bull is easy to get along with. It's unlikely that you'll have many quarrels or arguments.

Although he'll be gentle and tender with you, your Taurus man is far from being a sensitive type. He's a man's man. Chances are he loves sports like fishing and football. He can be earthy as well as down to earth.

Taurus love their children very much but try hard not to spoil them. They believe in children staying in their places. They make excellent disciplinarians. Your children will be polite and respectful. They may find their Taurus father a little gruff, but as they grow older they'll learn to understand him.

CANCER WOMAN
GEMINI MAN

Gemini men, in spite of their charm and dashing manner, may unnerve you. They seem to lack the common sense you set so much store in. Their tendency to start something, then out of boredom never finish it, may exasperate you.

You may be inclined to interpret a Gemini's jumping from here to there as childish or neurotic. A man born under the sign of the Twins will seldom stay put. If you should take it upon yourself to try and make him sit still, he will resent it.

On the other hand, the Gemini man may think you're a slowpoke, someone far too interested in security and material things. He's attracted to things that sparkle and dazzle. You, with your practical way of looking at things, are likely to seem a little dull and uninteresting to this gadabout. If you're looking for a life of security and permanence—and what Cancer isn't—then you'd better look elsewhere for your Mr. Right.

Chances are you'll be taken in by his charming ways and facile wit—few women can resist Gemini magic. But after you've seen through his live-for-today, gossamer facade, you'll most likely be very happy to turn your attention to someone more stable, even if he is not as interesting. You want a man who is there when you need him. You need someone on whom you can fully rely. Keeping track of a Gemini's movements will make you dizzy. Still, you are a patient woman, most of the time, and you are able to put up with something contrary if you feel that in the end it will prove well worth the effort.

A successful and serious Gemini could make you a very happy woman, perhaps, if you gave him half a chance. Although you may think that he has holes in his head, the Gemini man generally has a good brain and can make good use of it when he wants. Some Geminis who have learned the importance of being consistent have risen to great heights professionally. Once you can convince yourself that not all Twins are witless grasshoppers, you'll find you've come a long way in trying to understand them.

Life with a Gemini man can be more fun than a barrel of clowns. You'll never have a chance to experience a dull moment. He lacks your sense when it comes to money, however. You should see to it that you handle the budgeting and bookkeeping.

In ways, Gemini is like a child himself. Perhaps that is why a Gemini father can get along so well with his own children, indeed with most of the younger generation.

CANCER WOMAN
CANCER MAN

You'll find the man born under the same sign as you easy to get along with. You're both sensitive and sensible people. You'll see eye-to-eye on most things. He'll share your interest in security and practicality.

Cancer men are always hard workers. They are very interested in making successes of themselves in business and socially. Like you, he's a conservative person who has a great deal of respect for tradition. He's a man you can depend on come rain or come shine. He'll never shirk his responsibilities as provider and will always see to it that you never want.

The Cancer man is not the type that rushes headlong into romance. Neither are you, for that matter. Courtship between the two of you will be a sensible and thorough affair. It may take months before you even get to that holding-hands stage of romance. One thing you can be sure of: he'll always treat you like a lady. He'll have great respect and consideration for your feelings. Only when he is sure that you approve of him as someone to love, will he reveal the warmer side of his nature. His coolness, like yours, is just a front. Beneath it lies a very affectionate heart.

Although he may seem restless or moody at times, on the whole the Cancer man is very considerate and kind. His standards are extremely high. He is looking for a partner who can measure up to his ideals—a partner like you.

Marriage means a lot to the Cancer male. He's very interested in settling down with someone who has the same attitudes and outlooks as he has. He's a man who loves being at home. He'll be a faithful husband. Cancers never pussyfoot around after they have made their marriage vows. They do not take their marriage responsibilities lightly. They see to it that everything in this relationship is just the way it should be. Between the two of you, your home will be well managed, bills will be paid on time, there will be adequate insurance on everything of value, and there will be money in the bank. When retirement time rolls around, you both should be very well off.

The Cancer man has a great respect for family. You'll most likely be seeing a lot of his mother during your marriage, just as he'll probably be seeing a lot of yours. He'll do his best to get along with your relatives; he'll treat them with the kindness and concern you think they deserve. He'll expect you to be just as considerate with his relatives.

Cancer is a very good father. He's very patient and understanding, especially when the children are young and dependent and need his protection.

CANCER WOMAN
LEO MAN

To know a man born under the sign of the Lion is not necessarily to love him—even though the temptation may be great. When he fixes most women with his leonine double-whammy, it causes their hearts to throb and their minds to soar.

But with you, the sensible Cancer, it takes more than a regal strut and roar to win you over. There is no denying that Leo has a way with women, even practical Cancers. If he sweeps you off your feet, it may be hard for you to scramble upright again. Still, you are no pushover for romantic charm when you feel there may be no security behind it.

He'll wine you and dine you in the fanciest places. He'll croon to you under the moon and shower you with diamonds if he can get ahold of them. Still, it would be wise to find out just how long that shower is going to last before consenting to be his wife.

Lions in love are hard to ignore, let alone brush off. Once mesmerized by this romantic powerhouse, you may find yourself doing things you never dreamed of. Leos can be vain pussycats when involved romantically. They like to be cuddled and petted, tickled under the chin, and told how wonderful they are. This may not be your cup of tea. Still, when you're romantically dealing with a Lion, you'll instinctively do the things that make him purr.

Although he may be big and magnanimous while trying to win you, he'll let out a blood-curdling roar if he thinks he's not getting the tender love and care he feels is his due. If you keep him well supplied with affection, you can be sure his eyes will never stray and his heart will never wander.

Leo men often tend to be authoritarian. They are born to lord it over others in one way or another, it seems. If he is the top banana of his firm, he'll most likely do everything he can to stay on top. If he's not number one, he's most likely working on it and will be sitting on the throne before long. You'll have more security than you can use if he is in a position to support you in the manner to which he feels you should be accustomed. He's apt to be too lavish, though, at least by your standards.

You'll always have plenty of friends when you have a Leo for a mate. He's a natural born friend-maker and entertainer. He loves to kick up his heels at a party.

As fathers, Leos may go from one extreme to another with their children. Leos either lavish too much attention on the youngsters or demand too much from them.

CANCER WOMAN
VIRGO MAN

The Virgo man is often a quiet, respectable type who sets great store in conservative behavior and levelheadedness. He'll admire you for your practicality and tenacity—perhaps even more than for your good looks. The Virgo man is seldom bowled over by glamour. When looking for someone to love, he always turns to a serious, reliable woman.

He'll be far from a Valentino while dating. In fact, you may wind up making all the passes. Once he gets his motor running, however, he can be warm and wonderful to the right lover.

The Virgo man is gradual about love. Chances are your romance with him will start out looking like an ordinary friendship. Once he's sure that you are no fly-by-night flirt and have no plans of taking him for a ride, he'll open up and rain sunshine all over your heart.

The Virgo man takes his time about romance. It may be many years before he seriously considers settling down. Virgos are often middle-aged when they make their first marriage vows. They hold out as long as they can for the woman who perfectly measures up to their ideals.

He may not have many names in his little black book; in fact, he may not even have a little black book. He's not interested in playing the field; leave that to the more flamboyant signs. The Virgo man is so particular that he may remain romantically inactive for a long period of time. The mate he chooses has to be perfect or it's no go.

With your surefire perseverance, you'll be able to make him listen to reason, as far as romance is concerned. Before long, you'll find him returning your love. He's no block of ice and will respond to what he considers to be the right feminine flame.

Once your love life with Virgo starts to bubble, don't give it a chance to die down. The Virgo man will never give a woman a second chance at winning his heart. If there should ever be a bad break between you, forget about picking up the pieces. With him, it's one strike and you're out.

Once married, he'll stay that way—even if it hurts. He's too conscientious to back out of a legal deal of any sort. He'll always be faithful and considerate. He's as neat as a pin and will expect you to be the same.

If you marry a Virgo man, keep your kids spic-and-span, at least by the time he gets home from work. He likes children to be clean and polite.

CANCER WOMAN
LIBRA MAN

Cancers are apt to find Libra men too wrapped up in their own private dreams to be romantically interesting. He's a difficult man to bring back down to earth, at times. Although he may be very careful about weighing both sides of an argument, he may never really come to a reasonable decision about anything. Decisions, large and small, are capable of giving Libra the willies. Don't ask him why. He probably doesn't know.

If you are looking for permanence and constancy in a love relationship, you may find him a puzzlement. One moment he comes on hard and strong with declarations of his love; the next moment you find he's left you like yesterday's mashed potatoes. It does no good to wonder what went wrong. Chances are nothing, really. It's just one of Libra's strange ways.

On the other hand, you'll probably admire his way with harmony and beauty. If you're all decked out in your fanciest gown, you'll receive a ready compliment and one that's really deserved. Libras don't pass out compliments to all and sundry. If something strikes him as distasteful, he'll remain silent. He's tactful.

He may not seem as ambitious as you would like your lover or husband to be. Where you have a great interest in getting ahead, Libra is often content just to drift along. It is not that he is lazy or shiftless. Material gain generally means little to him. He is more interested in aesthetic matters. If he is in love with you, however, he'll do everything in his power to make you happy.

You may have to give him a good nudge now and again to get him to recognize the light of reality. On the whole, he'll enjoy the company of his artistic dreams when you're not around. If you love your Libra, don't be too harsh or impatient with him. Try to understand him.

Libras are peace-loving people. They hate any kind of confrontation that might lead to an argument. Some of them will do almost anything to keep the peace—even tell a little lie.

If you find yourself involved with a man born under this sign, either temporarily or permanently, you'd better take over the task of managing his money. It's for his own good. Money will never interest a Libra as much as it should. He often has a tendency to be generous when he shouldn't be.

Don't let him see the materialistic side of your nature too often. It might frighten him off.

Libra makes a gentle and understanding father. He's careful not to spoil children or to demand too much from them. He believes that discipline should be a matter of gentle guidance.

CANCER WOMAN
SCORPIO MAN

Some people have a hard time understanding the man born under the sign of Scorpio. Few, however, are able to resist his fiery charm. When angered, he can act like an overturned wasps' nest; his sting can leave an almost permanent mark. If you find yourself interested in a Scorpion, you'd better learn how to keep on his good side.

The Scorpio man can be quite blunt when he chooses; at times, he'll seem like a brute to you. He's touchy—more so than you— and it can get on your nerves after a while. When you feel like you can't take it anymore, you'd better tiptoe away from the scene rather than chance an explosive confrontation. He's capable of giving you a sounding-out that will make you pack your bags and go back to Mother for good.

If he finds fault with you, he'll let you know. He might misinterpret your patience and think it a sign of indifference. Still and all, you are the kind of woman who can adapt to almost any sort of relationship or circumstance if you put your heart and mind to it.

Scorpio men are perceptive and intelligent. In some respects, they know how to use their brains more effectively than most. They believe in winning in whatever they do; second place holds no interest for them. In business, they usually achieve the position they want through drive and use of intellect.

Your interest in home life is not likely to be shared by him. No matter how comfortable you've managed to make the house, it will have little influence on making him aware of his family responsibilities. He does not like to be tied down, generally, and would rather be out on the battlefield of life, belting away for what he feels is a just and worthy cause. Don't try to keep the home fires burning too brightly while you wait for him to come home from work; you may run out of firewood.

The Scorpio man is passionate in all things—including love. Most women are easily attracted to him, and the Cancer woman is no exception, at least before she knows what she might be getting into. If you are swept off your feet by a Scorpio man, soon you find you are dealing with a carton of romantic fireworks. The Scorpio man is passionate with a capital P, make no mistake about that.

Scorpio men are straight to the point. They can be as sharp as a razor blade and just as cutting. Always manage to stay out of his line of fire; if you don't, it could cost you your love life.

Scorpio men like large families. They love children but they do not always live up to the role of the responsible, nurturing father.

CANCER WOMAN
SAGITTARIUS MAN

Sagittarius men are not easy to catch. They get cold feet whenever visions of the altar enter the romance. You'll most likely be attracted to Sagittarius because of his exuberant nature. He's lots of laughs and easy to get along with. But as soon as the relationship begins to take on a serious hue, you may feel let down.

Sagittarius are full of bounce, perhaps too much bounce to suit you. They are often hard to pin down; they dislike staying put. If he ever has a chance to be on the move, he'll go without so much as a how-do-you-do. Archers are quick people both in mind and spirit. If ever they do make mistakes, it's because of their zip. They leap before they look.

If you offer him good advice, he probably will not follow it. Sagittarius like to rely on their own wits and ways whenever possible.

His up-and-at-'em manner about most things is likely to drive you up the wall at times. And your cautious, deliberate manner is likely to make him seem impatient. He will tease when you're accompanying him on a hike or jogging through the park. He can't abide a slowpoke.

At times you'll find him too much like a kid—too breezy. Don't mistake his youthful zest for premature senility. Sagittarius are equipped with first-class brainpower and know how to use it well. They are often full of good ideas and drive. Generally, they are very broad-minded people and very much concerned with fair play and equality.

In the romance department, he's quite capable of loving you wholeheartedly while treating you like a good buddy. His hail-fellow-well-met manner in the arena of love is likely to scare off a dainty damsel. However, a woman who knows that his heart is in the right place won't mind it too much if, once in a while, he pats her on the back instead of giving her a gentle embrace.

He's not very much of a homebody. He's got ants in his pants and enjoys being on the move. Humdrum routine, especially at home, bores him silly. At the drop of a hat, he may ask you to dine out for a change. He's a past master in the instant-surprise department. He'll love keeping you guessing. His friendly, candid nature will win him many friends. He'll expect his friends to be yours, and vice versa.

Sagittarius is a good father when youngsters are old enough for rough-and-tumble sports. But with infants, Sagittarius may be all thumbs and feel helpless.

CANCER WOMAN
CAPRICORN MAN

The Capricorn man is often not the romantic lover that attracts most women. Still, with his reserve and calm, he is capable of giving his heart completely once he has found the right partner. The Cancer woman who is thorough and deliberate can appreciate these same qualities in the average Capricorn man. He is slow and sure about most things—love included.

He doesn't believe in flirting and would never lead a heart on a merry chase just for the game of it. If you win his trust, he'll give you his heart on a platter. Quite often, it is the woman who has to take the lead when romance is in the air. As long as he knows you're making the advances in earnest, he won't mind—in fact, he'll probably be grateful. Don't get to thinking he's all cold fish; he isn't. While some Capricorns are indeed quite capable of expressing passion, others often have difficulty displaying affection. He should have no trouble in this area, however, once he has found a patient and understanding mate.

The Capricorn man is very interested in getting ahead. He's ambitious and usually knows how to apply himself well to whatever task he undertakes. He's far from being a spendthrift. Like you, he knows how to handle money with extreme care. You, with your knack for putting pennies away for that rainy day, should have no difficulty in understanding his way with money. Capricorn thinks in terms of future security. He saves to make sure that he and his wife have something to fall back on when they reach retirement age. There's nothing wrong with that; in fact, it's a plus quality.

The Capricorn man will want to handle household matters efficiently. Most Cancers have no trouble in doing this. If he should check up on you from time to time, don't let it irritate you. Once you assure him that you can handle this area to his liking, he'll leave it all up to you.

Although he's a hard man to catch when it comes to marriage, once he's made that serious step, he's likely to become possessive. Capricorns need to know that they have the support of their women in whatever they do, every step of the way.

The Capricorn man likes to be liked. He may seem like a dull, reserved person. But underneath it all, he's often got an adventurous nature that has never had the chance to express itself. He may be a real daredevil in his heart of hearts. The right woman, the affectionate and adoring woman, can bring out that hidden zest in his nature.

Although he may not understand his children fully, Capricon will be a loving and dutiful father, raising his children with strong codes of honor and allegiance.

CANCER WOMAN
AQUARIUS MAN

You may find the Aquarius man the most broad-minded man you have ever met. On the other hand, you may find him the most impractical. Oftentimes, he's more of a dreamer than a doer. If you don't mind putting up with a man whose heart and mind are as wide as the universe and whose head is almost always up in the clouds, then start dating that Aquarius who has somehow captured your fancy. Maybe you, with your good sense, can bring him back down to earth when he gets too starry-eyed.

He's no dope, make no mistake about that. He can be busy making some very complicated and idealistic plans when he's got that out-to-lunch look in his eyes. But more than likely, he'll never execute them. After he's shared one or two of his progressive ideas with you, you'll think he's a nut. But don't go jumping to conclusions. There's a saying that Aquarius are a half-century ahead of everybody else in the thinking department.

If you decide to say yes to his will you marry me, you'll find out how right his zany whims are on or about your 50th anniversary. Maybe the waiting will be worth it. Could be that you have an Einstein on your hands—and heart.

Life with an Aquarius won't be one of total despair if you can learn to temper his airiness with your down-to-earth practicality. He won't gripe if you do. The Aquarius man always maintains an open mind. He'll entertain the ideas and opinions of everybody, though he may not agree with all of them.

Don't go tearing your hair out when you find that it's almost impossible to hold a normal conversation with your Aquarius friend at times. He's capable of answering a casual question with an imposing intellectual response. But always try to keep in mind that he means well.

His broad-mindedness doesn't stop when it comes to you and your personal freedom. You won't have to give up any of your hobbies or projects after you're married. In fact, he'll encourage you to continue your interests.

He'll be a kind and generous husband. He'll never quibble over petty things. Keep track of the money you both spend. He can't. Money burns a hole in his pocket.

You'll have plenty of chances to put your legendary patience to good use during your relationship with an Aquarius. At times, you may feel like tossing in the towel, but you'll never call it quits.

Aquarius is a good family man and father. He understands children as much as he loves them.

CANCER WOMAN
PISCES MAN

The Pisces man is perhaps the man you've been looking all over for, high and low—the man you thought didn't exist. As a lover, he'll be attentive and faithful.

The Pisces man is very sensitive and very romantic. Still, he is a reasonable person. He may wish on the moon, yet he's got enough good sense to know that it isn't made of green cheese.

He'll be very considerate of your every wish and whim. He will do his best to be a very compatible mate. The Pisces man is great for showering the object of his affection with all kinds of little gifts and tokens of his affection. He's just the right mixture of dreamer and realist that pleases most women.

When it comes to earning bread and butter, the strong Pisces man will do all right in the world. Quite often they are capable of rising to very high positions. Some do very well as writers or psychiatrists. He'll be as patient and understanding with you as you are with him.

One thing a Pisces man dislikes is pettiness. Anyone who delights in running another into the ground is almost immediately crossed off his list of possible mates. If you have even small grievances with any of your friends, don't tell him about them. He will be quite disappointed in you if you complain and criticize.

If you fall in love with a weak Pisces man, don't give up your job at the office before you get married. Better still: hang onto it a good while after the honeymoon; you may need it.

A funny thing about the man born under the sign of the Fishes is that he can be content almost anywhere. This is perhaps because he is inner-directed and places little value on some exterior things. In a shack or a palace, the Pisces man is capable of making the best of all possible adjustments. He won't kick up a fuss if the roof leaks or if the fence is in sad need of repair. He's got more important things on his mind. Still and all, the Pisces man is not lazy or aimless. It's important to understand that material gain is never a direct goal for him.

Pisces men have a way with the sick and troubled. He'll offer his shoulder to anyone in the mood for a good cry. He can listen to one hard-luck story after another without seeming to tire. Quite often he knows what is bothering someone before that person, himself, realizes what it is. It's almost intuitive with Pisces, it seems.

Children are often delighted with Pisces men. As fathers, they are never strict or faultfinding. They are encouraging and always permissive with their youngsters.

Man—Woman

CANCER MAN
ARIES WOMAN
The Aries woman may be too bossy and busy for you. Aries are ambitious creatures. They can become impatient with people who are more thorough and deliberate than they are, especially if they feel such people are taking too much time. The Aries woman is a fast worker. Sometimes she's so fast she forgets to look where she's

going. When she stumbles or falls, it would be nice if you were there to grab her.

Aries are proud women. They don't like to be told "I told you so" when they err. Criticism can turn them into blocks of ice. Don't begin to think that the Aries woman frequently gets tripped up in her plans. Quite often they are capable of taking aim and hitting the bull's-eye. You'll be flabbergasted at times by their accuracy as well as by their ambition. On the other hand, because of your interest in being sure and safe, you're apt to spot a flaw in your Aries' plans before she does.

You are somewhat slower than Aries in attaining what you have your sights set on. Still, you don't make any mistakes along the way; you're almost always well-prepared.

The Aries woman is sensitive at times. She likes to be handled with gentleness and respect. Let her know that you love her for her brains as well as for her good looks. Never give her cause to become jealous. When your Aries date sees green, you'd better forget about sharing a rosy future together. Handle her with tender love and care and she's yours.

The Aries woman can be giving if she feels her partner is deserving. She is no iceberg; she responds to the proper flame. She needs a man she can look up to and feel proud of. If the shoe fits, put it on. If not, better put your sneakers back on and quietly tiptoe out of her sight. She can cause you heartache if you've made up your mind about her but she hasn't made up hers about you. Aries women are very demanding at times. Some of them are highstrung. They can be difficult if they feel their independence is being hampered.

The cultivated Aries woman makes a wonderful homemaker and hostess. She's clever in decorating and color use. Your house will be tastefully furnished. She'll see to it that it radiates harmony. Friends and acquaintances will love your Aries wife. She knows how to make everyone feel at home and welcome.

Although the Aries woman may not be keen on the responsibilities of motherhood, she is fond of children and the joy they bring.

CANCER MAN
TAURUS WOMAN

A Taurus woman could perhaps understand you better than most women. She is very considerate and loving. She is methodical and thorough in whatever she does. She knows how to take her time in doing things; she is anxious to avoid mistakes. Like you, she is a careful person. She never skips over things that may seem unimportant; she goes over everything with a fine-tooth comb.

Home is very important to the Taurus woman. She is an excellent homemaker. Although your home may not be a palace, it will become, under her care, a comfortable and happy abode. She'll love it when friends drop by for the evening. She is a good cook and enjoys feeding people well. No one will ever go away from your house with an empty stomach.

The Taurus woman is serious about love and affection. When she has taken a tumble for someone, she'll stay by him—for good, if possible. She will try to be practical in romance, to some extent. When she sets her cap for a man, she keeps after him until he's won her. Generally, the Taurus woman is a passionate lover, even though she may appear otherwise at first glance. She is on the lookout for someone who can return her affection fully. Taurus are sometimes given to fits of jealousy and possessiveness. They expect fair play in the area of marriage. When it doesn't happen, they can be bitingly sarcastic and mean.

The Taurus woman is easygoing. She's fond of keeping peace. She won't argue unless she has to. She'll do her best to keep a love relationship on even keel.

Marriage is generally a one-time thing for Taurus. Once they've made the serious step, they seldom try to back out of it. Marriage is for keeps. They are fond of love and warmth. With the right man, they turn out to be ideal wives.

The Taurus woman will respect you for your steady ways; she'll have confidence in your common sense.

Taurus women seldom put up with nonsense from their children. They are not so much strict as concerned. They like their children to be well-behaved and dutiful. Nothing pleases a Taurus mother more than a compliment from a neighbor or teacher about her child's behavior. Although children may inwardly resent the iron hand of a Taurus woman, in later life they are often thankful that they were brought up in such an orderly and conscientious way.

CANCER MAN
GEMINI WOMAN

The Gemini woman may be too much of a flirt ever to take your heart too seriously. Then again, it depends on what kind of mood she's in. Gemini women can change from hot to cold quicker than a cat can wink its eye. Chances are her fluctuations will tire you after a time, and you'll pick up your heart—if it's not already broken into small pieces—and go elsewhere. Women born under the sign of the

Twins have the talent of being able to change their moods and attitudes as frequently as they change their party dresses.

Sometimes, Geminis like to whoop it up. Some of them are good-time gals who love burning the candle to the wick. You'll always see them at parties and gatherings, surrounded by men of all types, laughing gaily or kicking up their heels at every opportunity. Wallflowers, they're not. The next day you may bump into her at the neighborhood library and you'll hardly recognize her for her sensible attire. She'll probably have five or six books under her arm—on five or six different subjects. In fact, she may even work there.

You'll probably find her a dazzling and fascinating creature—for a time, at any rate. Most men do. But when it comes to being serious about love you may find that your sparkling Eve leaves quite a bit to be desired. It's not that she has anything against being serious, it's just that she might find it difficult trying to be serious with you.

At one moment, she'll be capable of praising you for your steadfast and patient ways. The next moment she'll tell you in a cutting way that you're an impossible stick-in-the-mud.

Don't even begin to fathom the depths of her mercurial soul—it's full of false bottoms. She'll resent close investigation anyway, and will make you rue the day you ever took it into your head to try to learn more about her than she feels is necessary. Better keep the relationship fancy free and full of fun until she gives you the go-ahead sign. Take as much of her as she is willing to give; don't ask for more. If she does take a serious interest in you, then she'll come across with the goods.

There will come a time when Gemini will realize that she can't spend her entire life at the ball. The security and warmth you offer are just what she needs for a happy, fulfilled life.

The Gemini mother will be easygoing with her children. She'll probably spoil them and dote on their every whim. Because she has a youthful outlook, she will be a fun playmate for her kids.

CANCER MAN
CANCER WOMAN

The Cancer woman needs to be protected from the cold cruel world. She'll love you for your gentle and kind manner. You are the kind of man who can make her feel safe and secure.

You won't have to pull any he-man or heroic stunts to win her heart; she's not interested in things like that. She's more likely to be impressed by your sure, steady ways—the way you have of putting your arm around her and making her feel that she's the only girl in the world. When she's feeling glum and tears begin to well up in her eyes, you'll know how to calm her fears, no matter how silly some of them may seem.

The Moon Child, like you, is inclined to have her ups and downs. Perhaps you can both learn to smooth out the roughed-up spots in each other's life. She'll most likely worship the ground you walk on or place you on a very high pedestal. Don't disappoint her if you can help it. She'll never disappoint you. The Cancer woman will take great pleasure in devoting the rest of her natural life to you. She'll darn your socks, mend your overalls, scrub floors, wash windows, shop, cook, and do anything short of murder in order to please you and to let you know she loves you. Sounds like that legendary old-fashioned girl, doesn't it? Contrary to popular belief, there are still many of them around and the majority of them are Cancers.

Treat your Cancer mate fairly and she'll treat you like a king. There is one thing you should be warned about, though. Never be unkind to your mother-in-law. It will be the only golden rule your Cancer wife will expect you to live up to. Mother is something special for her. You should have no trouble in understanding this, for your mother has a special place in your heart, too. It's always that way with the Cancer-born. They have great respect and love for family ties. It might be a good idea for you both to get to know each other's relatives before tying the marriage knot, because after the wedding bells have rung, you'll be seeing a lot of them.

Of all the signs in the Zodiac, Cancer is the most maternal. In caring for and bringing up children, she knows just how to combine tenderness and discipline. A child couldn't ask for a better mother. Cancer women are sympathetic, affectionate, and patient with children. Both of you will make excellent parents, especially when the children are young. When they grow older you'll most likely be reluctant to let them go out into the world.

CANCER MAN
LEO WOMAN

The Leo woman can make most men roar like lions. If any woman in the Zodiac has that indefinable something that can make men lose their heads and find their hearts, it's Leo.

She's got more than a fair share of charm and glamour and she knows how to make the most of her assets, especially when she's in the company of the opposite sex. Jealous men lose either their cool or their sanity when trying to woo a woman born under the sign of the Lion. She likes to kick up her heels and doesn't care who knows it. She often makes heads turn and tongues wag. You don't have to believe any of what you hear—it's most likely just jealous gossip or wishful thinking. Needless to say, other women in her vicinity turn green with envy and will try anything to put her out of commission.

Although this vamp makes the blood rush to your head and makes you momentarily forget all the things you thought were important and necessary in your life, you may feel differently when you come back down to earth and the stars are out of your eyes. You may feel that although this vivacious creature can make you feel wonderful, she just isn't the type you planned to bring home to Mother. Not that your mother might disapprove of your choice— but you might after the shoes and rice are a thing of the past. Although the Leo woman may do her best to be a good wife for you, chances are she'll fall short of your idea of what a good wife should be.

If you're planning on not going as far as the altar with that Leo woman who has you flipping your lid, you'd better be financially equipped for some very expensive dating. Be prepared to shower her with expensive gifts and to take her dining and dancing to the smartest spots in town. Promise her the moon if you're in a position to go that far. Luxury and glamour are two things that are bound to lower a Leo's resistance. She has expensive tastes, and you'd better cater to them if you expect to get to first base with the Lioness.

If you've got an important business deal to clinch and you have doubts as to whether you can swing it or not, bring your Leo along to the business luncheon. Chances are that with her on your arm, you'll be able to win any business battle with both hands tied. She won't have to say or do anything—just be there at your side. The grouchiest oil magnate can be transformed into a gushing, obedient schoolboy if there's a charming Lioness in the room.

Leo mothers are blind to the faults of their children. They make very loving and affectionate mothers and tend to give their youngsters everything under the sun.

CANCER MAN
VIRGO WOMAN

The Virgo woman is particular about choosing her men friends. She's not interested in going out with anybody. She has her own idea of what a boyfriend or prospective husband should be. Perhaps that image has something of you in it.

Generally, she's quiet and correct. She doesn't believe that nonsense has any place in a love affair. She's serious about love and she'll expect you to be. She's looking for a man who has both feet on the ground—someone who can take care of himself as well as her. She knows the value of money and how to get the most out of a dollar. She's far from being a spendthrift. Throwing money around turns her stomach, even when it isn't her money.

She'll most likely be very shy about romancing. Even the simple act of holding hands may make her turn crimson—at least, on the first couple of dates. You'll have to make all the advances, and you'll have to be careful not to make any wrong moves. She's capable of showing anyone who oversteps the boundaries of common decency the door. It may even take quite a long time before she'll accept that goodnight kiss at the front gate. Don't give up. You are perhaps the kind of man who can bring out the warm woman in her.

There is love and tenderness underneath Virgo's seemingly frigid facade. It will take a patient and understanding man to bring it out into the open. She may have the idea that sex is reserved for marriage. Like you, she has a few old-fashioned concepts. And, like you, it's all or nothing. So if you are the right man, gentle and affectionate, you will melt her reserve.

When a Virgo has accepted you as a lover or mate, she won't stint in giving her love in return. You'll be surprised at the transformation your earnest attention can bring about in this quiet kind of woman. When in love, Virgos only listen to their hearts, not to what the neighbors say.

Virgo women are honest about love once they've come to grips with it. They don't appreciate hypocrisy—particularly in this area of life. They will always be true to their hearts—even if it means tossing you over for a new love. But if you convince her that you are earnest about your interest in her, she'll reciprocate your love and affection and never leave you. Do her wrong once, however, and you can be sure she'll call the whole thing off.

Virgo mothers are tender and loving. They know what's good for their children and will always take great pains in bringing them up correctly.

CANCER MAN
LIBRA WOMAN

It's a woman's prerogative to change her mind. This wise saying characterizes the Libra woman. Her changes of mind, in spite of her undeniable charm, might drive even a man of your changeable moods up the wall. She's capable of smothering you with love and kisses one day and on the next avoid you like the plague. If you think you're a man of great patience, then perhaps you can tolerate her sometime-ness without suffering too much. However, if you own up to the fact that you're a mere mortal who can only take so much, then you'd better fasten your attention on a girl who's somewhat more constant.

But don't get the wrong idea—a love affair with a Libra is not all bad. In fact, it can have an awful lot of pluses to it. Libra women are soft, very feminine, and warm. She doesn't have to vamp all over the place in order to gain a man's attention. Her delicate presence is enough to warm any man's heart. One smile and you're a piece of putty in the palm of her hand.

She can be fluffy and affectionate. On the other hand, her indecision about which dress to wear, what to cook for dinner, or whether or not to redecorate could make you tear your hair out. What will perhaps be more exasperating is her flat denial of the accusation that she cannot make even the simplest decision. The trouble is that she wants to be fair or just in all matters. She'll spend hours weighing both sides of an argument or situation. Don't make her rush into a decision; that would only irritate her.

The Libra woman likes to be surrounded by beautiful things. Money is no object when beauty is concerned. There will always be antiques and objects of art in her apartment. She'll know how to arrange them tastefully, too, to show them off. Women under this sign are fond of beautiful clothes and furnishings. They will run up bills without batting an eye—if given the chance.

Once she's cottoned to you, the Libra woman will do everything in her power to make you happy. She'll wait on you hand and foot when you're sick, bring you breakfast in bed on Sundays, and even read you the funny papers if you're too sleepy to open your eyes. She'll be very thoughtful and devoted. If anyone dares suggest you're not the grandest man in the world, your Libra wife will give that person a good sounding-out.

Libras work wonders with children. Gentle persuasion and affection are all she uses in bringing them up. Her subtlety sets a good example for them to follow.

CANCER MAN
SCORPIO WOMAN

When the Scorpio woman chooses to be sweet, she's apt to give the impression that butter wouldn't melt in her mouth . . . but, of course, it would. When her temper flies, so will everything else that isn't bolted down. She can be as hot as a tamale or as cool as a cucumber when she wants. Whatever mood she's in, you can be sure it's for real. She doesn't believe in poses or hypocrisy.

The Scorpio woman is often seductive and sultry. Her femme

fatale charm can pierce through the hardest of hearts like a laser ray. She doesn't have to look like Mata Hari (many of them resemble the tomboy next door) but once you've looked into those tantalizing eyes, you're a goner.

The Scorpio woman can be a whirlwind of passion. Life with her will not be all smiles and smooth sailing. If you think you can handle a woman who can spit bullets, try your luck. Your stable and steady nature will most likely have a calming effect on her. You're the kind of man she can trust and rely on. But never cross her—even on the smallest thing. If you do, you'd better tell Fido to make room for you in the doghouse—you'll be his guest for the next couple of days.

Generally, the Scorpio woman will keep family battles within the walls of your home. When company visits, she's apt to give the impression that married life with you is one big joyride. It's just her way of expressing her loyalty to you—at least in front of others. She believes that family matters are and should stay private. She certainly will see to it that others have a high opinion of you both.

Although she's an individualist, after she has married she'll put her own interests aside for those of the man she loves. With a woman like this behind you, you can't help but go far. She'll never try to take over your role as boss of the family. She'll give you all the support you need in order to fulfill that role. She won't complain if the going gets rough. She knows how to take the bitter with the sweet. She is a courageous woman. She's as anxious as you are to find that place in the sun for you both. She's as determined a person as you are.

Although Scorpio loves her children, she may not be too affectionate toward them. She'll make a devoted mother, though. She'll be anxious to see them develop their talents. She'll teach the children to be courageous and steadfast.

CANCER MAN
SAGITTARIUS WOMAN

The Sagittarius woman is hard to keep track of: first she's here, then she's there. She's a woman with a severe case of itchy feet. She's got to keep on the move.

People generally like her because of her hail-fellow-well-met manner and her breezy charm. She is constantly good-natured and almost never cross. With the female Archer you're likely to strike up a palsy-walsy relationship. You might not be interested in letting it go any farther. She probably won't sulk if you leave it on a friendly basis. Treat her like a kid sister and she'll love it.

She'll probably be attracted to you because of your restful, self-assured manner. She'll need a friend like you to help her over the rough spots in her life. She'll most likely turn to you for advice frequently.

There is nothing malicious about a woman born under this sign. She is full of bounce and good cheer. Her sunshiny disposition can be relied upon even on the rainiest of days. No matter what she says or does, you'll always know that she means well. Sagittarius are sometimes short on tact. Some of them say anything that comes into their heads, no matter what the occasion. Sometimes the words that tumble out of their mouths seem downright cutting and cruel; they mean well but often everything they say comes out wrong. She's quite capable of losing her friends—and perhaps even yours—through a careless slip of the lip. Always remember that she is full of good intentions. Stick with her if you like her and try to help her mend her ways.

She's may not be the quiet, home-loving woman you'd be interested in marrying, but she'll certainly be lots of fun to pal around with. Quite often, Sagittarius women are outdoor types. They're crazy about things like fishing, camping, and mountain climbing. They love the wide open spaces. They are fond of all kinds of animals. Make no mistake about it: this busy little lady is no slouch. She's full of pep and vigor.

She's great company most of the time; she's more fun than a three-ring circus when she's in the right company. You'll like her for her candid and direct manner. On the whole, Sagittarius are very kind and sympathetic women.

If you do wind up marrying this girl-next-door type, you'd better see to it that you take care of all financial matters. Sagittarius often let money run through their fingers like sand.

A Sagittarius mother may smother her children with love on the one hand, then give them all of the freedom they think they need. It can be very confusing.

CANCER MAN
CAPRICORN WOMAN
The Capricorn woman may not be the most romantic woman of the Zodiac, but she's far from frigid when she meets the right man. She believes in true love. She doesn't appreciate getting involved in flings. To her, they're just a waste of time. She's looking for a man who means business—in life as well as in love. Although she can be very affectionate with her boyfriend or mate, she tends to let her head govern her heart. That is not to say that she is a cool, calculating cucumber. On the contrary, she just feels she can be more hon-

est about love if she consults her brains first. She wants to size up the situation first before throwing her heart in the ring. She wants to make sure it won't get stepped on.

The Capricorn woman is faithful, dependable, and systematic in just about everything that she undertakes. She is quite concerned with security and sees to it that every penny she spends is spent wisely. She is very economical about using her time, too. She does not believe in whittling away her energy on a scheme that is bound not to pay off.

Ambitious themselves, they are quite often attracted to ambitious men—men who are interested in getting somewhere in life. If a man of this sort wins her heart, she'll stick by him and do all she can to help him get to the top.

The Capricorn woman is almost always diplomatic. She makes an excellent hostess. She can be very influential when your business acquaintances come to dinner.

The Capricorn woman is likely to be very concerned, if not downright proud, about her family tree. Relatives are important to her, particularly if they're socially prominent. Never say a cross word about her family members. That can really go against her grain and she'll punish you by not talking for days.

She's generally thorough in whatever she does: cooking, housekeeping, entertaining. Capricorn women are well-mannered and gracious, no matter what their backgrounds. They seem to have it in their natures to always behave properly.

If you should marry a woman born under this sign, you need never worry about her going on a wild shopping spree. They understand the value of money better than most women. If you turn over your paycheck to her at the end of the week, you can be sure that a good hunk of it will go into the bank and that all the bills will be paid on time.

With children, the Capricorn mother is both loving and correct. She'll see to it that they're polite and respectful and that they honor the codes they are taught when young.

CANCER MAN
AQUARIUS WOMAN

The woman born under the sign of the Water Bearer can be odd and eccentric at times. Some say that this is the source of her mysterious charm. You may think she's just a plain screwball, and you may be right.

Aquarius women often have their heads full of dreams and stars in their eyes. By nature, they are often unconventional; they have their own ideas about how the world should be run. Sometimes their ideas may seem pretty weird—chances are they're just a little bit too progressive. There is a saying that runs. The way the Aquarius thinks, so will the world in fifty years.

If you find yourself falling in love with a woman born under this sign, you'd better fasten your safety belt. It may take some time before you know what she's like and even then, you may have nothing to go on but a string of vague hunches.

She can be like a rainbow: full of dazzling colors. She's like no other girl you've ever known. There is something about her that is definitely charming, yet elusive. You'll never be able to put your finger on it. She seems to radiate adventure and optimism without even trying. She'll most likely be the most tolerant and open-minded woman you've ever encountered.

If you find that she's too much mystery and charm for you to handle—and being a Cancer, chances are you might—just talk it out with her and say that you think it would be better if you called it quits. She'll most likely give you a peck on the cheek and say "Okay, but let's still be friends." Aquarius women are like that. Perhaps you'll both find it easier to get along in a friendship than in a romance.

It is not difficult for her to remain buddy-buddy with an ex-lover. For many Aquarius, the line between friendship and romance is a fuzzy one.

She's not a jealous person and while you're romancing her, she won't expect you to be, either. You'll find her a free spirit most of the time. Just when you think you know her inside out, you'll discover that you don't really know her at all. She's a very sympathetic and warm person. She is often helpful to those in need of assistance and advice.

She'll seldom be suspicious even when she has every right to be. If the man she loves makes a little slip, she's likely to forgive it and forget it.

Aquarius makes a fine mother. Her positive and bighearted qualities are easily transmitted to her children. They will be taught tolerance at an early age.

CANCER MAN
PISCES WOMAN

The Pisces woman places great value on love and romance. She's gentle, kind, and romantic. Like you, she has very high ideals, and will only give her heart to a man who she feels can live up to her expectations.

Many a man dreams of an alluring Pisces woman. You're perhaps no exception. Even though she appears soft and cuddly, she has a sultry, seductive charm that can win the heart of almost any man.

She will not try to wear the pants in the relationship. She'll let you be the brains of the family. She's content to play a behind-the-scenes role in order to help you achieve your goals.

She can be very ladylike and proper. Your business associates and friends will be dazzled by her warmth and femininity. Although she's a charmer, there is a lot more to her than just a pretty exterior. There is a brain ticking away behind that gentle, womanly facade. You may never become aware of it—that is, until you're married to her. It's no cause for alarm, however; she'll most likely never use it against you, only to help you and possibly set you on a more successful path.

If she feels you're botching up your married life through careless behavior or if she feels you could be earning more money than you do, she'll tell you about it. But any wife would.

No one had better dare say one uncomplimentary word about you in her presence. It could set the stage for an emotional scene. Pisces women are maddeningly temperamental and can go to theatrical extremes when expressing their feelings. Their reaction to adversity or frustration can run the gamut from tears to tantrums and back again.

She can do wonders with a house. She is very fond of dramatic and beautiful things. There will always be plenty of fresh-cut flowers around the house. She will choose charming artwork and antiques, if they are affordable.

She'll have an extra special dinner prepared for you when you come home from an important business meeting. Don't dwell on the boring details of the meeting, though. But if you need that big idea, to seal a contract or make a conquest, your Pisces woman is sure to confide a secret that will guarantee your success.

Treat her with tenderness and generosity and your relationship will be an enjoyable one. A bunch of beautiful flowers will never fail to make her eyes light up. See to it that you never forget her birthday or your anniversary. These things are very important to her.

If you are patient and kind, you can keep a Pisces woman happy for a lifetime. She, however, is not without her faults. You may find her lacking in practicality and good old-fashioned stoicism; you may even feel that she uses her tears as a method of getting her own way.

Pisces is a strong, self-sacrificing mother. She will teach her children the value of service to the community while not letting them lose their individuality.

CANCER
LUCKY NUMBERS 2007

Lucky numbers and astrology can be linked through the movements of the Moon. Each phase of the thirteen Moon cycles vibrates with a sequence of numbers for your Sign of the Zodiac over the course of the year. Using your lucky numbers is a fun system that connects you with tradition.

New Moon	First Quarter	Full Moon	Last Quarter
Dec. 20 ('06)	Dec. 27 ('06)	Jan. 3	Jan. 11
3 1 9 4	7 2 5 0	0 3 8 1	1 5 8 6
Jan. 18	Jan. 25	Feb. 2	Feb. 10
6 9 9 3	3 7 1 0	4 4 6 1	0 4 2 5
Feb. 17	Feb. 24	March 3	March 11
5 9 6 1	4 7 2 7	9 8 4 7	7 5 8 3
March 18	March 25	April 2	April 10
3 6 3 6	0 4 9 2	2 6 9 7	7 1 5 8
April 17	April 24	May 2	May 9
8 3 6 6	1 0 6 8	6 6 4 7	7 2 5 9
May 16	May 23	May 31	June 8
3 0 1 9	9 7 2 5	9 3 6 1	0 4 8 2
June 14	June 22	June 30	July 7
2 5 9 5	7 4 8 2	7 3 7 1	0 5 8 0
July 14	July 22	July 29	August 5
2 6 2 4	8 2 1 8	1 6 9 4	4 7 1 5
August 12	August 20	August 28	Sept. 3
5 0 3 7	1 8 3 6	5 4 8 2	2 5 9 5
Sept. 11	Sept. 19	Sept. 26	Oct. 3
5 7 2 5	5 3 6 2	8 9 3 6	0 1 6 8
Oct. 11	Oct. 19	Oct. 26	Nov. 1
8 3 6 4	4 7 2 8	3 6 0 4	4 9 2 6
Nov. 9	Nov. 17	Nov. 24	Dec. 1
6 9 7 1	1 5 8 6	6 0 3 7	3 5 9 3
Dec. 9	Dec. 17	Dec. 23	Dec. 31
3 1 4 8	8 2 6 5	0 3 8 0	1 0 5 8

CANCER
YEARLY FORECAST 2007

Forecast for 2007 Concerning Business
and Financial Affairs, Job Prospects,
Travel, Health, Romance and Marriage
for Persons Born with the Sun
in the Zodiacal Sign of Cancer.
June 22–July 22

For those born under the influence of the Sun in the zodiacal sign of Cancer, ruled by the Moon, planet of feeling and fluctuation, 2007 will be a year of no gain without a degree of pain. While difficult at times, the resulting outcomes will be well worth the effort and sacrifices you make. The year ahead is a proving ground of whatever you've learned about money. For Cancers who pass the tests and trials, long-term financial security can be secured by the second half of the year. All twelve months are going to be fantastic for job opportunities. Work and career ambitions are now within your grasp, but you need to establish a solid base and then build up from there. Travel may not be at the top of your agenda. However, you can meticulously plan a future dream trip. Your health can be at risk simply because you refuse to give it sufficient attention. With so much on your plate at work, relationships will tend to suffer a certain level of neglect. If there just doesn't seem to be time or energy left for this extremely important area of your life, don't fret. Once Jupiter enters Capricorn, your relationship sector in late December, it should be a whole new ball game. Cancer singles can then find a partner, couples can renew romance and mutual appreciation, while families get the quality time they deserve.

Taskmaster Saturn has been turning your financial affairs into a sometimes forbidding experience. It's for your own good, if only you can see that. There will be some tough times, but hopefully that will scare you enough to force necessary changes to ensure your future long-term security. After all, you don't want to live on the edge forever. Whatever economies you are able to put into place this year should prove of enduring benefit. One of the main tasks of 2007 is lowering outstanding debt. This is important not just from your perspective, but in the view of your creditors as well. Borrowing simply has to stop, hopefully once and for all. Lessons learned now should last the rest of your life. Cancer people who are foolishly overextended may be at the mercy of rising interest rates. Try always to pay your way as you go and to avoid living on credit. The other side of this coin involves saving. Every time you spend on a luxury, put the same amount of money aside for that proverbial rainy day. That way your investment pool is sure to increase while unnecessary indulgences are reduced. In mid-2007 there is great opportunity to ramp up earnings to the maximum you're capable of generating. Don't hold back with low expectations matched by an equally low income. By year's end you'll be amazed at how your sustained effort in the right direction has paid off, creating an impressive bank balance and portfolio of performing investments. Stay on guard for parasitic types who want to feed off your hard work. While you may be remembered in a generous relative's will, don't rely on other people's money.

This is one of the best years on record for enhanced job prospects in your chosen profession. Change may come sooner than you anticipated, with leads from late last year turning into real offers during the first quarter of 2007. Despite any lingering doubts or anxiety on your part, the position may be just what you wanted. There's no excuse or reason for keeping an unsatisfying job and denying your profound need for vocational satisfaction. Do everything in your power to make the right choice, then let destiny do the rest. Be ready, willing, and able to take on larger responsibility and more authority. If in search of power in your working life, you are almost certain to find circumstances that offer it. However, expect rigorous testing to prove yourself in the line of fire. There's a chance to jump on the up escalator and ride all the way to the top. Effective productivity combined with a positive attitude can't fail to impress employers and clients alike. Many Cancers will be confronted with the need to conquer undermining mood swings in the workplace. Nobody wants to work with someone who often turns into the incredible sulk. You will get credit where credit is due, and super efforts will be suitably rewarded. When the power politics develop on the job, give no quarter and take no prisoners. Compassion and mercy on your part may only be seen as a weakness to be taken advantage of. If seeking an improved situation or promotion, prospects are best between March and May and again from August through September. Cancer business operators should be on the lookout for top-notch employees. If you need assistance, your prayers could be answered beyond your wildest expectations.

For some years, Cancer people have been experiencing a foot-loose and fancy-free period signaled by Uranus in Pisces. However, giving in to urges for change could be your undoing. Taking care of business and your own turf is of far greater importance now. The exhilaration of discovering new places and experiences in the wider world may have to be postponed. Although there are likely to be numerous invitations to travel, beg off and enjoy watching videos of the adventures. Interesting people who live abroad are sure to maintain ongoing contact and communication. Rather than making a long journey to meet them, use available technology to connect in cyberspace. Even trips that have already been arranged and booked may have to be postponed or canceled due to unforeseen circumstances. A brief trip in April might be a good chance for rest and recovery, which will renew your energy and spirits for the rest of the year. Keep your house open to visitors from overseas and traveling foreigners. The spirit of their adventure will rub off on you. And you'll have a long list of people to visit and places to stay in years to come. The last good chance for getting away presents itself in November.

Don't overlook wellness this year. An obvious culprit of ill health is likely to be workaholism. Whether you're in the best job or the worst one, overdoing can be physically harmful. This applies not only to high-powered executives or factory workers, but also to homemakers, students, and anyone who finds it hard to stop and take a break. Little mistakes and errors of judgment, such as inadequate nutrition, junk food addiction, and stressful stimulants like coffee, will take their inevitable toll. For Cancer people, eating is often a prime cause of physical upset. If you are facing a long period of work, prepare beforehand and adopt a lifestyle that accommodates hectic activity. That may mean going to bed earlier, eating right, and substantial regular exercise. Rather than fearing an illness, practice preventive measures. Schedule at least one thorough medical examination. Once you get the all-clear, it will be a huge relief, releasing a torrent of energy for activities other than worry. If there is a condition that needs treatment, you'll be in a position to receive the care you need for profound healing. Being too busy or too tired is not a valid excuse for letting yourself become run-down. Take good care of yourself rather than attending to other people.

Significant relationships can be shortchanged because of your ambition to get ahead financially and in your career. You may have become romantically disillusioned due to past failures or difficulties. While money and love often go together, it's not a matter of simply swapping one for the other. A life without love will be very lacking, no matter how successful you become. Work through past issues involving a former mate or partner. Otherwise the bitter taste of disappointment could linger for far too long. Remember to nurture the important relationships of your life with love, care, and quality time. Even determined Cancer singles need the relaxation and distraction of stimulating company and meaningful friendships. A major partnership is more likely to be ending than beginning. If that's the case, get on with it efficiently and in a dignified fashion. Don't pretend it's not happening to you. Couples who have been courting for a while may now be almost ready to tie the knot. Ideally, wait until late in the year or even into 2008 before taking that big step. Becoming a parent is foreseen for many by November. Singles who are players may want to sustain a solo status but will have a busy time meeting many potential candidates for love. As long as you're not expecting to meet that one special person, things will be fine. Your ultimate partner may not be revealed to you until next year, but meanwhile you can enjoy an active social scene.

CANCER DAILY FORECAST

January–December 2007

JANUARY

1. MONDAY. Spirited. Awakening to the first day of the New Year full of energy and with an urge to get up and go could take you by surprise after last night's celebrating. If you find yourself among strange company in unfamiliar surroundings you are sure to be disconcerted. Thinking fast on your feet might well be required in order to evade trouble or a heated confrontation. Being in a reclusive private sanctuary with your devoted partner or longtime companion fosters deep conversation. This serious discussion will help to focus relevant resolutions for 2007. Try to avoid contentious topics and opinionated hotheads, leaving you in peace to contemplate what's personally most important to you.

2. TUESDAY. Renewing. Today more properly marks the start of your personal new year because the Moon shines in your sign as it waxes to full. The focus of attention is on you, best seen in the mirror of your significant relationships. Go out of your way to honor the notable persons you rely upon. Rather than finding fault, praise those who butter your daily bread. Pleasing yourself remains the essence of the day, so make sure to look after number one. Any restlessness should be put to good use by connecting with people who matter most in your life. A normally penny-pinching person might shock you with an offer to pay for a movie or theatrical performance.

3. WEDNESDAY. Resolved. A setting Full Moon and a rising Sun straddle the horizon this morning, making a glorious sight for early starters. If you miss it, check out the reverse situation at sunset. This lunar event is of particular significance for Cancer people, putting you and your relationships in the glaring spotlight. Financial dealings and commercial negotiations can be hammered out, but the other parties will be determined and reluctant to even give an inch. Stand your ground against anyone who puts your convictions to the test. Connections in high places might pull strings in your favor.

Hired guns with special expertise should be employed to give you a needed advantage.

4. THURSDAY. Grasping. Wanting to do things your way may meet with indifference or fall on deaf ears. If you're not in a cooperative mood, arrange to work independently. Later in the day, settling accounts and paying bills could put a damper on your spending plans, especially if you are now counting the cost of a recent luxury purchase. Rather than worrying over the amount you paid, appreciate and enjoy what you bought. This is a good time to reassess and realign your needs and desires if happiness seems remote. Bringing joy to those you like and love could be more to the point. Share in the success of your mate or partner rather than competing or feeling threatened and left out.

5. FRIDAY. Energetic. Cancer businesspeople can expect a busy, profitable day. An enthusiastic attitude and glamour presentation will enliven routine proceedings, as well as doing wonders for the bottom line. Take advantage of advice and expertise offered to you. Of course, you may feel vulnerable by acknowledging your limits while relying upon employees, contractors, or experts. Yet a display of humility on your part encourages those working on your behalf to give their best. Asking for help is nothing to be ashamed of. Discuss any major purchase or expenditure with your mate or partner before proceeding any further. Your spouse is likely to understand if you must work late but don't let this become a habit.

6. SATURDAY. Constructive. Nothing less than commitment and dedication will do today. A huge amount can be accomplished if you are willing to roll up your sleeves and get your hands dirty. Tackle the big jobs, leaving minor chores for another time. Using the right tools can make all the difference. If you don't already own them, buy whatever equipment and materials are required, and make sure they're all high quality. Cutting corners on cost will prove financially foolish in the long run since you'll only get what you pay for. Hardworking employees definitely earn their pay, and you can have confidence in a contractor to do a great job. Building wealth is the overall aim to bear in mind, and earnest efforts will make it happen.

7. SUNDAY. Expansive. Despite being a day of rest, you may try to cover as many bases as possible. Obsession with order might motivate you to focus on your to-do list and then go shopping for appropriate home-office supplies. A mounting pile of paperwork has to be tackled sooner rather than later. This is a very good juncture to initiate a methodical plan. Just expect early glitches as you iron out the bugs. Running around town might involve your mate or partner's business or be at their request. However, don't let someone else's agenda drive you to the point of nervous exhaustion. Calls and visits could escalate later as the tempo picks up. An earnest individual hopes for a serious conversation with you.

8. MONDAY. Useful. Straight talking from the outset can save a lot of trouble, bother, and conflict. In any contest or negotiation, the wishes of the strongest party are likely to prevail. However, there's an opportunity now for a challenger to make a persuasive case. A convincing expression can sway the outcome. Lines of communication are open with your spouse or partner, offering the chance to even discuss difficult issues. Health or money matters require some practical attention. A physical checkup or a financial consultation can be confidently scheduled. Once you've been reliably informed of your status, you'll be able to take whatever action is deemed necessary.

9. TUESDAY. Upsetting. A bad mood or ill-tempered reaction could have physical consequences. This may just be a minor irritation like indigestion or a heahache. However, continuous daily stress may contribute to potential illness and disease of greater concern. Be careful of the responses you make under pressure, staying as calm and centered as possible. Keeping things in proportion definitely helps. Remember that it's a waste of energy to sweat the small stuff. If a coworker's behavior is habitually annoying, choose the right moment to address the issue. Keep communications clear and clean. Complaining simply will inflame tense situations. Peace and harmony prevail later, but only after expressive release.

10. WEDNESDAY. Happy. Warm love and cuddly intimacy in your familiar comfort zone makes it hard to leave the house early. Your relationship definitely improves when mutual affection overrules criticism or cold-hearted judgment. The healing power of real love shouldn't be underestimated. Even Cancers who are currently without a partner can exchange caring kindness with family members and pets. Happily puttering around at home would suit you, especially if there's fine company. Cancers who must leave the nest and go to work will find most interactions pleasant and helpful. An easygoing atmosphere in the workplace promotes productivity, and much can be achieved quite smoothly.

11. THURSDAY. Challenging. There could be trouble in paradise today. Even loving partners will want a reality check concerning commitment, joint resources, or survival issues. This serves as a reminder that maintaining harmony requires constant vigilance and continual adjustment to shifting circumstances. Dreams and plans demand practical steps to make them happen, or at least to start such processes. Utilize the tough attitudes and questioning of experienced individuals to motivate clear thinking and appropriate action. If their advice stops you in your tracks, that may be beneficial in preventing false moves and putting inflated fantasies in their true perspective.

12. FRIDAY. Rewarding. A playful mood descends on hard-working Cancer people. It's time to reward your recent effort with fancied personal pleasures. Uptight or conservative individuals may disapprove of your lighthearted attitude. Leave them to their responsibilities, while you do what's right for you. Pairing up with just one person might be a mistake now, since they could be hard to please and are likely to cramp your style. Even taking a break from your steady or spouse seems wise, although it could upset your relationship. Get out of the house this evening, and stimulate your senses with worldly temptations. It will be refreshing to simply do your own thing. Cancer singles are better off staying that way.

13. SATURDAY. Problematic. This will be a very social day as you meet many new people but get close to none of them. Spending time in the company of players leaves you no wiser as to their true nature. Coming to know and understand intimately is likely to be difficult. Although the attraction is there, along with shared interests, they may have something to hide. Certainly there's a mystery, which may not be easy to solve. If you have any doubts about an individual, err on the side of caution. Jumping into a relationship with someone you hardly know is likely to disappoint you, whether it's business or pleasure. Cancer parents may need to deal with a youngster falling into bad company. Be gentle, but wise them up.

14. SUNDAY. Rejuvenating. Greeting the day with a sober sense of reality can be a downer but will also be grounding. Perhaps it's nothing worse than a hangover after last night. Disillusionment is possible even for trusting and hopeful souls. Now is the time to put all that behind you and make this a day of meaningful accomplishment. Recovery can be swift if you are not emotionally stuck in a past full of bad feelings. A physical workout will do you a world of good. And you will feel even better once distasteful chores are faced and satisfactorily completed. Your mood gradually improves with the comfort of familiar routines and a hearty meal shared with enjoyable company.

15. MONDAY. Variable. Positive expectations can prove unsettling if what you hoped for fails to materialize, at least in the way you anticipated. A sense of humor helps ease the anxiety of disruption and turmoil. Rather than expecting the worst or the best, just wait and see. There's sure to be a surprise in store. Long-distance communications and technical equipment essential for a job might let you down. A journey is likely to suffer a temporary delay or other setback. For travelers, foreign customs and lifestyles can be uncomfortable, hard to understand or get used to. Adventurous diners and home chefs could be perplexed by exotic cuisine or curious recipes.

16. TUESDAY. Exciting. A firecracker of a day suits those of feisty spirit and indomitable purpose. Your drive for achievement is unmistakable. Don't hold back, give it all you've got! A project near to completion only needs to be signed off and settled up. Whether you're being paid or doing the paying, satisfaction is assured for a job well done. Vitality is high, and physical energy will seek relevant expression and appropriate exertion. Aim at a high goal. You're likely to hit the mark if you apply yourself. With emotions running high and romantic inclinations on the rise, now's the time to get together with someone irresistible and very desirable.

17. WEDNESDAY. Volatile. Relationships take on even more priority now that Mars has entered your partnership sector. This can lead to trouble with competitors, rivals, and open enemies, plus some liaisons you will welcome with open arms. Be aware that the advantage in any contest may now pass to your opponent, so come up with suitable strategies to offset this. Don't shut the door on flexible negotiations. Mutually satisfying agreements are possible where there's enough give-and-take. Of course, you're more likely to do the giving, while they do the taking. Paying for assistance from individuals with the right expertise and experience will be wise in circumstances that are beyond your capacity.

18. THURSDAY. Measured. Weighing the pros and cons of a partnership choice or decision could preoccupy your thoughts. This quieter time of the New Moon presents the opportunity to carefully consider the implications of a particular alliance. It might be business or personal, but it's likely that money and dreams are tied up with the situation. What someone else is promising or representing to you may seem quite wonderful. However, removed of all the gloss and glamour of projections, hopes, and wishes, you must decide if it is going to be real, reliable, affordable, trustworthy, and stable. Now's the time to pause and allow yourself to become certain of any impending move or deal.

19. FRIDAY. Perceptive. Use your crystal-clear thinking and sharp mental skills to good advantage. This is the time to take a long, hard look at financial accountability. Carefully review any situations involving money belonging or owed to other people, including loans, taxation, and insurance matters. A partner may be turn to you for advice about a major purchase or investment. Whatever you think, give it to them straight and don't sugarcoat your views. Honesty and integrity matter a great deal now in all of your relationships. You and a newcomer on the scene can come to know each other much more deeply, setting the stage for greater trust and intimacy. Reveal your hand, warts and all, and request the same of them.

20. SATURDAY. Bittersweet. Recent revelations and conversations with your mate or partner have brought matters to a make-or-break point. Love and money are difficult topics which can drive a wedge between you. One of you is likely to be overly romantic, while the other is excessively realistic and cautious. Choose to either agree to compromise and consolidate the relationship, or take a break from each other to seriously consider going your separate ways. There's the potential for faith and trust in each other, but equally there can be doubt and distance. Only time will tell which way your relationship will go. Face such concerns rather than denying the possibility or sweeping them under the rug.

21. SUNDAY. Challenging. An adventure will suit you today, especially with a robust companion who also relishes a challenge. Hiking and skiing are the sorts of outdoor recreation to get your heart and blood pumping. Strange environments and unusual destinations suit spirited Cancer explorers, but an experienced guide is worth considering before taking risks. Couples can have a fine day attending a cultural event of mutual interest. If seeking vocational direction, you may receive good guidance which steers you in the right direction. Find a person to do some repairs and maintenance through a recommendation or referral, rather than by choosing randomly in the phone book or by an Internet listing.

22. MONDAY. Outgoing. Meeting people is what it's all about today, so forget being shy, withdrawn, self-conscious, or private. Your current connections can open the door to better employment, health, and wealth. Don't hesitate to use the contacts at your dis-

posal. In legal and official concerns, who you know could make all
the difference to decisions and outcomes. If traveling, look up local
residents from your address book and pay them a visit. Even if it's
just someone who knows someone you know, a lot of good may
come from reaching out to them. A public presentation, publishing,
or a promotional venture can overcome technical hiccups and successfully reach your intended audience.

23. TUESDAY. Forceful. Joint decision making can be difficult
due to lack of cooperation. You're likely to receive little help. Cancers in leadership positions could be challenged by rivals who think
they can do the job better. This is no time to show weakness. Instead, lay down the law fast and get people to fall into line so that
you don't lose respect. Steer clear of aggressive types, especially in
public places where an encounter with a loose cannon is possible.
An argument with your mate or partner over money might embar-
rass you, especially if it's on view for others to witness. Purchases
and deals seem to be in the seller's favor, and prices will be high despite attempts at bargaining.

24. WEDNESDAY. Positive. Leave practical, hardheaded roles to
those best suited for such displays. Instead, use your initiative to
scope more imaginative and visionary directions. It will take
courage to stand up for your convictions and activate what you believe in. Nevertheless, this is a fine time to launch a well-considered
commercial venture, even if you must borrow money to make it
happen. Investment options look profitable, especially if you're
prepared to stay in for the long haul. General career prospects are
promising. Despite formidable competition or opposition, your experience and talent should help you prevail. By offering quality
service second to none, you will satisfy even the most discerning
customer.

25. THURSDAY. Unsettled. A friend's success could mean they're
going overseas to follow their fortunes. Or perhaps frustration with
limited local opportunities are forcing them to look for prospects
further afield. One way or another you will be saying goodbye to
someone you like. Don't worry, however, because a deeply forged
relationship will endure the test of time and distance. In addition,
you'll have another person to add to your list of contacts abroad,
giving you an even better reason to travel. A formal gathering offers fertile circumstances for Cancer singles in search of an eager
companion. Connections of convenience can be satisfactory but
lacking in passion.

26. FRIDAY. Upsetting. The company of people you recently met is preferable to the usual folks who are all too familiar. You are apt to feel bored with stubborn characters who seem reluctant to change and grow. Or it may be that they know you too well and understand your weaknesses, which makes you feel vulnerable in their presence. Whoever you're dealing with, trust seems at a low ebb and misunderstandings will be all too easy to generate even mistakenly. Fair-weather friends shouldn't be relied upon since they're almost certain to disappoint you and let you down. For your part, don't make false promises you have no intention or capacity to keep. Make sure any agreement is legal and purchases come with guarantees.

27. SATURDAY. Stressful. An unpleasant encounter could make you feel like going underground for the rest of the weekend. Whatever good intentions you have, it's unlikely that you'll be able to make loved ones happy, no matter how hard you try. This is probably no one's fault. Rather, it's impossible to expect people to always agree with each other and continually see things eye-to-eye, no matter how close they may be. Time alone is not such a bad thing now. Being undisturbed could be just what you need to get a clearer view of the bigger picture and totally recognize where you stand at this point. Besides, a partner may be too preoccupied with their own affairs to pay close attention to you.

28. SUNDAY. Stormy. Restlessness could be hard to ignore. You may feel like dropping everything all of a sudden and making a great escape. Time out from a relationship could be advisable and appropriate, but first talk things over with your mate or partner. Mutual agreement about the situation and a clear understanding of each other's perspective will be important. Unfortunately the best laid plans and structured strategies can't prevent chaos and unknown future events from happening, with unforeseen consequences. Try to stay loose and flexible, while attempting to maneuver toward relevant goals. Wild cards are in the deck, and some jokers also. Use self-discipline to stay calm and collected in the eye of the storm.

29. MONDAY. Suspenseful. Your keen intensity helps focus your energy and attention after yesterday's scattering winds. It's remarkable how necessity or even danger brings events into heightened definition. Current pressured circumstances motivate you to achieve and overcome. A trusted assistant or coworker is invaluable to your success and victory, especially in sealing a deal or satisfying a tough customer. Just bear in mind that thought must precede action. With an ongoing sense of change percolating in the atmosphere, carefully review the situation before committing to any specific course of action. Whatever is pending can actually wait until tomorrow. Bide your time for now and don't jump the gun.

30. TUESDAY. Rejuvenating. A bright, chirpy start makes a pleasant shift from the disturbed moods and inner tumult of the last few days. However, it won't be long before you encounter some sort of obstacle or roadblock. Whether it's a person or an event, it could take some fancy sidestepping to avoid a collision. Make your case for progressive attitudes and methods when faced with another person's conservative, traditional approach. Perhaps they're simply afraid of change and the new, or maybe they're scared of losing out financially. Although sticking to the rules might keep someone happy or secure in their safe predictability, it's a sure path to inertia and dullness.

31. WEDNESDAY. Inspiring. This in-between sort of day is best spent looking after yourself on your own terms. Focusing on your appearance and overall presentation can do wonders for employment prospects and an ongoing flow of profitable work. Diet and lifestyle can also make a huge difference to how you look and feel. However, don't make the mistake of just talking, thinking, or learning about it. Practicing what others preach is the only way to do yourself any good at all. If the knowledge is only in books rather than in your head, it's not worth much to you. A partner or friend may already be well on the road to a healthy lifestyle, and now it's time to follow their example.

FEBRUARY

1. THURSDAY. Expressive. Lunar energy is peaking, arousing Cancer people to a state of high alert. Loving sentiment and genuine regard for your mate or partner make a gift almost mandatory. You might even contemplate using your credit card in order to make a grand devotional statement. For those of a less generous disposition, a plea from your better half to loosen the purse strings may fall on deaf ears, especially if sticking to a tight budget seems more important. There can be demands made on your pay for less pleasant expenses, such as insurance, taxes, or the multitude of monthly bills. Schedule a health checkup or medical consultation for this month.

2. FRIDAY. Opportune. The period immediately following a Full Moon is generally positive, and today is no exception. Here's the chance to apply whatever it takes to make your dreams come true. Activate whatever is within your power to manifest a vision as well as your imaginative concept. Fortune favors the brave, and time waits for no one. Sail with the tides rather than against them. Commercial ventures and entrepreneurial endeavors are especially favorable, particularly for Cancers who have solid relevant experience and abundant energy. Your bravado and enthusiasm are sure to magnetize exactly the right support and resources that you will need to succeed.

3. SATURDAY. Exacting. The devil's in the details, or so they say, and you may find out that truth for yourself today. In all communications and instructions, pay close attention to accuracy. However, if you become too obsessed with nitpicking the fine print, you'll almost certainly fail to see the big picture. Missing the forest for the trees would be a classic error, somewhat like taking a grand sightseeing tour and reading about it while in transit instead of actually taking in the view. Cancer students can expect a challenging time wading through new material. Keep in mind that teaching and learning are a two-way street. You're entitled to ask relevant questions when you don't understand.

4. SUNDAY. Vexing. Applying the wrong knowledge will only take a situation from bad to worse. When it comes down to it, the classic case is garbage in, garbage out. A degree of chaos and confusion might temporarily reign, but that's no excuse to lose your head. Think from intelligent perception rather than anxious overreaction. Don't just act or make decisions for the sake of doing something. The appearance of understanding won't fool anyone for very long. There's no need to panic, because competent, effective aid is about to come your way. Dedicate quality time to someone personally important, leaving chores and outings for another day.

5. MONDAY. Insensitive. In your haste to get where you're going, it could be easy to upset fellow commuters or other drivers on the road. Thoughtlessness might lead to a heated confrontation if a troublesome individual gets rubbed the wrong way. A project can turn into a mess, or even a disaster, due to the absence of key personnel. Don't hand over responsibility for any job to people who have no idea what they're doing. A public pronouncement of your personal beliefs and opinions can cause you to receive criticism and negative reactions. This may or may not surprise you, but it will have a strong effect that influences further sharing of your views. Don't go looking for trouble.

6. TUESDAY. Positive. The well-being of family members may be on your mind, especially those living out of state or overseas. Sending them a gift or a note of affectionate regard is one way of letting them know you care. A female in-law could decide to make a surprise visit. No matter your attitude or response, your spouse will be happy for the visit and will enjoy the company. A family legacy or inheritance can help to solve a current budget shortfall, but that doesn't mean all of your financial problems will be solved. Don't ignore a realistic assessment which points to the need for decisive change. Home entertainment is favored tonight, with an exciting program streaming in from the wider world.

7. WEDNESDAY. Surprising. A sudden romantic attraction could catch you by surprise, but it won't be unwelcome. Single Cancers should make the effort to get out and about. Surprising magic can happen while in transit and at public venues, events, and gatherings. Couples will be well served by the romantic atmosphere and a mood of emotional risk. However, an argument with your current lover might push you into the arms of someone new on the scene. The attraction of forbidden fruit and glamour of the unknown could prove almost too enticing. A brand-new relationship will encounter obstacles or opposition. Don't expect a rival to welcome your interest or involvement.

8. THURSDAY. Enjoyable. New playmates should be enjoyed. Take pleasure in their quality company. Games of skill and physical exertion, especially one-on-one challenges, are good exercise and also release your competitive instincts. Flirtatious talk is likely, whatever you're doing. Humorous dialogue and sharp, witty responses can have pleasantly unexpected consequences. Business and other formal interactions will be more engaging than usual. People with experience and authority are generally well disposed toward you, offering whatever help and assistance they can. Your creative imagination peaks later, when just the right thoughts find easy expression.

9. FRIDAY. Mixed. You probably won't feel in the mood for working, and a worthy replacement shouldn't be hard to find. Tell this person all that needs to be done before you are lured away from practical concerns. Spontaneously going with the flow proves far more pleasurable than attempting to experience the unreality of idealized projections. Holding out for brittle hopes and futile dreams causes you to miss the real action. If your taste in movies, music, and entertainment does not match those of your companion, maybe it's better to go alone so you actually enjoy yourself. Playing around and deceiving your mate or steady date could take a heavy toll on the relationship, both in terms of money and trust.

10. SATURDAY. Sensitive. Make every effort to honor early commitments so that you don't disappoint those who are relying on you. While it may not seem important to you, other people may have a totally different perspective, especially those who are older or more conservative. In fact, they may be very hurt if you forget them or let them down in some way. There may be fakes and flakes you want to avoid, and that shouldn't be too hard. If you've lately been on an emotional roller-coaster ride, the guidance or example of a respected person can help you process your feelings and suggest how to pick up the pieces. Cancer parents need to support vulnerable youngsters who must face their insecurities and unfounded childish fears.

11. SUNDAY. Problematic. Attempting do-it-yourself maintenance and repairs could turn into a comedy of errors, or a nightmare, if the job needs more skill than you possess. Anything that isn't definitely broken should not be fixed today. Tampering with existing systems and well-worn routines will only force you into unnecessary exertion to restore the status quo. Putting book learning into practice can be harder than expected but will help you appreciate that only practice makes perfect. No matter how congenial hired hands may be, they're unlikely to perform at their best today and shouldn't be employed just now. Preparing for an upcoming journey is a big task since it will be hard to travel light.

12. MONDAY. Disenchanting. A busy day might emerge unexpectedly, as you find yourself rushing from social diversions and pleasantries to work commitments and routines. Marketing and efforts to promote a business may not reach the intended market or audience, despite quality products and sound management. Cancer students could experience a clash between classes and a part-time job. Many Cancers in regular employment may be envious of friends who are leaving on a vacation or traveling overseas. Intellectually, you know there's no security and reliable salary without putting in disciplined working hours. However, you'll still wish you were living a carefree existence without restraint and responsibility.

13. TUESDAY. Guarded. Letting your mate or partner direct affairs for the moment saves trouble. Every vehicle can have only one driver, and the same applies to many other life situations. Now it is their turn to take the lead. Perhaps they need to go first or initiate a plan, with you following them. Any issues you have with authority figures or with following orders should be discussed with the person concerned. Reaching an understanding will prevent conflict and disagreement. An important financial negotiation, deal, or purchase demands focused attention for the next few days. Before getting in too deep, make sure it's what you really want, and that the price, terms, and conditions are fair and reasonable.

14. WEDNESDAY. Promising. Leave money matters out of the picture for a change. Valentine's Day offers many other more pleasurable interests to consider. Your application for a well-paying job might have reached the interview stage. Remember that it is a competition, and you need to make a quickly favorable impression. Even if other candidates have more experience or better credentials, a show of robust enthusiasm could swing judgment in your favor. If you don't land this job, determine to keep trying. Surprisingly, you could come to respect an opponent. Starting out on opposite sides initially, you both naturally draw closer, as similarities and attractive qualities gradually are revealed.

15. THURSDAY. Restricting. Paying the bills can be a squeeze if your resources are depleted and accounts have run down. It's time to seriously plan a savings program to forestall future anxiety. Rather than lapsing into a routine of falling behind and running on empty, it would be more resourceful to reinforce good habits of providing for those inevitable unexpected bills. Your mate or partner's earnings may be combined with yours, but relying on them to pay for basic needs or become the lender of last resort won't do any good for your relationship over time. Come up with a way to provide for yourself. Then whatever remains can be lumped into a common pot for joint expenses.

16. FRIDAY. Complex. Optimists and pessimists are apt to be at odds, and the jury's probably out as to who is right. Whether things are coming up roses or going down the tubes, much depends upon perspectives and attitudes. If you're down for any reason, let another person's cheery good vibes buoy you up and bring a little ray of sunshine into the day. Pushing away the hopes and dreams of more idealistic individuals is just sour grapes on your part. There will always be events and experiences that are sad and beyond your control, but there's plenty to be grateful for as well. Spend just as much time counting your blessings, such as love, friendship, and health, as you do counting your net worth.

17. SATURDAY. Considerate. This morning the Sun and Moon rise together, marking a fresh lunar month. Pause and think carefully before embarking on any new plan or venture. Learn from recent events and experiences before making another move. That will ensure a step forward, instead of a step sideways or backward. Respect the views and suggestions of significant others. These may dovetail and complement your own, but you'll only know that by listening attentively. Your mood changes later, becoming better-humored and open to the world. An outing or cultural event holds greater appeal this evening. Do not put off a new beginning or fail to make an apology.

18. SUNDAY. Eager. Excitement and novelty are wanted today, and you're ready and eager. Cancer couch potatoes might opt to let paid professionals get the exercise while you stay in to watch sports and entertainment on television. However, that won't be the same as having the rush or thrill yourself. Timid Cancers should seek the company of risk-taking adventurers. Do something you've never tried before. Maybe it's time for your first parachute jump or downhill plunge on skis. Travel may tempt you beyond familiar borders. Despite a few mishaps or delays in transportation, courtesy of a currently retrograde Mercury, the exhilaration of different scenery and unusual companions makes it all worth the effort.

19. MONDAY. Twisted. A good mood can quickly sour when you don't get what you want. Greedy, grasping characters expose their hands today, so look and learn from such usually hidden behavior. Jealousy and envy of another person's success need to be avoided, especially in public. Pursuing romance in the workplace may readily incur the wrath and disapproval of superiors. Wearing your heart on your sleeve makes you vulnerable. The object of your desire may lead you down the garden path dancing to their tune. Guilt and manipulation are the weapons of choice for control freaks. Steer clear of them, no matter how tempting or compelling they at first appear.

20. TUESDAY. Variable. You might be all fired up about work and career prospects, feeling ready to take on the world all by yourself. However, you'll likely have to put on the brakes because a more cautious person with whom you're dealing wants to take no chances. Use all of your positivity and enthusiasm to motivate them

into taking action, before opportunities turn cold or pass you by.
Rather than going ballistic and burning all your resources in one
fiery blaze of glory, measure yourself for the longer haul. Aim to
achieve something that's lasting and of ultimately greater value.
Beware of generating enemies and opponents by not treading on
toes as you head to the top.

21. WEDNESDAY. Forceful. Confident force meets stubborn resistance today, and sparks are likely to fly. Anything worth doing often meets with significant obstacles on the way to accomplishment.
Sticklers for rules and regulations may attempt to trip you up or
slow you down, making you do it all by the book or wait for the
slow approval of distant superiors. Some individuals wield authority like a weapon, using it to hobble and frustrate potential rivals.
Don't let such people get you down. Despite their uncooperative
disposition, continue to produce. Go over their head if you must,
because your productive results are bound to impress higher-ups
more than their obstructive complaints.

22. THURSDAY. Principled. Friendship can suffer if a loan is involved. Whether it's a case of hurt feelings or financial distress, try
to recover the money before someone slips under the radar or in-
tentionally forgets their promise. A coworker or friend might be
having difficulty with family, career, or both. While you can't fix
their problems or change their fate, you can stand by them simply
because you care. In any group or team, there's usually one rotten
apple. Before this person contaminates others with their bad attitude or unhealthy habits, expose the issue for all to see. While you
certainly won't be loved for doing this, the rest of the crew should
be glad and relieved.

23. FRIDAY. Manageable. Turning former misfits into cooperative
players would be a great accomplishment. Use all the charms at
your command to win over strong allies and worthy accomplices.
Now's the time to build a team you will be proud to lead. In any
contest you can gain the upper hand by launching decisive blows
where they count most and by making moves at just the right moment. All seems fair in love and war. If you don't go after the top
prize you'll never win it. A cozy liaison might form between you
and a superior. You know it's dangerous territory, but it will be hard
to resist temptation. Once you get into such a situation you'll find it
difficult to extricate yourself.

24. SATURDAY. Challenging. This scrambled sort of day can easily make a mess of your original plans. Be prepared for mix-ups,

misunderstandings, and strange detours that make you wonder. Even when you thought you knew where you were going or what was happening, you'll quickly come to realize that you had no idea. Cancer travelers, drivers, and tourists should take special care to double-check directions and reservations. In any new gathering you will find it challenging to fit in with unfamiliar surroundings and exotic proceedings. You'll learn something, but probably nothing you ever thought you wanted to know. The safest option may actually be to stay in bed and just dream on.

25. SUNDAY. Stressful. Misinformation can cause unnecessary anxiety and stress, or even have worse consequences. Correspondence might prove inaccurate, proving to be exactly the reverse of what was communicated. Underhanded types can be spreading gossip and seeding scandal with the intention of undermining someone's reputation. Don't believe rumors or buy into any hate campaign. The fear of someone never returning is probably ill-founded, because it is likely they will come back despite how things look at present. Cancers who have strayed far from the beaten track must now cope with inner fears of being truly lost. The way out involves many twists and turns.

26. MONDAY. Renewing. Yesterday's trials fade away as conditions look more promising. Greet the world feeling more like your true self. Don't overdo it though, because those in charge won't appreciate having their authority usurped. Trying to do business with friends can create friction because of too many bosses and not enough workers. Arguments over who's supposed to be calling the shots can be resolved by referring to the rules or to a higher authority. Helpful connections occur with visiting foreigners and overseas contacts. Many Cancers will prefer to indulge in armchair traveling rather than actually leaving home. Browsing Internet sites may whet your appetite for a future trip.

27. TUESDAY. Successful. Make your mark with people who matter. There should be opportunity to impress or influence a larger group than usual. Without being stupid about it, do something that makes you sure to be remembered. Causes and political agendas are vitally important to you due to the influence of a humanitarian friend with similar ideals. Getting involved with a worldwide effort and comprehending the bigger picture can help you understand the world around you. An upcoming journey might be delayed by a financial shortfall or changes to your partner's schedule. Use this extra time to prepare even more thoroughly before eventually leaving.

28. WEDNESDAY. Balanced. Today you encounter a different face of planet Mars, which has recently entered Aquarius. Practical individuals with clear vision, strong ethics, and a grasp of technical matters can challenge you for leadership or control in the workplace. Customers and clients may prove infuriating, although they're trying to be logical. You'll collide with strong characters who contrast your style. Before you make a permanent enemy, try to appreciate their perspective and understand what they might have to offer. It may be that you're the one with sharp corners and rough edges. One way or another, even a difficult person might balance you out in a complementary fashion.

MARCH

1. THURSDAY. Trying. Credit card debt or other high interest loans drain your budget with their fees and charges. Consider finding a second job or putting in for overtime to earn money so that you can make higher repayments that will cut interest costs faster. The tendency to overdo could be strong, so use your good common sense when it comes to extravagant purchases and overindulgence. You don't want to work so hard that you start spending the extra money on self-gratification. A worried mood can descend later, so have a hearty meal and get to bed early tonight.

2. FRIDAY. Unsettled. Your plans can be disrupted when visitors arrive unannounced. If you feel that these people are taking advantage of your generosity, tell them they've arrived at the wrong time and that you have plans which can't be changed. In that way you'll relieve yourself of the stress and strain of putting up with them. An emotional confrontation that occurs between you and someone close can get out of hand if you become spiteful. If you can accept that there are always two sides, you might gain some insight into your own subconscious mind. It will be all too easy to say one thing but mean another. Keep your conversation clear and simple.

3. SATURDAY. Unpredictable. Today's Full Moon in Virgo brings an ongoing matter to a climax, which could be either chaotic or sublime. A feeling of waiting for the next event can color each moment with a sense of expectation and excitement. A conference or celebration may mean having to travel a long distance, pressuring you for time. However, don't let the circumstances influence you to speed because the possibility of an accident due to haste is high. A phone call could bring you some surprising news from someone at a distance, even a stranger. You might bump into a childhood sweetheart and feel proud that you were once close to this person. Consider that these qualities might just be a reflection of you.

4. SUNDAY. Easygoing. Tensions ease this morning, in contrast to the last couple of days, and the peace is sure to be appreciated by you. Working around your home can be relaxing, with the chance of a neighbor dropping in for a friendly chat. Catching up with old friends might mean lazing the day away with the phone attached to your ear, getting all the news from the four corners of the globe. If a friend calls who is in trouble with the law, be careful not to become implicated by getting involved even in a minor way. Cancer dieters could be tempted to take a day off and enjoy the sheer indulgence of doing whatever appeals most. It's up to you to make the choice.

5. MONDAY. Supportive. A male member of your family can help you solve a recurring problem once and for all. This is a good time to make out a will to ensure that your possessions go to the people you want to have them. A parent or other older person may need your help around the house. While you give them a hand, chat about what they want to do when running their own home becomes too difficult. It will be much easier if plans are in place before the time comes. An unusual person can stir your emotions and create sparks when you're together. This might be the start of a very passionate and committed romantic affair. Just be sure to think about what you really want before you get out of your depth.

6. TUESDAY. Positive. Advanced education could solve your career problems. If you need further study but also have to work to pay the bills, consider taking classes online. Structure your time well and you can achieve your desired goal. If you have the opportunity to buy your own home, don't let it slip away. Worry about rising interest rates and the world economy shouldn't put you off. Instead of paying rent, you will have an asset for your old age. Fame and fortune are in the stars, and everyone is entitled to their own fifteen minutes in the limelight. Today could be your moment. A promotion can mean less time for you at home, but the extra money will make it quality time.

7. WEDNESDAY. Reassuring. This is a favorable time to heal any rifts between you and your in-laws. They may be far more understanding than you think. Work on building a support network to balance your lifestyle with your commitments. Cancer parents may want to get together with other parents to share experiences and anecdotes. The more you get out into the community, the better your life as you gain the confidence to go after your dreams. Reflecting on an emotional issue would prove beneficial, as your true feelings for a special person become clear. If deeper understanding eludes you, it might be time to consult a down-to-earth friend or a trained counselor.

8. THURSDAY. Motivating. Mercury the planet of communication, goes direct today. Negotiations, contracts, and plans should start to move once again after a period of delays and frustration. An insurance claim might be approved, but the terms and conditions could prove disappointing. A gift from your sweetheart heralds a more committed phase of your relationship. This gift might be a valued family heirloom, a great honor to you but also a significant responsibility. Overseas travel is indicated. If you are due vacation time, book a trip now to receive a good discount and preferred accommodations. Cancer teachers might be offered an overseas post which includes career advancement and prestige.

9. FRIDAY. Rewarding. Pressure and expectations can put a heavy load on your shoulders. However, an optimistic attitude and willingness to work hard will get you through, rewarding you with a great sense of satisfaction and achievement at the end of the day. Champagne tastes on a beer income could be draining your savings and even putting you in debt. Take control of your life and finances. You'll be surprised how good it makes you feel to take the first step toward overcoming an addiction. The urge to take a sick day should be overcome. Your boss won't be pleased, and you could be unemployed for months all for one day of fun.

10. SATURDAY. Renewing. A minor health problem can turn into a major one if you don't notice and act on the warning signs. Eating disorders and laziness are both easy to live with, but they won't do your appearance or future health any good. Make an appointment to check for allergies, a correct diet, and a good exercise regime. You don't have to spend a lot of money or a large amount of time on your health. Just incorporate good habits into your everyday routine. Even a short walk during your lunch hour will be beneficial. If you're prone to overindulge, work on keeping your metabolism high so that toxins don't build up in your system.

11. SUNDAY. Active. Your normal routine is likely to be upset early in the day, with places to go and people to see being primary.

A long journey is indicated, as is public life. Whatever your plans, if you take extra care to avoid mishaps and misunderstandings you should be happy with the results. A garage sale can be profitable, not only making you extra cash but clearing out your old junk at the same time. Invite neighbors to join you, and advertise a monster sale to draw a crowd. Be choosy when selecting a pet. You value your freedom, so think about how much time and work a pet will be. Cats can be left at home alone for long periods, but dogs can't.

12. MONDAY. Insightful. A close encounter with a coworker could leave you feeling uncomfortable. You might have an idea that you cannot get out of your mind, to the point that seems to be controlling you. Look deeper and you may discover more about yourself than you ever realized. A thorough spring cleaning of your home could uncover treasures you forgot about. Discrimination could arise in the workplace. Rather than leaving yourself open to recriminations, it would be wise to turn a complaint over to the relevant authorities to sort out. Changing and updating your wardrobe can charge your self-esteem as well as attracting the right new people.

13. TUESDAY. Inspiring. Joint resources could be a sticking point between you and your mate or partner. Now is as good a time as any to have a heart-to-heart talk. Meaningful communication will give you both insight and understanding of your differing views. A technical problem may require fresh skills, and the challenge to learn something novel should be stimulating. If your loved one is feeling lethargic and burdened with too many responsibilities, go out together for some real excitement that proves life is for living, not worrying. You'll brighten your day as well as theirs. A new friend, perhaps from another country or culture, could introduce you to exciting concepts.

14. WEDNESDAY. Stimulating. You will benefit from being out in the world having as much contact with other people as possible. The opportunity to travel or to begin higher education can come through a friend. If your mate or partner's family lives far away they may pay for you to visit them. Talk to your employer about unscheduled time off if the trip seems important for your partner. You should be able to organize your vacation time to fit in with family plans. Just make sure to give plenty of advance notice. A legal matter should come to a successful conclusion, although you might feel that your lawyer has got more out of it than you considering the high cost of the legal fees.

15. THURSDAY. Healing. Without even thinking about it, you have a way with words and the ability to touch other people in a profound emotional way. Understanding what makes them tick or the underlying issues that are causing pain can be strong, as are your feelings of brotherly love. This will work the other way as well, with someone coming to your aid in a particularly stressful situation. Avoid romantic innuendos, which could transform into a too forceful advance and put you in danger. A risky investment that you have given up on could come through, delivering an unexpected profit. Don't let an impulsive urge to spend take away your gain.

16. FRIDAY. Taxing. Facing up to your responsibilities and commitments can get you down at the moment. You may feel that no matter how hard you try, you never really get ahead. There is always another dish to wash, another bill to take your money. Consider making partial payments on all bills each payday, making sure you have enough left over for some fun. Your mate or partner may have expensive tastes, putting you under pressure to buy expensive gifts. Change the situation around by purchasing unusual or sentimental items that don't break the budget. Make shopping for them more of a treasure hunt than a credit squeeze.

17. SATURDAY. Favorable. Your lighthearted mood makes it easy to get through the day. Charitable work might appeal to you. Working with and for other people for a good cause can be very satisfying. Humanitarian issues are likely to attract your attention. A cultural or environmental display or gathering could be very interesting as well as educational. Inner restlessness may have you longing to travel and see strange new places. Gather travel brochures and visit Internet travel sites to find a destination that's right for you. Keep a close eye on children or their boisterous play could lead to a mishap or emergency.

18. SUNDAY. Expansive. Mercury, the planet that rules all forms of communication, moves into Pisces and joins the Sun, Moon, and Uranus in your sector of travel and higher learning. This is an excellent time to sign up for a class in a specialized area that interests you and stimulates your mind. You might opt to work in the travel industry, earning money while you see the world. A zany friend may ask you to go along to a social event. This should turn out to be a great time, introducing you to a facet of society that you never knew about before. You won't be happy with everyday existence now, so explore new ideas to keep life from becoming boring.

19. MONDAY. Complex. The desire to get your work done could be undermined by a low energy level. Your thought processes may be so slow that you end up having to double-check everything for mistakes. Keep away from those who want to gossip and complain. They will only bring you down and could get you involved in something you regret. Nothing is quite what it seems, so do your own investigating rather than blindly trusting what you are told. A friend or colleague who is going through a tough time needs extra emotional support. No matter how pushed for time you may be, giving them your support will be appreciated more than you realize.

20. TUESDAY. Challenging. A lovers' quarrel is likely over money issues. If you're both willing to listen and be rational, you can find the common ground from which to arrive at a workable solution. If you take the criticism personally, however, you could make matters far worse than they already are. You are inclined to rush and could miss an important point, which will result in fruitless activity. Plan your day and take your time. In that way you can take advantage of all openings that come your way, while other people are madly rushing around. Travel for work is indicated. The traveling expenses paid to you may exceed actual costs, leaving you with some play money.

21. WEDNESDAY. Sociable. The Sun moves into Aries, your sector of career and reputation. Over the next month this will give you opportunity for advancement along your chosen path. Friends and colleagues support your ideas and needs. It might seem as if someone especially close can read your mind. If a friend is suffering from a serious illness, it can be hard to visit because you don't know what to do or say. Force yourself to stop by or at least call. This will clear your conscience and open the way to getting together more often to lend support. Your employer is seeing you in a favorable light, so show what you're capable of doing when given the chance.

22. THURSDAY. Irritable. This is not a favorable time for starting anything new because there is a strong possibility of being led astray by other people. Keep well away from illegal activities, and don't give in to an urge to lie. Otherwise you open yourself up to being found out and having to pay the price. Your self-esteem may be low, which makes it easy to feel offended or put down. Avoid this by being positive and by recognizing beforehand that it is only your mood and not a reality. This is a good time to examine unconscious issues seriously. In that way you can get control of that side of yourself which can sabotage your good work.

23. FRIDAY. Rejuvenating. With thoughts and ideas going round and round in your head, it's time to put them down on paper. A really creative project or understanding could be the result. Be prepared to spend a little more time alone so you can catch up on a backlog of work and give yourself a breather. A couple of days away, perhaps visiting a friend who lives out of town, will give you a break from the routine. Pretentious people could really annoy you. You might want to look into different spiritual or philosophical groups to find more meaning and purpose in existence. Get a book of wisdom by a renowned author, and relax while you absorb its message.

24. SATURDAY. Harmonious. No matter what comes your way today, nothing is likely to ruffle your feathers. You might seem to be in your own world to those around you, while you wonder why other people keep getting upset with you. Take a trip with the family to explore places you haven't been to before. A theme park could be a lot of fun and will give everyone a chance to forget all other worries. A day at the beach could be very healing as the sound of waves lapping on the shore and the smell of the clean air lull you into a serene and relaxed state. Enjoy a nutritious dinner, then go to bed early tonight. In that way you'll probably be able to avoid something unpleasant.

25. SUNDAY. Eventful. The need to change the structures of everyday life present a challenge. If you are starting a new job, or a second job, you will have to relax at unusual times. Working on Sunday can mean having to miss a major social event that all your friends are going to, making it hard to maintain close ties. People you take for granted can become rebellious, forcing you to pay them more attention to let them know you care. Visitors may arrive early and stay the night. While you will have a great time talking, household chores will take a week to catch up on.

26. MONDAY. Exciting. Positive change is in the air. You may want to give your appearance and environment a complete overhaul. New friends can provide ideas for reviving your wardrobe. A different hairstyle or color can make you feel like a new person. You could be on a few people's mind as you move ahead in your chosen career and make inroads with your innovative ideas. Relief in regard to the outcome of a legal battle is likely, leaving you feeling justified for taking the position you did. Emotions could fluctuate, though, and you might get unnecessarily angry if you speak without thinking first. Be prepared to accept the consequences for rude or boorish behavior.

27. TUESDAY. Helpful. The boss should be pleased with your ideas and willing to listen to what you have to say. Take this opportunity to bring up any workplace changes that need to be made for safety and worker well-being. If higher-ups are responsive, you'll be hailed as a hero by your workmates. You may have to change travel plans to avoid a country currently experiencing political turmoil or unrest. It might even be better to delay the entire trip until the trouble subsides, just in case it spreads to a neighboring country. A colleague might claim some of your good work as their own and gain a promotion for it. There may be nothing you can do about it this time, but make sure it never happens again.

28. WEDNESDAY. Subdued. Feelings of loneliness or depression are likely to overcome you. Cancers who recently suffered a loss may now be experiencing a sense of emptiness. An insurance payout can take care of the bills, but not a broken heart. A local support group where you can share your experience can be very helpful. Overwork leads to burnout if you are not careful. Stop being a workaholic and take some time off. Go shopping and enjoy the benefits of all your hard work. Replace an appliance that is worn out or outdated, eliminating the risk of a fire. This will also improve the look of your home and give you the feeling of prosperity.

29. THURSDAY. Mixed. A job change could be just what you need to renew your enthusiasm and creativity. You don't have to leave the one you're in until you find the right new one. Start sending out resumes to workplaces that inspire you. A situation you found very confrontational may have passed but left a bad taste in your mouth. Consider what you found so disturbing. Your personal values may need to be reevaluated to fit in with present circumstances. Try to avoid the need to borrow money in order to stay afloat. If you can get through a period of debt without adding more, you will be on your way to staying solvent permanently.

30. FRIDAY. Confrontational. Expect the unexpected and you will be well prepared for today's surprising events. A local community meeting can turn angry and confrontational when political factions get up on their soapboxes. Appeal to everyone's sense of fairness and understanding for the best outcome. Misunderstandings are likely, and messages could get lost in transit. To be on the safe side, confirm all of your correspondence to be sure it arrived and is being interpreted correctly. An art exhibit or local theater performance may be quite controversial but at the same time bring up ideas and concepts that broaden your horizons and liberate your mind.

31. SATURDAY. Expressive. Visiting friends and attending a social or sporting event may be on your agenda. You're apt to be more talkative than usual, so be careful who you tell what. Otherwise you could unknowingly hurt someone's feelings. A rowdy sporting match will give you a chance to let off steam, and you may even lose your voice cheering for your team. Computer nerds should take extra precaution on the Internet because an invisible new virus could be lurking in cyberspace. A new relationship may be romantic but seem like a lot of hard work. If you find it difficult to read this other person and therefore keep doing the wrong things, ask yourself honestly if you are right for each other.

APRIL

1. SUNDAY. Stressful. Having the courage to face this testing day means confronting a couple of issues head-on. One situation in particular will have to be dealt with once and for all. Honor both feelings and reason equally, then persevere privately. Coming to terms with disappointment regarding a financial resource might lead to private weeping regarding a stock or bond report. It's imperative not to force results. Instead, come to terms with reality and look for ways to create a firmer foundation. Manipulations or underhanded dealings will get you nowhere. Conserve your energy as you seek new abundance. An unusual perspective or an e-mail or phone call from someone at a distance might create a breakthrough in the nick of time.

2. MONDAY. Intrusive. Although lightening up and embracing a more social attitude is an admirable objective, today could see you dealing with limitations imposed by home versus career. Classic Mondayitis suggests stealing yourself away from loved ones in order to try to meet financial demands. Balance the two by streaking forward through the day, then reward yourself enjoying a cozy night. The outside world could deliver a surprise, reminding you it's not business as usual anymore. The cocoon of life is opening up to the larger world, asking you to care for those on foreign soil. Looking at more of the world's people as your family will help you accept the intrusions on your private life.

3. TUESDAY. Bright. Do your best to avoid limited thinking and nit-picking, which are possible byproducts of the weekend's challenges. Zest and determination are increasing, renewing your desire to move forward and overcome obstacles. The planet Mercury, governing thinking processes, is moving through your solar sector of overseas destinations and broad-minded investigations. There is also a suggestion of dreaming about faraway places, but longing for the resources to make travel happen. A delay may be unavoidable now, but put your dream on the wish list and factor in a realistic extra few months to achieve the goal. A romance heating up could shift your gears into overdrive, helping summon a much needed exuberance.

4. WEDNESDAY. Stable. Avoid wildly expansive thinking or promising more than you can possibly deliver. Attempt to remain on an even keel. Give yourself frequent reality checks, and seek expert guidance if necessary. An act of bravery is foreseen, but wanting to sacrifice for a cause greater than yourself can find you going overboard. An illusory romance that begins when a flirtatious glance comes your way is best avoided. Guard against mixing business with pleasure. Feeling empowered to go ahead thanks to support from a financial institution might make you feel anything is possible regarding a certain project. That is indeed the case, but you must come up with firm infrastructure first. Then proceed without further delay.

5. THURSDAY. Positive. Do not discuss finances this morning. Later on the lunar light of home and hearth provides you with new and progressive energy. There's a sense of wanting to move toward the future even for the most traditional Cancer. Becoming lost in unproductive yet enjoyable daydreaming is possible. Career matters are a poor second to the lure of faraway adventures and knightly pilgrimages. Be open to new influences as you learn from an unconventional teacher. A sudden change of scenery will inject a buzz of lively wakefulness. Socializing and indulging in creative activity might not produce funds today but will instill an inner richness that makes you feel truly alive.

6. FRIDAY. Tricky. Tightening up and coping with the realities of your job can rein in expansiveness, forcing duty to come before pleasure. Letting insults roll off you like water off a duck's back helps conserve energy for productive results. Opportunities abound for deep intimacy, although you need to avoid petty arguments. Mars is aggravating the energy flow, throwing barbs and challenges into the atmosphere for the unwary. Shutting the door and having much needed quiet time might be the answer, letting you refuel. Take time to get your environment perfect tonight. Setting the tone for an evening of color, scent, and mood ensures potentially blissful romance.

7. SATURDAY. Cooperative. Work-related socializing can be wonderful providing you don't overdo. A casual team get-together could create unusual problems regarding transportation and technology. Be on guard when traveling. Check the basics, such as oil and water and window-washing fluid for the car. It's the simple things you need that cause the most upsets. Once you arrive at your gathering, focus on core reasons for being involved with certain people. Share beliefs drawing you all together can potentially lead to more mutual projects. Working with those you love is favored. Retaining an open and flexible mind-set is key to being a successful team member.

8. SUNDAY. Buoyant. Needing rest could be secondary, as jovial Jupiter puts a spring in your step and the feeling that all's right with the world. The thought of work during the days ahead could be joyous for the entrepreneurial Cancer. Hardworking, stern Saturn flowing harmoniously with the Sun encourages a sense that your career is right on track. Emotions are intense but moving forward, with a vision as the primary goal. A few arguments are brewing, but nothing you can't handle. At least any enemies and antagonists are out in the open rather than hidden from your view. Just watch your step, and your mouth, in a fired-up crowd such as at a sports event or rock concert.

9. MONDAY. Fortunate. You could be downright lucky in a career sense, scoring a dream job involving the trendy young or the entertainment arts. A drive to accomplish comes naturally today. Anyone who tries to get in your way could be surprised to discover that you're not sympathetic to them and just want to be left alone. If you have felt a victim yourself, you should now have a sense of being on the comeback trail. Have the courage to face your fears. Keep going once you start climbing the mountain. It won't be as far to the summit as you think. While not reducing your own efforts, realize that help is also on the way.

10. TUESDAY. Manageable. A jealous or envious partner may need cheering up. Or you may have to redefine the boundaries of acceptable behavior. Partnership issues regarding money are highlighted. New negotiation may be needed. You'd think a loved one would be happy for you, but for some Cancers an upswing in status may necessitate taking a new, more assertive position. Fortunately any conflicts will soon pass. Paying for advice can help you if you feel oppressed by circumstances. Sometimes it takes another person to see what is invisible to those closest to the action. Drop any pride and isolationist tendencies in favor of accepting necessary assistance.

11. WEDNESDAY. Harmonizing. Cancer partnerships could receive a boost after the stress of yesterday. Socializing with friends or team members adds buoyancy to the day. Finances or subconscious issues that have been at a stalemate can now be resolved successfully. Handling dry but essential accounting details of an enterprise will keep you occupied for much of the day. Try to come up with a budget that's practical and reasonable. Cancers in the arts or working on an emotional level could sense the grace of supportive forces behind the scenes. Take a little time for tuning into the group psyche. A profitable day's work will emerge for writers or those in the healing arts.

12. THURSDAY. Rewarding. A tough situation involving resources needs strong and continuous focus. The buck stopping with you encourages resolving a difficult situation now rather than later. If it feels like the wound is being lanced, that's healthy. Escape could be tempting, so a personal reward is needed. Opt for a movie or favorite music indulged with a lover at the end of this challenging day. The past may rise up in the guise of a difficult memory, but it should be much less frightening these days. Someone whose company you seek may prefer to be left alone. View their choice as wholesome seclusion rather than an outright rejection of you personally.

13. FRIDAY. Compromising. Watching your back or having to cope with other people's suspicious behavior can limit your freedom and diminish your optimism. You might go searching for a new country to live in when bureaucracy tightens its officious grip. Family members could be pulling in a homeward direction, forcing you to juggle your emotions. To cope with change, let go of whatever is obviously not working. Going back to square one is the only way to explore exciting new vistas. Sudden travel plans and decisive action empower those with a keen sense of adventure. Keeping any such plans a secret will be hard.

14. SATURDAY. Surprising. Progressive and inventive energies surround you. Conditions favor absorbing a new culture or studying a foreign language. Charging off the beaten track provides an intriguing detour. Remain safe in your enthusiasm by double-checking routes and having backup gear on hand. The gypsy in you calls, so grab a backpack and go hiking, or jump on a bike to stay mobile. Give in to dreams, but be prepared for unusual challenges and sudden surprises. Your good intentions to accomplish a long list of outstanding chores are apt to be shunted aside in favor of excitement and spontaneous adventures. Unexplored realms beckon. Give the emotional side of your nature free rein.

15. SUNDAY. Active. A daring and different joint pastime can lead to more discovery, but family activities need to include an element of time for yourself as well. Doing your own thing for part of the day is vital. This will leave you open to meeting kindred spirits while pursuing a private interest. Quiet activities in a museum or behind-the-scenes at a gathering gets you away from the fray and lets the hidden, gentle side of your nature emerge. Any wheeling and dealing in an effort to get your way is likely to backfire immediately. Arousing and stimulating your creative energy is vital. Active learning in a field that interests you will keep potentially idle hands very well occupied.

16. MONDAY. Bracing. Get as much done on the job as you can, even if yearning for a long break. Building the foundation of your life adds stability that will not be easily washed away. That's sure to be a relief after the past few years. Looking good on the job is vital, giving you some publicity or more visibility. A media event to benefit charity can be more fulfilling than at first believed. Remain in tune with the collective mood. Gauge current trends in order to make the most of this potentially winning day. If you're in charge, lead by example. Don't let grudges or bias affect any of your decisions or judgments.

17. TUESDAY. Dynamic. With today's strong likelihood of gaining the camera's attention, focus on personal poise and great hair on the job. Being asked to take charge in some way, and having a dip into the fame game, casts your net far and wide. There are abundant opportunities to get a message out to the masses if you practice your excellent organizational skills. Consider propelling your message into the spotlight via the Internet, podcast, or publishing for a wider audience. You need to be quick-witted in order to make the most of your opportunities. Steamy undercurrents may percolate in a group. Under cover of the New Moon tonight, a secret rendezvous has a much better chance of remaining that way.

18. WEDNESDAY. Frustrating. Coping with yesterday's success leads to more tasks on your to-do list. Glitches in cooperative endeavors are bound to be frustrating. Keep in mind the old adage that no one cares more about your project than you. Expansion calls for to-the-penny budgeting and thorough teamwork. There is good potential to make new contacts and blaze forward. Resources appear stretched, however, and you must keep running to catch up with good fortune. Double-check to be sure a new business colleague is as good as his or her word. An aspiring someone may stretch the truth to the breaking point. An outsider is likely to remain on the outside, while tight exclusivity dominates in a group.

19. THURSDAY. Stimulating. Renew yourself behind the scenes, working out of the public eye. This encourages regrouping in the inner sanctum with a core team of like-minded, trusted individuals. Power is still available, allowing you to dare something worthy. It's a matter of seizing the day or days. The ante is upped as some less committed associates drop away. The need for integrity is strong to counter the temptation to rely solely on Cancer charisma. Conserve your energy and aim the arrow deep and true. Burying yourself in workplace activity may not last long as you are disturbed by sweeter diversions. A desire to taste forbidden fruit can overwhelm you in an instant, to be regretted almost as quickly.

20. FRIDAY. Cautious. A romantic behind-the-scenes interlude calls siren-like this evening. However, balancing work and social agendas brings challenges. An electric but unstable energy abounds, with a need for sharp alertness. The thought of throwing caution to the wind after the pressing demands of this week can send you into reckless daredevil behavior unless you center yourself and your energies. Be prudent with speed while traveling. Look for freedom in healthy ways by not overdoing it, either on the road or while indulging in deserved pleasure. The Sun in Taurus brings a refreshed appreciation of the senses and the natural world. Enjoy alone, with one other person, or with the whole world.

21. SATURDAY. Volatile. This morning brewing passions and potential emotional dramas unfold, with secrets exposed for the dishonest or indirect. Unraveling the hidden motivation of someone close to you can bring out the detective in you. Reason returns in the afternoon, ramping up the atmosphere. Party invitations dovetail with practical times, moving your personal interests to number-one position. Give yourself a nurturing treat at the spa or healing time out from the streak to completion. The Moon returning to your own home sign fulfills needs you had to put on the back burner. Communication with loved ones from a distance makes you think about foreign climes.

22. SUNDAY. Streamlined. Be guided by your perceptive intuition on a feeling level. This will fast-track emotions to instant knowing and simple decision making. Being eager to act one way or another leads you to shun people and situations you have been overly patient in handling. Only Cancers who really want to help themselves will make the grade with so many important responsibilities. Such clarity might even lead you to think you can't lose, but don't get too headstrong. Meditation and concentration are vital to ensure you are aided by kindred spirits and synchronous grace. Profiting fully from current supportive influences allows you to shift gears downward.

23. MONDAY. Changeable. The undertow of shifting moods and atmospheres lends a wave-like tone to the day. Don't let this play havoc with your self-esteem or affect the solid gains made last week. Having events become increasingly curious may drive you to aim for definite structure in life, from morning coffee to your best clothes. Whatever works, use it to cope. Straightforward communication may be difficult in the workplace, with a need for extra clarity. Aiming for easily accomplished tasks you can achieve independently will make this a most productive day. Being self-reliant is the best policy since support, other than from your guardian angel, is a little hard to come by.

24. TUESDAY. Vexing. Financial considerations and a proud mood tussle with the fixed attitudes of friends. A little disharmony could have you ducking and weaving to avoid the fray. Opening incoming bills may feel like delving into the proverbial can of worms. There can be a painful need to come to grips with an unhealthy situation. Focusing on abundance with a grateful attitude is sure to magnetize good things to you. Attempt to get to the bottom of repetitive economic issues. By confronting existing circumstances and openly sharing fears or wounded pride, you'll gain better understanding of a situation. This will finally enable you to release the problem and then restructure a realistic solution.

25. WEDNESDAY. Unsettled. Concentrating on heavy-duty jobs on your to-do list puts unavoidably serious tasks on your agenda. Preparing tax forms, facing age-related issues, or coping with temporarily limited resources could make you feel lonely. Reminding yourself that this too will pass is a must to get through this emotionally chilly day. Clinging to work you relish can create a hard-fought opportunity, yet there's a need not to sign any important document while Neptune clouds your vision. A con artist could be present, adding general confusion. For best results, step back and assess all choices from a logical perspective. Proceeding carefully and steadily will see you eventually succeed.

26. THURSDAY. Successful. Firing up the courage to blast jobs to completion allows your success potential to skyrocket. Detaching from pressing love-related issues frees you up emotionally to concentrate on business and to energize important projects. Taking aim and then massive action is fully supported. It's likely that a large number of people will benefit from your hard-won product or wisdom. Getting around in your neighborhood and bumping into pleasant acquaintances adds to the heady mix and thrill of being in the thick of today's action. Sharpen communication and upgrade your e-mail, telephone, and teleconferencing skills. Make sure you're aware of water-cooler gossip so that you can benefit from strategic knowledge.

27. FRIDAY. Upsetting. A neighborhood dispute leads to everyone taking sides and splitting hairs. Prepare for sudden upsets, with change the only constant. Stories and conflicting points of view will be lacking cold hard facts. Minding your own business for the better part of the day might be a wise idea. Otherwise you may have to defend every point of view. Clearing your in tray and dumping old papers or files calls for sorting out and clarifying. A new health program should begin successfully and could be the start of a new image with Saturn blessing Venus. The disciplined high road is the one that will make you look and feel fabulous.

28. SATURDAY. Searching. Venus sailing behind the scenes magnetizes you toward following your desires and venturing far beyond the mundane. Consider traveling to exotic locations where you can relax at outdoor cafes, enjoy yogic monasticism, or hide away in an old bookshop. There's a strong need to get away from irritating circumstances in your current environment. Suddenly hopping on the last plane out of town, or driving away on the open road heading for a cozy wilderness cabin, would see you escape successfully. Explore a potential hero's journey of some kind. Ancient artifacts and an age-old code could keep you busy in a reflective, interesting way. Keep searching until satisfied that you have found what you want.

29. SUNDAY. Gracious. Hosting a colorful feast is a perfect way to channel the sensuous Taurus and Libra energy now in the air. Lush scents and anything which invites the good life should be brought out of hiding to indulge the senses and inspire witty, delightful conversation. Giving up something for someone could see you making a sacrifice for a cause close to your heart. This is a wonderful day to use your money to support a charity benefit. A fund-raising occasion will be fun as well as rewarding for the cause. Put on your best and shimmer. Children will enjoy today's buoyant energy, perhaps putting on a play to entertain older folk.

30. MONDAY. Happy. Continuing on with the theme of living life to the full, today promises to be social and packed with adventure. Cancer wordsmiths will have an easy time writing or finishing a puzzle. Floating down the main street in the latest creation, the Libra energy inspires creative Cancers to maintain a happy frame of mind. Skate over the surface of problems to find joy with a light heart. Make sure to notice flowers and all things bright and beautiful. The Libra Moon is still shining in full glory. Keeping the day light is key. Jupiter is encouraging a mood not to overwork, so expect to extend your lunch hour and don't promise to be back at your desk by a certain time.

MAY

1. TUESDAY. Challenging. Someone in the workplace could be trying to undermine you or take credit for your good work. Stay alert for underlying innuendos, and let your intuition guide you to find this person. Unselfish behavior is second nature to you at the moment, but don't fall into the trap of playing the martyr. Besides not being very rewarding personally, doing this will greatly annoy your coworkers. Blended families could be in for a struggle of wills, as the kids work out the pecking order. Parents shouldn't get involved except as referee. Otherwise they could end up fighting it out alongside the kids. Your travel plans may be upset due to illness or work commitments.

2. WEDNESDAY. Unsettled. Everybody is going to want to have his or her say, but no one will be listening. If you can remain silent, you'll learn a lot about the other people, especially a few handy insights into what makes them tick. If you don't have a current will or living trust, look into how to protect your children's inheritance and ensure the distribution you want. Do some research on the subject by speaking to a lawyer or surfing the Net. You'll come up with the best solution for your individual circumstance. An exciting evening could be in store, even if you're staying home. You might see the best movie ever on television or the best political debate.

3. THURSDAY. Advantageous. Accept the job of spokesperson if it's offered, to you. You will undoubtedly do a really good job. Sociability and entertainment give this day a pleasant aura. Meetings and group discussions should pass all motions without any real argument, although there may be one issue that's more important than anybody realizes. By being thorough and examining all issues in depth, you'll do your boss a big favor, one that might well be worth a raise. Health issues are highlighted later in the day. You might even decide to cancel an evening's outing because you're excited about starting a new diet or health program.

4. FRIDAY. Productive. You need good health and ample vitality to live life to the full, and you should have both right now. Cancer sports people should use common sense to know when enough is enough. In your enthusiasm you could overdo, possibly causing a sprain. Your income level will be rising. If this moves you into a higher tax bracket, see an accountant or make an investment to offset earnings. An inquiring mind, or the desire to start a job in teaching, might be the key to enrolling in a higher education course. One extra advantage of this can be forming alliances that strengthen your social network.

5. SATURDAY. Enjoyable. A richness of feeling, combined with a sense of achievement, will imbue everything you do today with pleasure. Even ordinary, everyday tasks take on a unique flavor. Much can be achieved if you put your mind to it. Finishing off repairs such as plumbing could be made easier with expert advice from a friend or neighbor who works in the field. Changing old habits comes easily. All you have to do is start initiating new habits with commitment. Plans to go visiting may have to be called off due to car trouble. If you need to stay home and look after somebody who is ill, you'll be able to play the role of nurse to perfection.

6. SUNDAY. Guarded. An experience in your love life can be very intense and may lead to indiscretion if you're not careful. Cancer singles might be followed around by someone who is totally fascinated but not fascinating. You may dread going out or answering the phone in case it's that person. Ask a friend to accompany you if you're worried or feel you are being stalked. Cancer couples need to remain aware in order to avoid minor issues upsetting the relationship. You may even need to take the role of counselor, letting your mate or partner pour out their heart. If you just make sure not to judge what you're being told, the end result should be very rewarding. Guard a secret by not telling a soul.

7. MONDAY. Manageable. When a love affair becomes routine and stale, it's often time to start over again or at least try to revive the relationship. Because of your need for stability and security in life, you will probably opt for one more try. Your own high ideals can make it hard to accept that your mate or partner is simply human, but love will inspire you to keep trying. Use caution if tempted to unload your troubles onto a friend. Some people don't know when to keep quiet and maintain a confidence. A legal matter that has gotten bogged down in bureaucracy may be starting to cost too much money. Get an expert's advice on how to hurry up the process before it stalls altogether.

8. TUESDAY. Creative. Venus, planet of love and creativity, moves into your sign of Cancer today, bestowing her glorious gifts of attractiveness, elegance, diplomacy, love, and art on you. Feeling good and looking great will put you in a positive frame of mind, making it easy to achieve what you're trying to do. People may notice you from across a crowded room, and you could receive a few social offers. Be choosy now, because you can. This is a favorable time to turn to your bank for financial help, which is highly likely. Personal inhibitions should be ignored. Start a creative project and release the artist within you.

9. WEDNESDAY. Motivating. Intense frustration can lead to pulling out all the stops in an attempt to get things moving positively. Coming up against domineering or power hungry people can get you angry, stirring up your inventiveness in an effort to outmaneuver them at their own game. A business deal can be saved with some extra negotiation and understanding. Get to know what the other party really wants from the deal, then you'll know how to approach it successfully. A romantic attraction can make you question what you really value in life and how well that fits with the outside world. Just don't leap ahead to thoughts of marriage on the first date.

10. THURSDAY. Surreal. Expect a dreamy start to the day. Fuzzy thoughts and being overly sensitive to other people can make you reclusive and even elusive. Strange thoughts and fantasies move through your mind, leaving you with fresh ways of thinking. An accidental brush with a colleague may seem arousing and inviting, then leave you wondering if you didn't just imagine it. Sharing a ride to work could turn into the ultimate nightmare, as you experience a string of close calls along the way because the person driving can't stay focused on the road. The day promises to improve, and the evening should bring love and laughter in comfortable surroundings.

11. FRIDAY. Distracting. Contact with a foreign exchange student or overseas tourist can add a new dimension to your worldview and open up an avenue of work that you never thought about before. The need to make a difference on a global scale can be strong. Contact with a humanitarian activist might turn into a vigorous and insightful debate regarding philosophical issues. Keeping your mind on the job or on demanding studies could be the last thing you want to do. The urge to resign from your job and head off on an adventure could become almost overpowering. A nervous reaction should be treated by a physician to make sure it doesn't worsen or develop into a chronic complaint.

12. SATURDAY. Turbulent. Actions based on emotions are usually impulsive and can have widespread repercussions. To avoid negative reactions, think before you act. Overwork leads to burnout, so start planning a vacation. Make sure you head to a destination that will relax and rejuvenate your love for life. Your social life could be at a low ebb, or you may be mixing with the wrong crowd. People who are fashion slaves, addictive personalities, or just plain selfish will only bring you down, then move on when your usefulness to them has been exhausted. Do yourself a favor by following your dreams, not the crowd. This approach will prove far more rewarding in the long run.

13. SUNDAY. Subdued. The desire to stay home and do your own thing might clash with a need to meet your social obligations. Compromise and do both, by staying home longer and arriving later. You're sure to come up with a believable excuse. A female relative could be trying to boss you around, using all types of emotional blackmail to get her way. Agree with everything she says, but don't do what is expected. She may not notice until it is too late. An attraction to beautiful things could deplete your bank balance but add prestige and elegance to your home. Check the authenticity of expensive art before purchasing to ensure you are getting what you are paying for.

14. MONDAY. Promising. Your reputation as a high achiever and a good sport puts you in line for an award or recognition of some sort. You are likely to act first and think later. Although this is somewhat risky, your intuition will steer you straight. Speaking up for an underdog might end up saving your company a lot. Don't let this person be hounded into depression and unemployment. A group of coworkers may be planning a trip together and ask you to join in. It should be a fun adventure, securing bonds of friendship for years to come. You're in a good position to secure a loan for a large and promising investment.

15. TUESDAY. Progressive. Mars, the planet that rules action, moves into Aries and your career sector today. This gives you greater aggression and assertion to fulfill your ambitions and reach your goals. The boss could get on your case and expect more than you ever bargained for. However, you have energy in reserve right now, so show what you're made of and you might get a promotion. A good friend may ask you to go along to a lecture of some sort. The opportunity to meet influential and interesting people shouldn't be missed. Listen to the advice of a friend when it comes to a risky new investment. They may not be an expert, but their intuition could be precise.

16. WEDNESDAY. Auspicious. Dedicate the morning to consolidating plans and ideas for a new project. Later on you may have to present your work to a group. The more thoroughly prepared you are, the better your ideas will be received. A group project can be started now, but try to be sensitive to the ideas of other people so that it is a truly cooperative venture. You could be asked to take charge of a charity fund-raising event. This will be a great way to improve your organizational, marketing, and leadership skills. With your strong competitive spirit and urge to get ahead, this is a chance not to be missed. Any temptation to be underhanded or manipulative should be avoided.

17. THURSDAY. Good. This is a fortuitous time for Cancer students to catch up on studies and absorb complicated concepts and ideas. If you are having trouble grasping a subject, don't hesitate to contact the teacher and ask for some extra help. They are sure to appreciate such interest. Solitude will produce your best work, as research and reflection help the flow of independent, original thinking. The urge to get away could be irresistible. Plan a weekend retreat in the great outdoors with someone you love, allowing you to revel in the sheer luxury of being alive. You may have to counsel a brother or sister if they ask. Although their problems might upset you, you can help them find a solution.

18. FRIDAY. Difficult. The desire to stay home from work to avoid an office troublemaker is understandable. Sometimes people can be very smart at manipulating and controlling, and there's nowhere to hide. These types are recognized by their lack of compassion and empathy. If you come up against such a person, seek help through a personnel counselor rather than just complaining in general. Your health needs extra care. Listen to what your body is telling you, then act accordingly. Get more rest and don't go out tonight. Contact your friends and cancel any prior engagement. You're sure to feel much better and be able to party tomorrow if you look after yourself today.

19. SATURDAY. Cooperative. You should feel really up today. Your need to belong and to relate to friends and loved ones will be satisfied fully. With the Moon in your sign of Cancer, the next few days are a fine time to refocus on your goals. Devotion to a community project may require visiting friends and neighbors to drum up more involvement in the cause. An attractive demeanor is bound to tip whatever you're doing in your favor, well rewarding your activities. A friend in need might unload their worries on you, making you privy to a dangerous secret. Be very careful if you're tempted to repeat what you're told in confidence.

20. SUNDAY. Changeable. A sensitive mood can scare you away from a large crowd or disruptive people. Pamper yourself with the sort of treatment you'd give someone you love. Don't worry about the cost, tomorrow is another day. Artistic pursuits are likely to please you. A class in painting, pottery, or even Asian cookery could be exciting. Travel plans may be more expensive than you can currently afford. Perhaps by deferring the trip for six months you won't have to settle for second best. A friend, relative, or even a psychic may not tell you what you would like to hear. Be discerning and don't believe everything you're told.

21. MONDAY. Confident. Cancer salespeople are likely to have a bumper period, with the best sales yet. Your mood is more confident and assertive without being belligerent or pushy, and the results will speak for themselves. There may be a considerable amount of driving involved with your job. Make the trip more enjoyable by taking the scenic route and listening to your favorite music. A talent for leadership could surface during an emergency or dangerous situation. You're prepared to take a calculated risk and to trust your instincts more than usual. Finances should be on the up and up. Fulfilling a desire to donate some money to a good cause might mean more to you than an expensive purchase.

22. TUESDAY. Responsible. Worry and stress are the two biggest enemies of good health and well-being. It's all too easy to push a problem under the carpet, but the knowledge of it still stays in the back of your mind. Take control over your destiny and confront nagging issues head-on. Contact creditors and work out a manageable repayment plan, or come up with a budget you can live with. A problem that involves another person requires approaching them sensibly. If you feel the other party is not reasonable, look around for a competent mediator, one who knows you both well enough to understand all the issues. You might not solve your worries overnight, but they'll no longer continue to haunt you.

23. WEDNESDAY. Intense. Understanding the motives behind the actions of workmates could make even the smallest change very interesting. Just be very careful of sticking your nose in where it's not wanted though, as it is likely to get you in big trouble. A friend's outgoing, chatty exterior could hide a very private interior, so don't assume too much. If your father or another close male relative is not well or is recuperating from a recent illness or accident, it may be tough to get the time for a visit. Make a phone call and at least chat for a while. Knowing you care enough to listen will go a long way to cheering them up and speeding their road to recovery.

24. THURSDAY. Expansive. A vacation abroad can sound like lots of fun, but Cancer people need to feel personally secure. Any doubt as to safety and security on the trip should be addressed before you depart. Call ahead to the cities you're going to be visiting. Find out how well English is understood, the cost of living, and crime statistics. Read relevant stories by fellow travelers on the Internet and other literature. Then you can head off knowing exactly what circumstances lie ahead. A restless mood could make you more touchy than usual, so think twice before arguing or complaining. This evening promises some exciting entertainment.

25. FRIDAY. Adaptable. Your powers of persuasion are in top gear. If you are in the market for a new car, you might be able to beat the salesman at his own game. An offer of a low-interest loan could be too good to refuse. Even if you didn't plan on borrowing money at this stage, it might turn out to be a gift from heaven. You may have overlooked a bill, and now the debt collector comes knocking on the door. Use your wiles to gain another chance before you are penalized or served with a summons for court. Take this as a lesson to get paperwork tidied up and in order, so important papers won't get lost in the clutter on your desk. Stay home tonight.

26. SATURDAY. Private. Home renovation projects take precedence over the outside world. With the Moon occupying your sector of home and family, and the Sun in your sector of solitude and privacy, you might not even want to open the front door. Get your family to give you a hand and generally share the day with you. Cancer travelers are likely to feel homesick, possibly spending hours on the phone or Internet talking to loved ones. An ambition to be in the public eye could be achieved by first working behind the scenes, getting to know how everything works. Take over new roles little by little, so that in time your confidence will be up to any test.

27. SUNDAY. Domestic. A shopping trip around antique and thrift stores is sure to be a great success. Practice your haggling skills and you could bag a bargain. Redecorating your home to suit lovely old furnishings is a challenge that you are equal to. An investment can pay a large dividend, boosting your savings. However, don't let this go to your head. Risky investments are just that, and you always need to do the homework first. You have been working hard lately, and your physical fitness is testimony to that fact. Start an exercise program or take up a sport to maintain this level of fitness in the future. Pick an activity that can be practiced into your old age.

28. MONDAY. Creative. A clandestine love affair could start to become a social fact, and soon you may be able to declare this love publicly. You might now set a wedding date, and celebrate your engagement with a big party for all your friends. Cancer parents may have to help their child finish homework. Try instigating a reasonable timetable to help youngsters learn to organize their time more effectively. Work and play are both a vital part of life and should be balanced out. Working pays the bills. However, an entertaining hobby you can enjoy on nights and weekends, one that provides fun and laughter and new friends, would give you relaxation without having to work hard at it.

29. TUESDAY. Surprising. What starts out as a potential problem can turn into exciting opportunity. Try not to judge things too early, developing a set attitude. By approaching everything with an open mind, lateral thinking will kick in and could change everything. What were problems may now become solutions. The boss may ask you to defer time off, but if you have everything planned and paid for, you will have to refuse. Don't let them use a power play to break your resolve, because you won't be fired. Relatives from out of town might be staying with you. The excitement is likely to wear off if you don't define your personal boundaries. Talk about your feelings once everyone is comfortable.

30. WEDNESDAY. Exciting. Developing a talent into a career may mean having to skimp and save to get by. However, you should not have to struggle for as long as you might think. The artist within you is very strong, just needing the right training to excel in your chosen field. A change of heart regarding a love affair can have positive and far-reaching effects, altering the way you look at the world, your values, and how you view yourself. Be careful not to allow other people to influence you. You'll naturally make the decision that's best for you. A teaching post could offer a job change, giving you the chance to broaden your horizons and learn more about the world.

31. THURSDAY. Exacting. Working outside allows you to get away from other people and give full scope to your own ideas. Gardening or landscaping, or even just mowing your lawn, suits you better than working in an enclosed space. Today's Full Moon in Sagittarius highlights the need for freedom of thought and movement at work. If such requirements are not being met at the moment, you might be tempted to quit on the spot. Overindulgence is also possible. Fattening foods can ruin your diet, and too much alcohol can seriously loosen your tongue. Take a walk at lunchtime to enjoy solitude and reflection as you plan your dinner menu and contemplate love.

JUNE

1. FRIDAY. Fulfilling. During this Full Moon period, many Cancer people have reignited enthusiasm for developing a healthy, fulfilling lifestyle. There are many available avenues of exploration, which can seem overwhelming because of so many options to choose from. Discerning the one that's right for you can be a tough challenge. Trying out many of them won't help because of the time you'd need. Although numerous paths are available to achieve your objectives, stick to one and you'll arrive at your destination. For instance, from a smorgasbord of educational courses, pick the one that has most relevance and practicality, so that earning a good living becomes a reality.

2. SATURDAY. Useful. Throw yourself into weekend chores first thing today. A lot of work can be dealt with quickly and effectively. Even big jobs can be handled despite your initial misgivings. Putting unpleasant or tedious tasks off until later would be a mistake. A difference of opinion is likely with a cautious, older individual. Try to be respectful while nevertheless expressing yourself honestly and authentically. Cancer shoppers are unlikely to find too many bargains. Striking a deal that you can afford might require tough negotiations over a period of days or weeks. Spending time in the company of people with business skills and experience can teach you a great deal about commerce.

3. SUNDAY. Upsetting. Yesterday's respect and patience could be in short supply today. Anyone who stands in your way or might damage your reputation is sure to be on the receiving end of your wrath. Arguments with parents or in-laws can be short, sharp, and to the point. Say what you really mean and get things off your chest. This is not the time to hold back or to indulge in brooding resentment. Expect other people to be equally blunt with you. Be prepared to hear their issues and complaints, especially those that concern you personally. If you can't stand the heat, get out of the kitchen. And if you can't take a dose of your own medicine, stop dishing it out to anyone else.

4. MONDAY. Uneasy. Who or what you love could seem distant or difficult to attain. You may have been saving long and hard for a desired purchase, only to realize it remains as out of reach as ever. Either adjust your goal to make it realistically achievable, or continue on the chosen path with solid determination. Sadness or loss experienced by your mate or partner can make your relations seem remote and cool. Gently express kindness and support. A relationship could be drifting apart, perhaps because you're both concerned with similar issues but from opposite points of view. If you're both too wrapped up in your own perspective, it's unlikely there will be much togetherness or eventual agreement.

5. TUESDAY. Satisfactory. When it comes to medical professionals, you're only likely to receive the quality of care you pay for. Be glad if you have adequate health insurance, affording you whatever is needed in the way of appropriate counseling and treatment. This is an optimal day to schedule a consultation or diagnostic procedure. If surgery or therapy is essential, go ahead without delay or anxiety. The outcome looks positive and favorable. A general checkup is likely to give you the all-clear. An attempt to negotiate an enhanced employment contract with improved work conditions and level of pay should be successful. Both sides are likely to be fair and rational, pleasing everyone with the win-win outcome.

6. WEDNESDAY. Demanding. Try not to let the heavy, relentless demands of survival overwhelm your dreams of a better life. Maintain a clear vision of what you want most, and where you want to be several years down the track. You may struggle with bills as usual, and find this process disheartening. Or you could be holding back on a relationship commitment or proposal because you now have insufficient resources for such a major step. Whatever seems to be restraining you or dampening your prospects needs to be analyzed, then dealt with positively and constructively. Seek consoling or counseling if you're starting to lose hope or can't see any light at the end of a long, dark tunnel.

7. THURSDAY. Excellent. Today is ideal for taking off on a vacation or business trip. Either planning a journey, or leaving on one, should result in what you hope to enjoy or accomplish. Not only can you learn and experience a great deal, you can also make wonderful connections with people in distant locations. All forms of correspondence are sure to reach the intended destination and hit the mark. Cancers seeking an audience for creative expression, or wanting to promote a product to a broader market, should grab the stage and become the center of attention. This will succeed best if you know exactly what you're doing and can deliver the goods as promised.

8. FRIDAY. Stimulating. Many Cancer people are ready for a change of routine and deserve a break. Further attempts at getting ahead in the world can go sideways or fall flat today. Pushing harder won't necessarily accomplish anything more, so why not slip out quietly and get away from it all. Leave work early and enjoy a long weekend. Your departure won't be noticed or create a fuss. However, if a getaway becomes too hard to organize easily, let off steam this evening instead. Avoid your usual associates and habitual hangouts. Go somewhere you've never been before, taking part in unusual activities that lift you out of your comfort zone and stretch the range of your experience.

9. SATURDAY. Rewarding. The opportunities and initiatives for making money that come your way today should be grasped. Motivation stemming from purchasing a home might fuel energetic efforts to earn more. Initiating a search for better employment can be fruitful in short order. The right job is waiting, unless you're already in it. Spending in general is today's theme, as if you are rewarding yourself for a job well done. Shopping for household furniture and decor allows you to express your artistic eye. However, this might cost more than intended unless you keep control of the budget. Romantic appreciation of a special person may inspire a beautiful gift of love, and you're likely to spare no expense.

10. SUNDAY. Courageous. You have energy to burn, so don't resist the impulse to get physical at every opportunity. Competitive games of strength will test your skills and stamina. There's a chance to show what you've got, establishing a reputation that is apt to endure. Fortune favors the brave more than ever. Backing a large plan or project can pay off handsomely. A powerful romantic attraction could sweep you off your feet and prove to be lasting. This is no time to resent anyone who exhibits the positive attributes that you lack. Instead, determine to develop the strengths that are needed to rise to new heights in your world.

11. MONDAY. Disenchanting. Affording all that is on your most recent wish list of desirable purchases seems unlikely at the moment. Your tastes for fine quality are apt to outstrip your capacity to pay for them. Window-shopping, browsing through catalogs, and dreaming are more likely your speed. Enjoy the idea and maintain the intention, even if it's currently out of reach. A social outing or extended family gathering can be costly and also take you away from your work. Being happy with what you've already got may seem hard. Recent success has probably not satisfied you in the way you expected. It's possible that you're looking in the wrong places for what you really want. Meeting up with friends this evening should cheer you up.

12. TUESDAY. Mixed. Some areas of life can be relied on now, but other matters need close scrutiny and fine discrimination. Career ambitions and business goals are on fire, with unstoppable progress being made at a full-throttle pace. What you put time and effort into earlier in the year is now on the way to providing you with deserved rewards. Don't be shy about going public with what you've accomplished, even if you are doing your best work behind the scenes. Make sure that any payments made or owed are what you're worth or what was agreed. It could be easy for a dishonest individual to defraud you in some way, or to take credit for your efforts. A false friend may be undermining the whole group.

13. WEDNESDAY. Thoughtful. Be grateful for a very welcome opportunity to take time off today. The chance to be able to do just what you want is sure to raise your spirits and lift your mood. Spend this period wisely by attending to personal affairs that really matter. Even just getting in touch with yourself, being able to listen to your inner voice, may prove to be a revelation. Resist the temptation to invite anyone else into your sanctuary. Company will cause static and disrupt an intensely private experience. Cancer writers and thinkers have easy access to free-flowing ideas. Prayer and meditation will lead to deeply calm awareness. Be smart on your own behalf.

14. THURSDAY. Extraordinary. Providing you are prepared to get out of your own way and let events unfold naturally, this can be a sublime New Moon period. Quietly go about the day's necessary routines. Don't become overly involved in what's going on, either in the workplace or at home. Instead, observe the world spinning around you from a detached perspective, seeing it clearly for what it is. Rest while wheels already set in motion take care of themselves. By remaining open and receptive, visionary potentials can infuse your mind's eye, giving renewed hope for future fulfillment of your hopes and dreams. Sticking to a schedule and droning through an ordinary day is just not possible now.

15. FRIDAY. Focused. Determination to be your own person will help you resist manipulation or pressure from coworkers who want you to toe the line. Perhaps someone on the job is trying to cut corners and you don't agree with their tactics. Nagging anxieties about the state of your health will prove unfounded. The more you march to the beat of your own drum, the better you'll feel. Ideas and plans that have occurred to you when alone should now be communicated to other people. They are likely to find your thoughts of great interest, while you receive the benefit of their opinion. Any personal view that you want to make public or raise with officials can now confidently be expressed.

16. SATURDAY. Expressive. This can be a period of brainstorms for many Cancer people. You may be fixated on one really big idea, perhaps a book or publication of some sort, a performance, or a website. Appropriate incorporation of technology is critical to the project. You could flit from one activity to another, as a flurry of interests grab your attention. Educational avenues and foreign destinations figure prominently in certain considerations. Whatever is at the center of your attention, no further progress is possible for the present. A period of review and digestion must happen before the next step is taken, even though you are eager to proceed.

17. SUNDAY. Easygoing. This quietly uneventful day offers the chance to rest and gather your wits. The shadow of work to be done in the week ahead may hang over you, making it all the more important to take a relaxing break. Disturb your surrounding environment as little as possible so there will be nothing to distract from peaceful ordinariness. Ignore any problems for now, because tomorrow's another day. This afternoon the mood shifts, with a little more enthusiasm injected into coping with necessary housework and preparations for what lies ahead. Budgeting future activity could involve preparing spreadsheets or going back to the drawing board more than once.

18. MONDAY. Joyful. Love comes to town in a big way today. Taking yourself too seriously would be missing the point. When passion and affection create a heady atmosphere, it's wise to act right away. The chance to express your true feelings for someone you're attracted to shouldn't be missed. The fear of rejection or of being ridiculed might inhibit you from making the first move, but keep in mind nothing ventured, nothing gained. In hindsight you'll probably come to realize it was mostly your own self-consciousness getting in the way. On the commercial front, workers can have more fun than usual making money. Employers will get great value from happy staff and satisfied contractors.

19. TUESDAY. Intense. Aim at transforming dreams into reality. For Cancer entrepreneurs, this is a red-letter day. Plans start to take shape, even if the green light is still some time off. A determination to commit to a large project can set you up in business for the foreseeable future. Check all practical considerations thoroughly at the outset, because once things are in motion there will be no turning back. If you have the drive to build an empire, there is unparalleled opportunity. However, people in high places need further convincing. Don't become discouraged or jump to conclusions simply because a proposed venture isn't immediately taking off.

20. WEDNESDAY. Informed. Curiosity can unearth a lot that is of interest if you're asking the right questions or questioning the right people. Feel confident about making inquiries of official organizations and dealing with political representatives. The environmental and social impact of development can be a hot topic of local concern or public debate. The return of a well-known wanderer to the old neighborhood lends a surreal sense to the current scene. Chatting together and filling this person in on the latest gossip makes the hours fly by, while hearing stories of their travels makes you hunger for your own adventurous journeys of discovery. You two have more in common than you may realize.

21. THURSDAY. Troublesome. Gremlins are hard at their mischievous work, so expect a few bugs and breakdowns in systems at the moment. Problem solvers and help desks could be rushed with requests for assistance. The same is likely for repairmen and mechanics, who will probably be booked weeks ahead. Everybody might want their equipment fixed yesterday, but there's little doubt that a wait will be in store. Cancer workers in the travel industry, and those responsible for the smooth running of schedules, could be tearing their hair out amidst a chaos of delay and reorientation. An impulsive trip begun now may be regretted, whether it's just a short drive or a crazy jaunt overseas.

22. FRIDAY. Enhancing. Loving attention given to your family members, and taking care of affairs on the domestic front, can pull you away from consuming personal interests. Try not to react or become grumpy if it's not possible to forge ahead in splendid isolation. You may be feeling quite independent, but the network that forms the basis of your life shouldn't be neglected or ignored. Putting the finishing touches to home maintenance or decorative effects may be troublesome, and getting things just right can seem frustrating. Perhaps one last purchase will bring it all together. If you shop with resolve you might turn up exactly what you are looking for and at a bargain price.

23. SATURDAY. Auspicious. Finding comfortable stability in your private life needs to be a priority. The opportunity to establish a home-based business should be given serious consideration, especially if you must be home a lot of the time for domestic duties and family care. Loving regard for those you live with is foremost. Such ties will go a long way to smoothing any temporary ruffles or differences within the household. A dynastic enterprise involving a network of blood relatives could create worthwhile employment. It's an added bonus when the profits are returned to everyone instead of fattening the bank account of some unrelated boss or investor.

24. SUNDAY. Stormy. A tense standoff won't last long before it erupts into an outright battle of wills. Confronting bossy in-laws might send accusations and sparks flying freely. And you may wish you'd bitten your tongue when put on the receiving end of verbal, or even physical, blows. Discretion will definitely be the better part of valor. Don't regard politeness, forbearance, or tolerance as a show of weakness or inadequacy. Rather, it's the mark of politeness and civility. When differences or disputes come up, step back. In hindsight you'll be glad that diplomacy and tact prevailed over an impulsive reaction.

25. MONDAY. Pleasant. You may wish today was a holiday. If social inclinations feel stronger than your will to work, extend the weekend for another day. A little bit of what you long for is sure to do a world of good for sensitive Cancer souls. And after all, it's your birthday month. You may feel lucky enough to gamble on a risky outcome or become a winner by backing the favorite and following the crowd. A forum or learning exchange can stimulate your ambitions for further education, or cultivate a taste for the latest popular travel destination. Invitations to intriguing happenings keep you on the hop, flitting from one pleasurable experience to the next interesting encounter.

26. TUESDAY. Variable. If you're in the mood for more fun, get out early for recreation and playtime. Incorporate flexibility in your routine by taking a different route to your destination. Appreciate any touch of spontaneity or humor that lightens the day. If youngsters want immediate attention, don't put them off, because you may be preoccupied later. Pleasure seeking comes to an abrupt end when serious issues demand close attention. It could be depressing to leave toys and playmates, but you'll land in trouble if you don't. Self-discipline is key. Don't jump to negative conclusions concerning money or relationships. Be realistic, and avoid sweeping things under the carpet in hopes they will go away.

27. WEDNESDAY. Strenuous. Work mode is fully engaged and in gear from the get-go today. Whether it's the housework or running a multinational corporation, you need to be in top form and ready to handle a heavy workload. On the bright side, you are certainly in a position to earn a bonus and turn a handsome profit. However, it will take a major effort to handle everything that comes your way. Stick to your specific functions and perform one task at a time. Attempts at coordinating with a group may be inconsistent and disjointed, so don't make that a priority. Socializing this evening would be stretching the limits of your physical endurance, and may fail to live up to your expectations.

28. THURSDAY. Motivated. A wave of enthusiasm could propel you at the outset of the day. Jump on board and don't look back. Certain personal plans may not be making the progress you'd like, but don't dwell on what's not happening unless you like to make trouble for yourself. Rather, give total attention and commitment to what can and must be done. When the working day is over, you'll want to look back with a sigh of relieved satisfaction, not with an exasperated sense of wasted time. The measure of current success should be demonstrated by a growing bank balance. If not, you're probably doing something wrong or irrelevant. Searching for a new job should turn up promising potentials.

29. FRIDAY. Successful. It's the end of the workweek, and it would be a shame to let down now. One last mighty effort could be what it takes to crest the hill. Then you can relax for a well-earned break, and sleep peacefully knowing you've given your all. Taking pride in your accomplishments and skills is part of the deal. When kudos, approval, and praise come your way from customers, colleagues, and superiors, you're doing something right. Once the job is done, stop to savor what you have achieved. Workaholics should temper any tendency to overdo or there could be negative health consequences. A deep level of vocational satisfaction may prove addictive.

30. SATURDAY. Unstable. The Full Moon setting at sunrise is a stirring sight in this summer solstice period. A neglected partner may not ask for attention and quality time but still crave it. Don't wait for a loved one to plead for what they actually deserve. Make the first move to show how much you care. Maybe buy a gift as a peace offering or a gesture of care and regard. Certainly be prepared for a lengthy and serious discussion on the state of your relationship. One way to relieve any tension or distance is by going out together in the company of fun-loving, good-humored friends whom you both know well and enjoy. Their influence in a more relaxed atmosphere can thaw frozen feelings and blocked expression.

JULY

1. SUNDAY. Tense. Avoid focusing on purely material aspects of your romantic relationship, especially if you are involved with a separation or divorce. Doing so will produce confusion or lead to evaluating resources in a limited manner. Back off from any decision making until the dust has settled. Sharing your feelings through heated debate with a group and expressing yourself to the whole world take top priority. You are likely to receive extra attention. Part of you is caught in the twilight of hidden feelings and secret motives. Aiming for clarity and transparent actions will save you a battle later on when a crucial fact is no longer a secret.

2. MONDAY. Stormy. Your feelings and your ideas are competing for attention, making you feel out of rhythm. Connecting with like-minded or sympathetic friends might be soothing later in the day. You may be in a mood to argue with the group, with a dispute over principles and philosophies causing a flare-up of tension. Silencing your lips is a good way to avoid the unpleasantness that comes from fixed sides and opinions which are unlikely to change, at least for today. Channeling tension into martial arts or physical fitness can add energy for personal achievement. It's best to stick with controlling your own patch of ground, which will be more than enough for today.

3. TUESDAY. Worrisome. Everyday activities you can practically do with your eyes closed are likely to prove unfulfilling if your only focus. There are hidden personal mysteries to be solved, to place a piece of the jigsaw into the subconscious picture. Stern Saturn could weigh on your mind long enough to arouse a painful old memory. An older family member could be the worry. Gaining valuable support from a trusted friend can share the burden, evoking a more positive reaction. Try not to take on another person's worries as your own, or you won't be much help to them. From now on vow to have more love and happiness amidst the daily struggle to survive. Being part of a community can give you the sense that it's not just you and the bills alone.

4. WEDNESDAY. Renewing. The Pisces Moon lends heightened inspiration to your thoughts, giving you the ability to be present in a deep and open space. Wanting to get on with the job refuels you for action, jump-starting the holiday with an assertive attitude. Center yourself as soon as you wake up to raise your spirit upward, then pour yourself into all that matters. Family members or friends support your feeling nature, and changes or upgrades to your home or community give a sense of moving forward. You may receive a loan regardless of the past week's negative reactions when you first broached the subject.

5. THURSDAY. Uplifting. Being willing to take off on a detour can excite the day with unknown options involving travel. Or you may approach a larger-than-life subject with expansive wonder. Keep an alternative plan handy, in case of transportation delays or another glitch in the system. The Sun and Moon in harmony suggest change is not too much of a problem personally, and might lend excitement to any activity on your agenda. Schedule accounting for another day. You need to leave room for spontaneous decisions, business as unusual, and lightning fast reactions. Today it's an option to suddenly decide to fly to Paris.

6. FRIDAY. Cautious. Keep unique idiosyncrasies to yourself and observe personal boundaries. Go about your business carefully. Work could be demanding, with changes lending an air of dissatisfaction to the proceedings. Upgrading and rerouting come with stress attached, and there's also less trust in spontaneously fulfilling outcomes. The Moon hurtling into Aries invites you to prepare for people telling you how it is in a manner that is not entirely pleasant. Your image may be challenged by someone in the workplace, so make sure you have protective shoulder pads or a classy business suit as the first line of defense. Schedule time later when the real you can come out to play.

7. SATURDAY. Mixed. Being expansive and sporty could get you out into the fresh air after yesterday's stress and intrigue. To make the most of the fun atmosphere, delight in the company of friends who are open, trusting, and adaptable. Even catching up on weekend study should be easier than normal thanks to your interest in the subject rather than operating from the pressure of necessity. Cancer people who are searching for a job could be fortunate today. Updating your resume can reveal you're more skilled than previously thought. An angularity of Sun and Moon shows tension between soft option and hard. Get work out of the way and leave room for a stimulating get-together with friends.

8. SUNDAY. Fortunate. Getting the ball rolling in the right direction will produce a stable and happy day. There isn't much to hold you back. Even finances appear to add up. The art of voluntary simplicity will come more naturally, gracefully stretching the dollar like multiplying fishes and loaves. Streamlining personal office space or deciding on a change in work methods looks positive and without drama, even putting more money in the coffers eventually. Pluto's positive charisma could see other people telling you you've got the right stuff. Your ability to use charm to get what you want will steer you in the right direction and help in the love stakes tonight.

9. MONDAY. Bold. There could be an urge to run off and escape into the wild blue yonder. Jupiter is throwing an odd angle to the Moon. There are traps for the unwary, although you may manage to heal old woes related to a group and their activities. Let off steam with a good physical workout at some point during the day. Prepare for strong emotions erupting at a late afternoon or early evening meeting. Hard attitudes and assertive feelings will vie for dominance, and people will be sticking to their guns. A predominantly male way of acting and reacting makes for an attitude of my way or the highway. Apply your charm but don't back down.

10. TUESDAY. Uneasy. Unexpressed feelings could give you a headache. Turning the music up a notch louder to deflect tension this morning is a beneficial option. Someone is refusing to budge from a stubborn position despite your logical arguments to the contrary. Don't say boo to today's budget. Just get on with getting through the day as best you can. Peak experiences will be hard to come by. Later on, a butterfly Gemini Moon helps to soften concrete attitudes. Get ready to expand out into the comforting territory of supportive energy. Moving forward will be a lot more fun tonight, with the chance for artistic Cancers to tune into far-out wavelengths.

11. WEDNESDAY. Unsettled. Guard against going overboard emotionally regarding your feelings about behind-the-scenes activities or your private world. Jupiter is inspiring an over-the-top approach of expansive feeling. Reason might not prevail for some time. In fact, the Uranus vibe later in the day can stimulate profoundly eccentric feelings all around. Malfunctioning computers, cars, and technological gadgets are foreseen, so brace yourself. With your diminished powers to adapt emotionally outside your comfort zone, make sure you don't stretch yourself a little too much. Dwell on what's normal before you run off to join the circus.

12. THURSDAY. Exciting. Pay attention to your feeling nature as aspiring Neptune urges you to reach higher for soul contact. Stability of reason and purpose, modulated by teacher Saturn, suggests you're making good choices behind the scenes. Your soul life is making sense emotionally. However, an impulse for a transformative makeover can cause a tumultuous ending or beginning, challenging your emotional resilience with compulsive, passionate instincts. Timid Cancers may not be able to hide in the past or the familiar. A romantic or strong figure wants the best from you, not just the shiny surface. Embrace all that is new and exciting.

13. FRIDAY. Bright. The Moon returning to her own sign shines attention on your personal projects and the need to have quality time to work on your own. Cooking, gardening, and just puttering are all positive. A Leo flair for romance, lingering not so subtly in the background, fans the fire for a relating drama. It's up to you whether the movie in which you are starring is positive or negative. Handling a relationship's limiting qualities along with an upgrade in values can be purification by fire. However, this can strip creative talents to bare bones at the same time. Aim to expand your learning capacity. Being open to all that is new while still nurturing your cozy corner means you can have the best of both worlds.

14. SATURDAY. Nurturing. Playing close to home remains on the agenda as the New Moon sojourns in restful Cancer. A fresh breeze of freedom blows cobwebs away, with an open mood still benefiting you. Spending time with friends and acquaintances can be pleasurable after a day of feathering your nest. You may open up your home as a refuge for weary friends. The world sees boundaries disappearing and reappearing with an intriguing rhythm, and life at home follows suit. An older relative could need some time and attention from you, a repayment of past loyalty. Any energy you put in today will buffer you from the coldhearted world for the entire weekend.

15. SUNDAY. Independent. Venus moving into Virgo heralds an independent streak. A visit to the grocery store without family or a solo trip to the mall should help you find emotional space. Leave room in the day for doing your own thing. Activities involving health could spark your interest. A sale of great gymnasium equipment or graduated weights might be just what you need to raise your energy level. Travel is likely to be short and to the point. Using the morning to get chores done offers fulfillment in checking off your to-do list and getting mundane affairs sorted out. A calming dinner at home with friends and family members around the dinner table brings a harmonious end to the day.

16. MONDAY. Fiery. Dramatic tension is in the air, with a dancing Leo Moon promoting fabulous clothes and sparkling jewelry. Dancing to the rhythm suggests a bright social day dressed in all your finery. Just watch a tendency to dominate the space. There will be many people competing for attention, one who is sure to represent the A-list or nobility. It could even be you, so accept any and all invitations. Jupiter encourages optimism, sport, and action. Don't take conflict too seriously. A debate of some sort, then making up, could be all it takes to remind you that life's fantastic amidst the pressured drama of it all. Give it your best and you'll relish the rewards.

17. TUESDAY. Harmonious. The Moon in harmony with Venus holds out the prospect of gentle interaction with your neighbors and friends. Keep to simple tasks, creatively tidying up life. A village atmosphere of greeting neighbors and having time for quick chats makes for a pleasant day. At work, you may long to break out of office restrictions, seeking fresh air and open space. Jupiter calls Cancers to buy a lottery ticket or indulge in a small business risk. Using entrepreneurial skill at work helps tie up loose ends. Just make sure not to overextend yourself. A good-humored atmosphere encourages taking time off and not being a slave to constant responsibilities.

18. WEDNESDAY. Energetic. A dynamic interplay of Uranus energies unsettles and charges the atmosphere with jittery nervous energy. Settling down to the job at hand might be difficult unless you first make a short journey and adopt straightforward approaches. Group action will be successful if everyone takes aim and shares goals. Be prepared to figure out people's emotions and adapt to approaches that suit each individual. Cancer workers can air views even though a few revolutionaries are present. Focus on projects requiring courageous leadership. Much can be accomplished in a short space of time. Children may demonstrate an independent rebellious streak. Show them a safe way to proceed, then fly the coop yourself for a while.

19. THURSDAY. Tense. Changes in the workplace are likely to give rise to tension in general. Competing energies can be very annoying while you attempt to center yourself in the potentially neat Virgo Moon. Search for the balance between work and play. Do whatever is hard first, confronting petty jealousies or tangles in the emotional fabric. Power plays are foreseen, and you will need to negotiate. Your personal appearance could be a subject of discussion at work. Make sure your clothes, hair, and posture contribute to how you're projecting yourself. Later in the day a Libra Moon potentially eases conflict. Harmonize your surroundings with soothing colors and scents.

20. FRIDAY. Positive. Spending time decorating your home, perhaps adding trendy updated furniture and wall coverings, can exercise your flair for creating. There are possibilities of overseas visitors arriving in connection with friends or with a group you belong to. An assortment of companions makes for an interesting day. It looks like all systems are go, with deepening insight into how you're living. Just watch a tendency for your mind to battle your emotions. Inviting a healing energy into your home, or clearing cluttered energy, gives a positive base from which to refuel yourself. Working from a home office, or reorganizing it more to your liking, can make you glad you're not hoofing into a city office.

21. SATURDAY. Contented. Even with a tinge of the unpredictable on the home front, Neptune lends dreams and a flow of contentment to the day. You will be in the mood for a harmonious day on a deep level. Cancer songwriters and artists flourish in the Libra lunar atmosphere. Feeling at peace with the world and being able to deeply concentrate on an emotional level brings contentment. There's not too much tension in the air, giving you many options. Work and play have the chance to merge. Enjoy everyday activities and prepare for a pleasantly social evening. Inviting people to your home allows peaceful sharing and relating during the evening.

22. SUNDAY. Bracing. Today's different set of energies requires you to change gears. The Scorpio Moon inspires passionate creativity, while minor matters are on hold due to a lack of energy. Sharing thoughts and feelings is favored, so be locally social and roam the neighborhood helping with chores and stopping to chat. Home life contains its fair share of tension. Get out of the house and circulate in the world, letting your energy rise. Factor in a little love for the evening after a time of playing it safe. It's not so much calm you're searching for but a charge of excitement. Stay creative despite any and all disturbance.

23. MONDAY. Uneven. Handling a potential conflict related to a group you're involved with demands that you be prepared for conflict of some sort. Challenges to the way you create, deal with children, or use the time and resources available to everybody may produce a no-win situation. This begs you to reconfigure to the positive. Friends or influences from overseas and a broader perspective open the cautious Cancer to progressive future possibilities and fun. Of course, some of this will be illusory. There's the potential to yearn for fantasy, but caution is advised. Put your whole heart into a sport or outdoor activity, but remember to play it safe.

24. TUESDAY. Unstable. Getting a grip on the day is like tying down a tent in a gravitation-free zone. Neptune misting up contacts with friends and associates throws potential confusion or charlatans into the mix. Make sure people are the real deal. Positive lines of clear energy and productivity can work efficiently. The result will be abundant resources and cash coming back to you if you are able to stick to the facts. Intrigue is certain to be on some people's minds, gliding like an underwater stingray. Duck and weave to keep things level. Take time out to spoil your loved one with a delicious treat. Utilize your private and hidden world to find sanctuary among the madness.

25. WEDNESDAY. Expansive. Take time to relax. Work from a position of joy and abundance. Your businesslike mood for creating something from nothing turns the volume up on trends, happenings, and beautiful people. Remain open to connections at the right place and time. Consciously feel as one with the stream of people and good flowing into your life. Minor tangles or adjustments in communication and presentation require a tweak here and there, but it's nothing that can't be fixed quite easily. Mainly small healing changes are needed in your thinking, especially regarding subconscious wounds. Be willing to forgive, forget, and move on.

26. THURSDAY. Strong. Taking massive action describes today, with its definite ending and beginning. You could be putting your energy and passion into leaving a job or beginning a new project. Either will take all the energy and commitment you can muster. Avoid half measures. A little positive aggravation is likely, but it could be the thorn in the side that makes you take action. Face and resolve a problem with a friend or group which is incompatible with the harmonious outcome you're seeking at this stage. Working hard can give you almost instant rewards. Infrastructure that you set up today could last the distance, to be copied and envied in the future.

27. FRIDAY. Organizing. Looking for a partner, or working with one, is a highlight of the day. Being out and about with a friend or loved one, enjoying activities in the neighborhood or concentrating on a local concern worthy of your attention, conveys a theme of duty. This is a results-oriented day. Frustration regarding a financial or real estate issue is apt to continue unabated. Arguing may get you nowhere. There are competing needs, and all of them must be catered to and eventually met. Draw up a list and be creative in resolving outstanding issues. Define values and goals plus where you're not happy. Then don't agonize but organize.

28. SATURDAY. Significant. Aim for unity of purpose as a priority. A desire to work with other people becomes a juggling act, with projects also needing time on your own. Having an innovative attitude and mixing it up a bit can dissolve tension and help you remain open to spontaneous solutions. Late in the day socializing with interesting friends and colleagues arouses excitement and stimulation, blowing the dust off partnership cobwebs. Group dining at a favorite restaurant, or a gathering of friends at a favorite bar, will lead to energized debate and laughter. Write down some of the genius ideas that are sure to be exchanged while you think outside the box.

29. SUNDAY. Conservative. Someone could be setting a tough standard, with an argument over money or resources hard to avoid. Standing up for yourself becomes important. Taking an in-depth look at how to better organize your finances or real estate needs courage. Mercury, planet of thinking, is in your sign, encouraging the cautious and conservative, especially with a Saturn Moon waxing to full. Take it easy on yourself. Factor in a special treat or visit to a nurturing friend to offset the limited, dutiful atmosphere. Even friends in the neighborhood might be stressed out.

30. MONDAY. Emotional. Taking a long, hard look at yourself and contacting unspoken needs can draw you into a feeling world that dominates reason. Cancer actors and artists can let loose with a creative, if messy, emotional drama to be played out on the stage of life. Avoid overdoing in any area or with any substance or drink. There's the potential to go overboard in a quest for a surreal state. Facing truths about situations could be difficult. Watch a good movie to see others play out darknesses in your own emotional life. Fixing boundaries for yourself could be uppermost in importance, especially if you feel that people are mistreating or taking advantage of you. Rest and be gentle with yourself.

31. TUESDAY. Variable. Tensions and aggression in the atmosphere suggest people may feel trapped and ready to lash out. Money, or lack of it, may prey on your mind, producing a mild bout of depression. You need to be resourceful and to cultivate survival instincts. To enrich your emotional life, cultivate perseverance and joy, regardless of outward circumstances, and then move on. Keeping on going is the way to move forward. Exotic travel could be an escape from your current troubles. Keep planning the trip of your dreams with the person of your dreams. There is no reason to settle for second best.

AUGUST

1. WEDNESDAY. Unpredictable. Traveling offers a few surprises for the unwary. Have an alternative in mind in case a plane is delayed or a sudden long-distance travel plan changes. You may find yourself longing for the open road as a spiritual yearning leads you to a devotional retreat seeking elusive Shangri-la. Try to avoid making irresponsible or exaggerated promises even as a Jupiter-unbounded Pisces Moon encourages out-there actions from even the most rational Cancer. Be safe by not indulging in overly risky behavior. You could find on office environment much too restrictive with energies like these. Get plenty of fresh air and factor in the random nature of events.

2. THURSDAY. Fruitful. Getting a message out and presenting your image to the world can definitely work. Being in tune with publishing and the wide world of overseas contacts could feature strongly. This is a communicative day. Jupiter shining in tune with the Sun sends happy entrepreneurial sparks flying. It's also a great day to launch a fashion show, magazine, or an event which gets you immediate cash. However, there's a chance the green-eyed monster is in the wings at work. Guard your back and then press on, deflecting petty jealousy from the insecure. Concentrate on your own talents for a results-driven day. Romance is secondary to achieving career goals.

3. FRIDAY. Enthusiastic. Successful career dealings and presenting a good image help you forge ahead in style. You are poised to succeed as a new opportunity unfolds. Utilize your fiery and enthusiastic side to explore with pioneering imagination. Your drive, desire, and determination to achieve will take you a long way. A new job or second stream of income looks positive, and financial backers or institutions should be easier to deal with. Receiving extra attention or publicity for your job can put the assertive Cancer in a prime position, showing the rest of the world how it's done. Keep up with late-breaking news.

4. SATURDAY. Helpful. Contact with a large group of people can spark the weekend with excitement related to a work or service project. Mercury, planet of communication, isn't doing anyone any favors however, especially when it comes to friends and social activities. Make sure your foot isn't in your mouth when speaking. An older person can give you an opportunity or a financial hand up.

It's important to recognize and be grateful for all the energy older relatives have given you over time. Their generosity will hopefully be repaid by you in the future. Dealing with a backlog of correspondence can take a chunk out of the day but is sure to make the week ahead easier.

5. SUNDAY. Connecting. Getting your social needs met shouldn't be too hard. Your sector ruling friendships, social connections, and humanitarian interests is ready for action. Being open to what's new and experimental leads to trying new places and connecting with new groups. The key is moving on from an obsession with the state of your resources. A positive transformation is possible as a degree of anxiety goads you to find and form a supportive community. If you review your independent lifestyle and find it lacking, reach out and establish new connections. Groups that appeal to you will welcome you as a new member.

6. MONDAY. Careful. Having to deal with current limitations can put a damper on yesterday's expansive feelings. Getting on with the job and waiting for the mood to pass can help you make some headway in a persevering way. Relationships can take on a sense of competition, forcing you to stick up for the underdog. A fight could brew within a team, club, or humanitarian interest group this evening. The fixed attitude of someone in a leadership position can bring on a confrontation. It's unlikely that offering the olive branch of peace or a neutral option will work. Sticking to your defined principles, and fighting the good fight head-on, seems to be the best choice.

7. TUESDAY. Emotional. The Moon swimming through the Cancer sector of secrets brings your lunar side to the fore. You may feel minor sunburn of the soul if you're too out there, making you crave escaping big-time. Create a sanctuary if you can, a place to experience the mysterious and the divine. Writing, painting, or an art form can channel your lush emotions and confrontational energies. Conflict is in the mix for lovers of romantic drama. A strong creative tension needs to be released in some form, whether meaningless argument or constructive challenge. If you are able to surmount the emotional tests you stand to gain financially as you make something solid from the energy.

8. WEDNESDAY. Significant. Be willing to participate on the fringe of society and lend a helping hand to those less fortunate than you. Stretch yourself to fit in with weirdly eccentric people, including artists. Be adaptable and ready to lend a nonjudgmental ear. You may not save a soul but you could help someone escape the present and find safe, calmer waters. The dark side can be painfully obvious and the workplace is apt to be stressful. Aligning to a personal compass point is crucial to maintaining emotional balance as this day reaches a crescendo. What you achieve can be of real value, making you stronger and wiser. Keep your light around you and go under the radar.

9. THURSDAY. Rewarding. You will perform well in tasks needing verbal dexterity and a flair for the future. Hitch your sail to a trend and follow an intuitive map of the road less traveled. Keep a good sense of the practical uppermost in your mind. Taking on a second job for additional income is possible. Look into work which involves personal freedom, where you're able to be yourself. Feeling like you have to adapt and change for economic reasons can sting your soul. Extraordinary people are sure to inspire you. Cultivate optimism despite negative appearances. Go for what you love, which could involve packing a bag as a positive form of fate comes calling.

10. FRIDAY. Challenging. Expanding a limited attitude is possible if you explore ways to rethink your life positively. Reorganizing joint finances or rethinking approaches to economic security can be challenging. However, doing so will help you face issues you've been intending to confront for quite a while. An unusual quirky side to the day could charge you with a radical sense of humor, breaking the tension of facing your fears. Go easy on yourself. Be ready to adapt the way you present yourself. Arrange to spend some time on personal projects. Find space to relax and recharge your batteries. Being at a favorite nature spot can refill the waters of your soul and put life back into you.

11. SATURDAY. Auspicious. The action planet Mars charges the atmosphere with assertiveness, making you ready to contribute resources and things of value. Look at real estate or new job possibilities with a behind-the-scenes approach, playing detective and checking out the lay of the land. A feeling of buoyant optimism will be replenishing. Your ship is coming in again in the tide of good fortune. Remain open to cheerful, progressive people who can help you on your path. You may bump into the right contact thanks to a coincidental meeting. Cultivating faith can tune you to a happy wavelength of success. Cancer lovers can enjoy a break getting away from it all. Be adventurous even if you only go on a drive in the country.

12. SUNDAY. Exciting. Head and heart are joined, combining to produce idealized decisions in the realm of moving or evaluating your current position. Just guard against seeing the world through rose-colored glasses. The fantasy is great, but make sure you also clearly see illusions. Gearing up for an elevation of your role in a life drama gives you a feeling of increasing excitement. There's the chance this week to play the lead instead of being a supporting actor. Dramatic and lively people attract you. Visiting the theater, a museum, or a photographic exhibit chronicling the best of an era can inspire a peak experience. Cancers in love can be over the top as plans come to fruition almost immediately.

13. MONDAY. Disquieting. Meditation or prayer can nullify some of the effects of the nurturing Moon meeting haughty Saturn. Usually this produces some sort of limitation, with doses of fear and loneliness for good measure. Luckily Venus is here too, suggesting relationships can go one way or the other. A breakup may occur, but strong commitments can be made as well. Do whatever it takes to ward off feelings of isolation and panic. Movies, ice cream, and remaining with centered friends are all possible tactics. So is being brave and doing what you have to do successfully. Use whatever hero's myth works for you to build courage. Just don't sign for anything on the dotted line.

14. TUESDAY. Unsettling. Time out to look at the birds and butterflies might be the break your mind needs. Avoid taking risks with property or being overly trusting with financial decisions. You need all your wits about you to navigate the twists and turns of the day, especially while traveling. Sudden detours or changes to familiar routes can challenge your good humor. Make the most of a disorganized environment by focusing on what you are able to control. Writing projects could benefit from your crazy energy if you adopt the right attitude. Scale down to your local turf and only take baby steps.

15. WEDNESDAY. Magnetic. Despite tensions in your neighborhood, a work opportunity can upgrade your property and give you additional items of value. An increase in income coupled with an out-with-the-old, in-with-the-new approach, can lead to transforming your environment in an exciting way. Get dressed up in your fabulous best and find your share of the limelight. Presenting yourself in a colorful manner adds life to all you encounter. Convince other people that you need to be blessed in fine style. Just be careful as you shine charismatically that you don't become manipulative. If you're at ease with your energy and pass the abundance test, you'll be given more than if you sell your soul.

16. THURSDAY. Rewarding. Plan on working from home or on a domestic project. This will combine your need to work quietly behind the scenes with being creative from your home base. A productive day is foreseen if you stay connected to the stream of information you need from a mother ship of some kind. Using design skills in a practical way for a second job or for a labor of love will be intensely exhilarating. Working with artistic flair, art, and dramatic colors can uplift and enrich any project. A friend may instill extra positive input, taking you further faster. Whatever you work on today, there's an understanding that two heads are better than one. Realizing you're not on your own is working wonders for your finances.

17. FRIDAY. Insightful. Strong intuition is possible as the planet of deep perception touches the planet of the mind. As you see perceptively into a situation and gain clarity, you'll touch on more than a few home truths. Play detective in any situation to discover its essence. When it comes to resources, property, or income, you can find the information you need. Cancer lovers and couples can have a fairy-tale evening of beauty and relaxation at home. The positive Neptune mood is playing your song, and a deeply healing experience thankfully occurs between you and that special person. Remain open to the subtleties of relating to each other. Create a harmonious mood, then float away.

18. SATURDAY. Focused. Dealing with everyday realities is big on your agenda. Being self-reliant and using what you have at hand will lead to making something out of almost nothing. Waste not, want not could be the mantra of the day. Ideas that come to you for the smoother running of everyday systems will help where most needed. Home and organizational duties must not be ignored. Tighten your belt and embrace a more frugal style. You could be working into the evening, when Saturn lends the mood for working late or a quiet dinner rather than tripping the light fantastic. Seriousness is the new mode.

19. SUNDAY. Powerful. Remaining open to unusual options can bring electrifying freshness and new ways to express yourself emotionally and creatively. A potential love interest from overseas can recharge you with unique inspiration, showing you a different approach to life. Being in the now and releasing past attitudes brings abundance. Keep alert for new projects as you're chatting with acquaintances. The opportunity to have resources come easily is potent, so give thanks. Gratitude will bring happiness and fill the coffers. You may want to test the waters in tussling arguments that wring out private secrets. Someone may know your soul better than you thought.

20. MONDAY. Mixed. Two sets of desires are playing out on this organizational Monday morning. Going with a soulful upwelling of feelings will produce its own agenda. Find balance by putting energy into your job or monetary issues. Allocating time to function in two gears can tweak the day into the most successful outcome. Escape is high on your emotional wish list, but guard against alcohol or substance abuse, or giving your all to fantasy. Make sure safety clauses are included in anything you sign or undertake. Keep receipts for any purchases and avoid giving in to a pressured sales pitch. Confronting fear is part of today's test. Keep your environment clean and nurturing to balance all of the challenges.

21. TUESDAY. Cautious. Getting through the day without an emotional drama of some sort can be a miracle when fiery Moon does combat with feisty Mars. Get the conflict out in the open in a safe way, and turn the heat down if an argument is escalating into the stratosphere. Argumentative moods might provoke everyone. Going off to a martial arts lesson, or letting off steam in some other healthy way via exercise, can channel the edginess in the air. Leave plenty of time to travel safely. Be aware that business as usual is unlikely. If determined to get work done, be sure your plan is realistic and watertight. Avoid taking expensive risks since today's not the day.

22. WEDNESDAY. Inspiring. Unusual energy on the work front forces you to adapt to a sometimes crazy agenda of stops and starts. Being inspired by a new health regime can be uplifting thanks to your resolution to become healthier and to renew and reinvigorate your life force. Finding an art object of your dreams can complement your living space and give you a feeling of deep connection. The struggles you've been involved with in the wider society serve to enhance and reinforce your basic beliefs. Take advantage of broad horizons calling and be ready for an adventure. Systems might not be the highest priority, but being fully alive is. Wrap yourself in the arms of love tonight.

23. THURSDAY. Volatile. Visionary philosophy overrides the day. Be prepared to operate from your most deeply held beliefs rather than everyday consciousness. Expect a creative and intimate day lived out at a compelling personal level. Let go of old attitudes and embrace all that is new. Getting better acquainted with people at work, and linking up to the greater good, begins a new phase of your work life. You may opt to leave your job or let go if feelings of fulfillment and satisfaction aren't present. Brace for a fiery, adventurous day. Home's coziness might be a low priority for the moment. Children understand that you have to pursue a life vision and will give you necessary space.

24. FRIDAY. Positive. Working dutifully with a partner on down-to-earth tasks affords an opportunity for a grounded day puttering around the neighborhood. Being dedicated and businesslike rules the day. Attention to detail is important. Check off the to-do list as you go, and feel a sense of satisfaction. Jupiter is tempting an over-expansion of some sort. Getting away for a walk in nature at lunch, or taking a ride to a satellite village, can clear the cobwebs from your brain and stretch the synapses for more work. You and your mate or partner may encounter new friends this evening. Welcome a bohemian element of enjoying the arts rather than perceiving this as threatening your current boundaries.

25. SATURDAY. Deceptive. Be careful not to go overboard in a shopping spree or when making any solitary purchase. Stick carefully to your budget. Listen carefully to the salesperson when making big purchases. Do not cave in to an appeal to your pride in keeping up with the trendy family down the street or to your image. It's unlikely you need the purchase all that much. Writing or educational projects and general communication can lead to debating how much to tell other people. This comes as the result of Mars still journeying through your secret soul sector. Playing it safe for one day can free up energy to have fun when the coast really is clear later.

26. SUNDAY. Healing. Reviewing your deep subconscious needs presents an opportunity to have memories or dreams fit like a piece of the puzzle into your personal jigsaw. Understanding a past event with the assistance of a talented interpreter can relieve you of old emotional burdens and invite healing to begin. Quietly work on projects close to your heart. Natural energy is coming from the passion you feel for the plight of kindred spirits communicating similar experiences. Respect grief that may come from darkened emotions. Feelings brought to the surface can launch the healing process once communicated. Being at one with other people going through similar circumstances makes for a profound day.

27. MONDAY. Restricting. Limitations with finances are the main aspect hindering a desire to dive in and take a chance. For the moment you're being asked to make the most of what you have, despite being willing to max out your credit. However, doing so would only come back to haunt you like an illusory ghost of fear. So buckle the belt and instead dream of ways to make something from nothing in an attitude of thankfulness and creativity. You're rich in artistic talent and the more positive Neptune fluidity will assist you to realize your cup runneth over. Do what you love and the money will eventually follow.

28. TUESDAY. Surprising. Hearing stories from close relatives, extended family members, or neighbors can pepper the day with elements of the bizarre. Remaining flexible is vital because of today's sudden breakdowns in communications, transportation, or e-mail. Going with the flow might be appropriate, except it's more a case of brace for the sudden event. Keep your light around you while traveling. Be extra cautious even when driving locally. Take care of nerves with a possible soothing treat at the day spa, or whatever calms you on a frenetic day. Do all that you can to avoid aimless gossip. Ignoring meaningless events can shore up your energy and give you added raw life force to pour into what truly matters most.

29. WEDNESDAY. Uneasy. To cope with this amazing day, plant yourself firmly and stay focused. The lightning excitement of astro contacts keeps you on the go. Use your inventive energies positively. Observe plenty of caution while on the move, and sit tight until a particularly electrifying storm passes. Do your own thing when it comes to studying, lecturing, or publishing. You may feel the stirrings of a brave new world just waiting for you to join in. Discernment and productivity will steer you toward creative success. Going under the radar, and having fun in the uprush of it all, sees your crabby sense of humor well utilized with friends.

30. THURSDAY. Opportune. A buoyant widening of your emotional mood concentrates attention on career matters. Present yourself in a professional, happening manner. Be ready for opportunities to take you to the next level. Be aware of the positive impact from being in the flow of cool trends and harmonizing with life. Taking an energetic, assertive position in regard to your professional intentions can lead to a successful scenario unfolding. There's a need to work behind the scenes linking up with people who can positively support you. Keep on working as the next chapter is written. Romance is in the cards for Cancer singles staying in the light of their own path.

31. FRIDAY. Fortuitous. Be ready for actions on the career front to harmonize with what you value. You are building something solid and of worth. Available energy is determined and deep, helping you go for what you want in a concentrated way. Make the most of today's vibes on which you can solidify your reputation and recent gains. Changes to your routine can be made gracefully. Prepare to charge forward with positive professional influence and public recognition. A friend or acquaintance from an alliance with a favorite group may offer an opportunity after spotting your obvious talent or gift. Have a happy day working hard and feeling supported in a beneficial way.

SEPTEMBER

1. SATURDAY. Satisfactory. The company of a few close friends is likely to be far more enjoyable than a large gathering of acquaintances. The dawn of a new realization can shake you from complacency and cause you to question your true purpose. Any opening for you to help someone else will provide great satisfaction. You might start to think about volunteering for a charitable organization. You may need to reveal a well-guarded secret to a person you can trust, just to get the worry off your mind and obtain feedback about the best action to take. Traffic delays can be a real headache, so stay close to home and experience the delights of your own neighborhood.

2. SUNDAY. Confusing. Emotional reliance on a close friend could make you demand more of their attention than usual. You might even find yourself getting jealous if they show someone else extra attention. If so, let the feeling go and move on or you may fall prey to all sorts of self-delusions and manipulation. You are likely to be very sensitive to the moods of other people and could pick up mixed messages as they say one thing but do another. Sports activities would be refreshing. Exercise prompts good feelings, and the social contact allows for impersonal conversation. The less you stew about your own problems, the better. Look ahead with confidence.

3. MONDAY. Rejuvenating. Concentrate on what you must do today and don't worry about anything else. Many small achievements combine to make your day productive and personally satisfying.

This is a favorable time for writing and for all forms of mental work. Cancer students can make significant headway with assignments and research. If a neighbor is not feeling well, a visit from you might cheer them up. You may even be able to fulfill a need that they cannot handle alone. If you yourself aren't feeling up to par, it is probably because you're trying to do too much. Reduce your to-do list and allow your body to relax while recharging your batteries.

4. TUESDAY. Uplifting. You could lose yourself in whatever you are doing, becoming so immersed that the hours fly by unnoticed. Working behind the scenes suits you. You can get your best work done in private, without the doubts and questions of fellow workers or friends imposing on your plans. Start walking or jogging not only to keep fit or lose weight but also as a way to lift your spirits by getting outside in the fresh air. If you don't seem to have enough hours in the day, get up a little earlier and create time. It will only take you about three weeks to change a habit, so start implementing desired changes now. Before the a month is over you'll be right on track.

5. WEDNESDAY. Buoyant. The Moon moves into your own sign this morning, making this an opportune time to focus on your personal appearance and environment. Your mind and body will be especially responsive to the feel of clothes on your skin and the colors that surround you. You may need to go shopping for new clothes and accessories. Your favorite store could have some original and creative designs that appeal to you and are just what you're seeking. Look at your home environment also. Reflect on your mood in different rooms and consider changing the colors to the most pleasing hues of your choice. Gather the family for a delectable meal to be savored together.

6. THURSDAY. Liberating. The chance to break your daily routine and experience something different can be refreshing and inspiring. Some doubts and fears may nag at the back of your mind. However, when you actually confront them and take a close look, they are apt to prove unfounded and disappear from your conscience. Cancer students may receive a surprise result on an exam or assignment. This will make a positive difference to the way you feel about yourself. Teachers will be happy to discuss questions or problems, so don't hesitate to make an appointment with them. If traveling, your thoughts could turn to home. Make contact to ensure that everything is going smoothly.

7. FRIDAY. Bright. Fun and laughter fill your day, making the world rosy. If you are inclined to carry out practical jokes, be careful who you play them on. A neighbor might not think you are very funny, then go out of their way to make life hard for you. Your self-esteem may be on shaky ground, more reliant on what other people think of you than is really healthy. Keep in mind that they could be jealous of you and therefore exaggerating what they find annoying, so don't take everything to heart. Buying a beautiful item could make you feel better, although you may not be able to afford what you actually want most. Call a friend you can rely on and laugh together. Happiness is priceless.

8. SATURDAY. Exciting. Good feelings hold sway throughout the day. Indulge in all the things you love, but just be careful that you don't let these good feelings influence your better judgment. There are underhanded manipulators out there waiting for some trusting fool to fall into their trap, and you don't want it to be you. Electrical devices and gadgets may go on the blink. Take precautions if using older appliances or machinery. Romantic urges help to rekindle the lustful embrace of your love's early days. Cancer singles might start to think about where to go to find love. A large concert or social event will be memorable in more ways than one.

9. SUNDAY. Productive. Intense emotions give you that extra push to fix and eliminate problems from your life. Health matters might need to be dealt with by making renewed commitment. It's no good saying you ought to do something. You must muster up the resolve to actually do it. Now is the time to make changes and stick to them. Storage could be a big problem at home. Look into innovative ways to create space, and enjoy being creative and practical at the same time. Items such as shelves that fit on doors and under-bed storage boxes can be effective. Or you might even lower a ceiling and create extra space up high.

10. MONDAY. Independent. Debating different ideologies can turn into an argument if you feel that other people are trying to impose their beliefs on you. Now that Venus is moving direct again, self-esteem and your creative side are picking up and starting to have a positive effect. A special talent might be developed into a business, allowing you to start making money doing what you like best. Check out all the financial angles of a business before you start. It might be beneficial for you to become incorporated or to obtain a small-business loan. Talk to experienced people in your area for their stories and you will learn a lot.

11. TUESDAY. Dynamic. Today's New Moon in Virgo makes this a favorable time to initiate negotiations or to sign a contract. Cancers who are in the market for a new car should make the rounds of automobile showrooms and scan newspaper ads. Don't buy the first model that appeals. Do your homework in order to find a real bargain. With computer technology changing rapidly, keep your finger on the pulse by looking into groundbreaking software and hardware. If you have your own business, doing this can give you an edge over competitors. A nitpicking neighbor could overstep the limits and force you to speak up.

12. WEDNESDAY. Mixed. Refinancing a personal loan or your mortgage is a good idea if it will allow you to pay off your debt faster. Research banks and other lenders before making any decision. Excessive fees and charges can be avoided if you do the homework. A family discussion may become emotional, with thoughts and feelings misconstrued or misunderstood. Keep in mind that heart and mind are two separate functions. It can be very hard to put feelings into words, since what you are thinking isn't necessarily what you are feeling. A brother or sister can offer great support when it comes to dealing with one of your parents.

13. THURSDAY. Promising. Write your thoughts down rather than speaking them out loud. When your thoughts are on paper, you might view them quite differently. Professional Cancer writers may have trouble with publishers, so shop around. You might find another outlet for your material that cuts out the middleman. Travelers may wind up in an unusual motel or hotel this evening, either a very expensive one or one that offers champagne luxuries for the price of beer. An inheritance may mean that you can finally do what you've dreamed about all your life. Set the wheels in motion without delay.

14. FRIDAY. Unsteady. Your private life is likely to be taking up the majority of your time, with work coming last. You may be going through a break from the job and not missing it. Cancer absentees may find that coworkers think you're fooling the boss. They may resent that you are getting paid but not having to work. These are normal responses and won't last. Look after yourself first and let the future take care of itself. Court proceedings might turn up a surprise witness. If you are called to testify, tell the whole truth and nothing but the truth, or you may end up suffering the consequences. Avoid making any legal threat.

15. SATURDAY. Intuitive. A choice between the sacred and the profane is a dilemma that only happens now and then. Nonetheless, this is apt to be one of those times. You might be better off not making any decision at all for the present. The concept of winners being the losers could start to take on significant meaning for you. Your energy level could be lower than usual, and implementing a personal project may seem almost impossible. Focus on your physical well-being. Once you're in tip-top shape once again, the project will proceed without a hitch. Take a chance on a long shot today. Your intuition should be providing some extremely reliable information and feedback.

16. SUNDAY. Romantic. Love is in the air. That special someone in your life might be a next door neighbor or a friend's brother or sister. Stop looking for love and let it find you. You won't be disappointed. You are apt to be easily influenced by those around you now, so think twice before making any life-changing decision. An artistic project could cost more than expected, but the eventual outcome might prove better than anything money could buy. Experience and understanding can put you in a position to rapidly advance your life's goals and ambitions. Sign up to take a course in a cultural subject in order to expand your horizons.

17. MONDAY. Stressful. Underlying tensions are accentuated by pressing deadlines and unexpected delays. You may not be feeling sufficiently up to par to deal with the extra workload. Taking time out might make it worse for everybody else. However, in your current mood if anybody takes you by surprise you could lose it. Let everybody know how you feel, and don't try to do more than you must. In that way you can pace yourself. An elderly relative or neighbor could be getting to a stage where they really need round-the-clock assistance. Though stubborn, they may be asking for help all the time. A decision will have to be made eventually, so talk to their doctor or a close relative now.

18. TUESDAY. Carefree. You should be feeling much better today, with something exciting to look forward to. Cancer students should study hard for an important exam. Sharing ideas and discussing topics with fellow students will be effective as a learning exercise. You might work with a person who really turns you on, the sensuous enjoyment of being together making the day fly by. This is a favorable time for those planning to travel and to find a job in the country of destination. This should help to take the guesswork out of the trip, allowing you to relax and simply anticipate the adventure that lies ahead. Try to keep all of your plans open-ended.

19. WEDNESDAY. Powerful. Intense emotions are the order of the day. Much can be achieved if you put your mind to one task at a time. You might have to play the role of psychoanalyst at work in order to diffuse a potentially explosive situation between two co-workers. Be sure not to judge or you could end up being judged yourself. Car trouble may leave you stranded, changing the course of the whole day. Remember to check gas, the oil, and water before leaving on a long journey. You can rely on support from a family member if you need help to get out of a tough situation. A brother or sister might be willing to give you an interest-free loan. Draw up a repayment plan and get them to sign it for your mutual peace of mind.

20. THURSDAY. Creative. Unconscious urges could be a creative force in your life. Just guard against falling prey to pretentious people and believing nasty gossip. Your inner thoughts and feelings should be honored and given the attention they deserve. Otherwise you will be only reacting to outside forces and may miss the chance to harness your own potential. A relationship has reached a turning point where you either both go out of your way to fix it, or you both go your separate ways. Try putting romance back into your life. Visit a counselor for some guidance before you swap one situation for another that might be worse. Legal proceedings can be settled out of court if you give in just a little.

21. FRIDAY. Mischievous. A neighbor or relative could be meddling in your affairs, carrying tales back and forth between you and your mate or friend. This is a favorable time for meaningful communication, so talk about what has actually been going on. Then you'll be able to cut the third person out of your affairs once and for all. Bargaining can work in your favor now. If you feel undervalued by your employer, negotiate for better pay or more benefits. You might be able to reach a deal. Just make sure to read the fine print in any contract or agreement that you are about to sign since there may be something that you were not told about beforehand.

22. SATURDAY. Supportive. A family member may need extra-special attention. If you are worried about their health, get them to a specialist who is able to give a positive diagnosis. This should put any worry to rest. If the person seems withdrawn and depressed, take them out to do something fun together, then enjoy seeing the smile on their face once again. A joint resource should be starting to yield dividends. This is a good time to start looking at new investment opportunities to help your savings grow even faster. Cancer singles may meet somebody destined to be a partner for life.

Couples can strengthen their romantic bonds with candlelight and playful fun.

23. SUNDAY. Intuitive. Don't let other people talk you into changing or rushing a creative project. By trusting your own inner feelings you will maintain your own high standards. If preparing for a medical test or surgery, follow your doctor's advice regarding diet and exercise. Don't let other people influence you into drinking or overindulging in any way that could harm a positive outcome. The Sun enters Libra today, shining its light into your sector of home and family. Over the next month you can make positive changes to your personal security by giving more time to family members. Also focus on making your home the kind of place you have always envisioned.

24. MONDAY. Expansive. The admonition to act globally but think locally is very appropriate today. You are apt to be politically minded and want to do something to help ease the plight of suffering people in distressed countries. Apart from going overseas yourself to help, the best way to bring about change is by joining a group of like-minded people. Together you can take part in a promotional campaign to raise the consciousness of your neighbors and colleagues. Cancers who married into another culture may often be misunderstood because of cultural differences. Instead of expecting other people to understand you, start off by learning about them. In that way you will feel more welcome and expand you mind at the same time.

25. TUESDAY. Invigorating. The best way to defuse tension is through relaxation. If you let the stress build up, you won't be able to think straight and do the right thing. Practice some form of meditation or other relaxation technique to help you deal with problems before they become too big for a simple solution. People around you could attempt to take advantage of your easygoing attitude, getting you to do all the hard work for them. Be aware of what is being asked of you, and only take on what is right for you. Once you get on top of problems and stand up for your rights, you'll gain a new lease on life. Travel is indicated, possibly involving study or work.

26. WEDNESDAY. Sensitive. Your time and attention are being sought after by many people, giving you little freedom to think about your own problems. This can be a blessing if you are seeking to escape, but of course you won't fix your problems this way. Set aside some private time for self-examination and analysis. Some-

times one person's problems can get confused with those of someone else. When you allow yourself time, you could find that your
own issues aren't really quite so serious. Practice good time management. By doing so today everything will get done and done well.
Your parents or other relatives may have a disagreement and ask
you to act as go-between. Enlist the help of another family member
so that you can't be blamed for anything.

27. THURSDAY. Opportune. A new job opportunity could open
up, and it would be in your best interests to put your name in for it.
Last-minute details of a large project can be held up due to a communication glitch. Keep your computer hardware up-to-date and
your security software also, in order to protect valuable investments of time and money. Recognition for a good deed might put
you in a position of leadership. To get the most out of the situation,
it might be a smart idea to take a short course in management skills
so that you can get ahead quicker. A new circle of friends could develop through an outside interest that takes you in a different direction altogether.

28. FRIDAY. Lively. The chance to join a group, organization, or
club should not be missed. Although you may feel it is out of your
league, it will give you the opportunity to learn a new skill or develop a talent that you didn't know you had. A child can present a
challenge, and you might need to have a serious talk. Treat youngsters with respect and you will probably gain valuable headway. A
good way to break down barriers would be to take them to a theme
park or play a game together. In this way you set the scene for enjoyment. Although you may be in a talkative mood, watch what you
say and to whom. What you think is funny, another person could
take as an insult.

29. SATURDAY. Active. Mars, the planet of energy and assertiveness, moves into your sign today, which should raise your energy
level noticeably. The urge to be independent and explore new fron-
tiers makes this an excellent time to start a fresh project of your
own. If other people try to push you around or tell you what to do,
you'll be inclined to lose your temper. Your budget is in danger due
to impulsive shopping and group activities. Beware of trying to
keep up with the proverbial Joneses instead of living within your
means. When you take stock of your own situation and are true to
yourself, you can't go wrong.

30. SUNDAY. Private. Self-motivation is your prime mover and
shaker. There shouldn't be any trouble turning people away in or-

der to focus on your own pet project. If you get the chance, a long walk in a scenic location would clear your mind and invigorate your body. A neighbor could be particularly annoying, dropping by to borrow something or just generally wasting your time. If that's the case, take the phone off the hook and don't answer the doorbell. This person should then get the hint without you having to lose your temper. Travel plans almost complete, give some thought to the security of your home while you will be away. The evening will go especially smoothly for you.

OCTOBER

1. MONDAY. Enthusiastic. Getting out and roaming the outdoors could be the best way of overcoming a confined situation. Your thinking processes are sharp and clear, giving you the ability to get to the bottom of any problem. Something bizarre or uncanny about the day could have you road-testing your intuition or coping with a surprising behind-the-scenes development. The mood is present to live life at a high level, with a mystical aura pervading the day. Just make sure you don't go too far outside your comfort zone if someone asks for more than you can or want to give. Tonight is wired for a larger-than-life, exotic experience. Spending time alone carving an artistic niche can birth something radically unique.

2. TUESDAY. Determined. Reviewing the past to learn from mistakes can lead to discarding long-held beliefs or feelings. This is an all-or-nothing day. You could end an association that has outlived its value. Perhaps it's time to move on. Making peace with hidden enemies might have forgiveness at the top of the list. In the afternoon, coming out of your Cancer shell might be appropriate. The action planet Mars inspires going for it wholeheartedly. A personal project gets the green light and your self-confidence soars. Just be sure that arguments aren't meaningless or low on tact. Friends on the receiving end of your sharply worded point of view can feel the sting of your tongue.

3. WEDNESDAY. Confident. Your ability to produce what you need dovetails with your increased charisma. Being enthusiastic and expansive inspires other people to share your vision and also allows creativity to unfold. Staying on the good side of popular and progressive types comes easily now for the shy Cancer nature. You could receive a beautiful gift or artistic work to add to your collection. People are increasingly aware of your original side. Look to the future and align your goals with your talents. This will help take the pressure off conflict arising at home. The key is to keep moving forward with determination. Being more empowered to handle challenges is sure to increase your confidence in all arenas.

4. THURSDAY. Uneasy. The way that you're prioritizing your plans and interests could be at odds with workplace demands. Scheduling time for yourself as you usually do might not be acceptable to demanding colleagues. Attempting to stabilize your own life can make it seem you're unwilling to grow and stretch. With pulverizing Pluto traveling through your work sector, be extra cautious in fulfilling work duties properly. Brace for changes or upgrading, and look for security from other sources. Cancer romantics may be too busy to take a break until evening. Schedule intimate time with your mate or partner over a leisurely dinner, when fiery romantic energies call to you and your lover.

5. FRIDAY. Lucky. Devoting time to a second job will take time away from creative pursuits or family recreation. However, this is a great day for taking an opportunity to the next level. A promotion or lucky break should give you the feeling that Lady Luck is on your side. Be ready for an opportunity to shine in publishing or teaching. Don't take a backseat to anyone. Push your interests to the limit. Home and family life are blessed with harmony. Concentrating on those for whom you're bringing home the bacon will produce extra appreciation for your efforts. Be careful not to try to do too much or proceed with too little. Despite luck, this is not the day to try anything radical.

6. SATURDAY. Risky. Personal spending and financial planning need extra care. Keep all receipts. Avoid signing any document or being talked into a quick decision. There's a risk of dishonesty, of things not being what they seem. You may be eager to be free of annoying work demands or your current job. Venus, planet of good times, suggests abundance available for the careful. Champagne taste on a beer income could limit you. Sleep on new plans before doing anything concrete. A reality check won't be a problem if what you want to do is for real and you have a solid plan. Cancer romantics can look forward to an affectionate time thanks to a poetic declaration.

7. SUNDAY. Manageable. Catch up with outstanding correspondence. Answer e-mails, return phone calls, and reply to faxes. Use the organizational Virgo Moon to full advantage. Meeting and greeting neighbors and enlarging your circle of casual acquaintances can make the morning go quickly. Take advantage of the existing work ethic, but reduce accompanying stress by planning your day well. Duty and results are the order of the day. Mentally creative endeavors and writing reports are favored. Personal affairs turn to down-to-earth matters in order to see if needs are being met. Some Cancers may be lonely, but others can be ready for a marriage proposal. Romance is high on your partner's agenda even if fireworks are absent.

8. MONDAY. Tricky. Unexpected ups and downs can make or break a relationship, with many wanting to do their own thing. Having time to yourself might be necessary if your mood is at odds with the desires of your partner or family this morning. Time for sport in the fresh air can channel your dynamic, willful energy. Be cautious while traveling locally in a car or on foot. Home base looks cozy and welcoming. Take advantage of the easygoing artistic Libra Moon to invite friends to socialize in the nest. A rebellious spirit can have bohemian Cancers airing views and taking interesting positions. Unconventional types could be on their high horse, unwilling to settle down.

9. TUESDAY. Argumentative. With the Moon in fussy Virgo early in the day, try not to worry about unnecessary stresses. After dealing with details, focus on new opportunities to expand your world. These will come from inspirational friends and generous mentors. It could feel like everybody wants a piece of you, but try not to bow to the pressure to be all things to all people. You've got lots to accomplish of your own and need ample space at the moment. Surprise yourself by how fast you can complete a project you've been keeping under wraps. Later in the day use the discernment that comes from the Libra Moon to calm choppy waters. Everyone's impatient today, including you.

10. WEDNESDAY. Easygoing. This is a good day to lie low and recuperate from the recent busy time. Sometimes it's wise to stay silent and observe from the sidelines. Conserve your energy and stay adaptable. Family members will be eager for your attention. Feelings run deep, and there's a lot to be gained by giving your mind a rest and tuning into the deeper side of life. People may see you in a different light as you seek original ways around difficulties. As a Cancer you are an excellent entrepreneur, so remain confident. Calmness stemming from the backing of a special someone will go a long way toward inspiring security. Enjoy fine food, calm surroundings, and a night of love.

11. THURSDAY. Uneven. Working quietly and not pushing too many personal plans suits you at the moment. This is a low energy time of the New Moon. Backtracking over old issues regarding a lover or a creative pastime can lead to gaining closure. The communication planet Mercury slips a gear for the rest of the month. As a result, be ready for challenges to your travel plans. Keep family cars in tip-top shape. Be extra organized on all levels. Avoid becoming too soft or emotional. Tending to home and hearth will keep you busy, yet there are mysteries to solve behind the scenes at work. Seek truth and it will set you free, providing fresh energy. Keeping your head down and working will be most productive and will help you avoid trouble.

12. FRIDAY. Positive. At home under Scorpio lunar rays, you may unearth interesting secrets as you go over the past. Working extra hard and polishing your demeanor can encourage new admirers. A new get-fit phase can work wonders for you. The marathon of life goes on, and you continue to make great progress. Keeping your sense of humor, no matter how zany, will give you joyous energy to make a fresh start. Feeling secure is key to more abundance of all kinds, so be sure to nurture yourself. Idealistic love could be cause for joy with someone very special. Lift up your heart and you'll reach seventh heaven, or is it cloud nine?

13. SATURDAY. Exciting. Be cautiously disciplined while focusing on an educational project or hobby demanding strict attention to detail. Intensely powerful feelings vie with the need to be dutiful and conscientious. Love and creativity are open to novel situations. Excitement is in the air, but guard against going overboard for the wrong type of person. You are apt to seek to break free of restrictions and in the process become attracted to someone not your usual type. If flirtation is in the ethers, check out your intended's emotional history to make sure they're on the level. You don't have to go overboard. A relationship not currently working out can experience coldness or distance, with a breakup possible.

14. SUNDAY. Demanding. An older person may need attention during this busy day. Try to remain compassionate despite the stress of activities. You may feel the need of a health and diet checkup, even a new approach. Put the body in for servicing of some kind. Extra work and responsibilities can dim the Sagittarius Moon's free-flowing spirit. Settling down to your responsibilities may not come easily. However, you can get a large amount of work out of the way. Just make it clear you can't do anyone else's jobs for them. There's enough on your own plate. A quiet evening suits you, with tiredness a natural outcome from the day's demands.

15. MONDAY. Adventurous. New business propositions and ventures offer the thrill of fresh territory yet to be explored. You're in the mood to run with the ball and to act quickly once decisions are made. Remember to double-check facts and figures in the rush to make a dream come true. Sports and games of good-natured competition can be fun and will help you blow off steam. Misunderstandings could occur with close loved ones due to differing points of view. Quirky overseas friends can be hard to contact. Speaking with them privately for a while might be a good idea, either by phone or e-mail. Close to home turf, you have a better chance of keeping things organized the way you prefer.

16. TUESDAY. Challenging. Gearing up to change your job or upgrade thanks to a promotion can have you moving on emotionally from a stale work situation. If boredom has occurred, it's probably time to seek out fresh challenges. Restful nurturing of your overall health and nerves can calm overwrought emotions. Aim at balancing home and work life. People in general are passionate about their convictions, making tonight's dinner a hotbed of varying views and beliefs. Relationships pick up with your devoted partner staying close to home. Participate in gentle activities after dark. Go easy on yourself throughout this challenging week.

17. WEDNESDAY. Harmonious. You need to fit in with some person's plans and expectations. Today's opportunity to work out a conflict of desires or interests with a love partner, associate, or colleague promotes a potential win-win situation. However, you have to be careful. Someone feels their needs are not being met. It is important for you to be dedicated, practical, and ambitious for your partnership coupled with a caring and emotional approach. The foundations of Venus-inspired harmony are yours for the asking. Taking the law into your own hands should be avoided. Legal formalities suggest doing nothing too unconventional. Stick with what has worked for you in the past.

18. THURSDAY. Active. Willingly become part of a more progressive situation in order to keep balance in a special relationship. Foreign contacts can be positive and easy to connect with. Broadening your emotional references can produce fresh influences. If feelings are a little stale, getting out of a rut should be easier. Incorporate the new in your dealings with other people, and be in tune with futuristic and original trends. The action continues, with you being social and giving the world your utopian thoughts. Stay flexible with family members despite some preoccupation with your own interests. Your options can be a little wilder without losing the basic plot. Make yourself the main character in any drama.

19. FRIDAY. Manageable. Dealing with rigid timetables put forth by family members could have you stretched thin and madly juggling your activities. Getting up earlier and multitasking where necessary can help you beat potential stress with good organization. Focusing on future economic security, joint finances, or emotional matters can be at odds with your desire to have more fun in a love affair and to be creative. It's important not to practice hindsight budgeting, which is spending big and fantasizing about how you'll ever pay the bills. Nurture yourself without breaking the bank. Stick to fabulous creative efforts after working out your finances. Look for thrift-store bargains and avoid mall mayhem.

20. SATURDAY. Magical. True adoration is calling, but much of the energy is behind the scenes. This suggests a private, magical day. Keep gambling and joint finances well apart. It's dangerous to be seduced by a get-rich-quick scheme or a too-good-to-be-true scenario. A well-researched, well-calculated risk can pay off, however. By remaining centered you can take advantage of the day's balance between home and work. Changing your routine comes easily today. Working from home base leads to achieving a lot. Being in tune with your feelings puts your progressive humanitarian attitudes ahead of the pack. Be sure to maintain some distance from world problems. You need to conserve your energy and pace yourself.

21. SUNDAY. Joyous. Home and family affairs, including extended family, are likely to take up much of the day. Beautifying or working on property to create more value can be successful. Redecorating can be achieved without too much fuss. Home entertaining can be a pleasure. Financing a building addition or to buy new furniture or collect antiques should proceed without a hitch. Late tonight, dancing or dreaming can take the sensitive Cancer off to the stars. Communicating your feelings on a deep level comes easily, with the chance for a perfect romantic moment near a lake or the ocean. Take advantage of the subtle Pisces Moon this evening to indulge in a mystical state with your mate or partner.

22. MONDAY. Mixed. Planning a vacation or a long journey for pleasure or business may be limited in some way. Far-off horizons can have unusually wild weather patterns. There's a probability of veering off the beaten track, even if you are only being an armchair traveler. Your faith could be tested by having to adapt to unforeseen conditions while on the road. Cancer students have the ability to create a sudden turnaround, favoring those who move on and widen their scope. Romance contains pressure-cooker moments of a stalled attraction followed by a sudden breakthrough. For a few lucky ones, a bolt of love from the blue could knock your socks off in the best possible way.

23. TUESDAY. Mystifying. Being in the mood for intimate sharing in a love affair, or indulging in a big romantic gamble, produces the possibility of a larger than usual emotional risk. Rising to a challenge could also lead you to indulge in extreme sports of some sort. You may solve a mystery about a romantic attraction after events take on an aura of intrigue. Try to remain honest in all dealings, and resist any temptation to play dirty. Biting off more than you can chew in a situation requiring cloak-and-dagger tactics has the chance of backfiring. A child could be born or figure prominently in your day thanks to creative fertility.

24. WEDNESDAY. Cautious. Guard your image while the Moon travels through your career sector. Appearing too much at odds with your professional image will detract from your carefully built reputation. Find the middle ground between being assertive and passive in the work sphere. Irritation can develop unless you take extra care. Cancer lovers may find it's all work and no play, with career matters drawing all the energy away from home and hearth. Appearing before the public can mean critics aren't far away, complete with comments on your position in the world. Be ready for a bite-size piece of information that can change your day.

25. THURSDAY. Changeable. Personal relationships have a stop-start quality, with breaks in communication likely. Be adaptable and resourceful in dealing with other people. Expect changes to your plans. A teacher or mentor could light the path for your career. Following a trail to success can have a straightforward quality. You possess a lot of drive to get things done, and you'll also be impatient for results from helpers. Balancing the time you spend in your career and at home presents a challenge. Working from home base or successfully juggling your responsibilities is key. The Full Moon in Taurus this evening whets appetites for quality indulgence, prompting celebration with fun friends.

26. FRIDAY. Starred. Time spent with a group or club produces stable results. Gathering people together to fulfill responsibilities comes naturally. Concentrate on getting a desired outcome and you are sure to be pleased with the large amount of work achieved by day's end. A vibrant get-together with friends offers an enjoyable, energetic time. Jump at a chance to get to the bottom of a mystery at home. Clearing out a closet could bring to light a piece of jewelry or art you haven't seen for a while. If beautifying or entertaining in your own space, focus on color and design. New curtains or rearranging the furniture in a room will get the green light.

27. SATURDAY. Confusing. Working out who's on top in a group or club can have you confused. Someone could be showing their good side, but it's up to you to work out whether they're being totally truthful. Challenges can seem to be coming from all directions. Try to keep the day simple by avoiding too many complicated situations. You may long to stay home, away from social responsibilities. Making the best of things can involve just getting through the day, until you find time and energy to do your own thing. Try to gain peace in the midst of annoying demands. A day spa treat, utilizing the sensual Taurus Moon atmosphere, cheers the soul.

28. SUNDAY. Restricting. Taking the phone off the hook and getting much needed quiet time is important. There is also a potential for loneliness. Current circumstances can feel generally restricting. Writing behind the scenes, or coping with unusually erratic conditions, requires mental and emotional dexterity. Be prepared to do your own thing and work within existing limitations. Relationship issues involving individuality and self-expression encourage you to make conscious choices about personal needs. Social interaction with strange characters could be testing. Spending time with harmonious friends with whom it's easy to relax is favored.

29. MONDAY. Significant. Seeing a foreign movie, or dipping into cultural waters, can provide needed time alone coupled with a Gemini Moon's drive for communication. Be careful of recklessness or extravagance in your quest to overthrow yesterday's restrictions. Being quick-witted and adaptable within your private life can lead to a situation reaching a point of no return, Focus on beginnings, even in the face of an important ending. Restructure any feelings of persecution and look for a way out. You may be ready to end an association with a teacher, mentor, or counselor. Visiting a spiritual retreat to gain perspective can be subtly fulfilling.

30. TUESDAY. Dynamic. Self-interest energizes personal plans and makes achievement of goals more tangible. Airing frustrations comes naturally, with Mars contacting the Moon in your home sign. This is not an easy day, but at least you are free to communicate your feelings. Playing competitive sports or toiling physically will ease aggressive attitudes. Working on a project in the neighborhood is favored. Romance may contain a fight, but also an ability to make up creatively. Cancer artists have the potential to find a breakthrough after a period of struggle. Stay open to all that is unusual and progressive, and don't be afraid to express your more original side.

31. WEDNESDAY. Emotional. Finding time to relax and recharge your batteries may be difficult unless you find an escape through a labor of love. Spending time on a personal project can be very rewarding. Review job obligations and restrictions. There are also domestic chores that need to be done well. The planet Mercury traveling through the home sector encourages redecorating to create extra studio space or to make your living quarters more attractive generally. Rearranging heirlooms or mementos of the past can make your home warm and nourishing. Being sentimental about the past comes easily today. A sense of nostalgia brings loved ones closer in your heart, if not physically.

NOVEMBER

1. THURSDAY. Vexing. Business and pleasure don't mix easily today, so it's probably best not to try. However, if you can't resist the temptation, remember to pay continual attention to the bottom line. Cancer gamblers and speculators could lose some recent profits all too easily by being greedy or foolhardy. If your attitude is easy come, easy go, be prepared to watch it go. Kids could cost a lot, even older ones you would expect to pay their way by now. Pursuing a love interest may be tantalizing, yet the expense may not be equivalent to your heightened expectations. Sports and other recreational activities are great for your social life but a strain on your wallet.

2. FRIDAY. Rewarding. An ideal solution to a current financial problem may be right in front of your nose. It would be wise not to turn down any offer or gift. Don't delay taking advantage of grand opportunities if they come your way. This can be a special chance to create wealth. All it really takes is loads of perspiration and a dash of inspiration. Dreamers and schemers often get the mix completely wrong, forgetting the labor and sweat and replacing that with wishful thinking. Do not make this mistake or your dreams of economic freedom will quickly fade and disappear. You can find required backing for a visionary venture if you have a prototype or a workable plan to present.

3. SATURDAY. Dutiful. Taking care of the older people in your life should be your prime concern. Their mobility may be an issue, requiring extra effort on your part to drive them to the local shopping mall or to an appointment with a professional. Or they may require a hand around the house with maintenance and chores that have become difficult for them to manage as they once did. An absent relative will appreciate a call from you, even if it's brief and to the point. An ex-partner might contact you, and it should be enjoyable to catch up for old time's sake. However, you'll both be clearer than ever that what's over is definitely over.

4. SUNDAY. Liberating. A restless urge could find many Cancers out the door and off for an impulsive outing. With Mars currently in your own sign, physical movement such as biking and hiking would be the most beneficial way to go mobile. Even a walk in an unexplored park will aid your circulation and respiration, not to mention the sheer exuberance of being in the open air surrounded by natural beauty. Let go of any thoughts or worries about housework and other chores, which will all be there when you return. Take things as they come in a freewheeling, spontaneous way. Big expectations and plans are likely to topple in a frenzy, but don't go down with them!

5. MONDAY. Upsetting. Although you seem emotionally on top of things, someone else's foul mood could ambush you and temporarily cause a storm. This person may be envious, which is sure to make you feel uncomfortable. Succumbing to manipulative tactics by reacting will only feed their perverse agenda. The best strategy is to do nothing at all. Simply ignoring them should drive them wild. Any revenge you may be contemplating for recent hurts is best taken when you're less vulnerable and more detached. Dangerous liaisons are in the air for lusty Cancers with an impulse to hook up instantaneously. Keep in mind that it takes two to tango, so don't force affection upon an unwilling object of your desire.

6. TUESDAY. Sensitive. A day at home suits those who can afford it, but you won't be lazing around and taking it easy. If you aren't able to actively do your thing, a grumpy mood can overcome you. Being short-tempered won't do anything for peaceable relations. However, fortunately for you, other people appear reasonable and tolerant. Relatives and neighbors, in particular, are sure to understand even brusque treatment and sharp words. If you're angling for a fight you'll get one, when you finally go too far. Stress and strain in a lovers' exchange can erupt, especially if jealous insecurity and emotional frustration are part of the mix.

7. WEDNESDAY. Idyllic. You can turn lemons to lemonade, concocting uplifting refreshment. Don't fitter away precious time rehashing recent upsets. Let bygones be bygones, and move on into the present. Romantic themes and seductive overtures can calm a previously stormy and frustrating relationship. Home is where the heart is for Cancer people, and this is more true than ever in this period. A courtship will progress smoothly, with meaningful keepsakes and heartfelt communications. It doesn't do any harm to tell that special someone you know what they want to hear. Find some delicious recipes or an outstanding new restaurant to top off this perfect day.

8. THURSDAY. Expressive. Shop for household provisions first thing this morning. Also take care of other minor errands while you're at it, getting them out of the way and unburdening your mental to-do list. Problems at home involving how to share domestic duties or other persistent annoyances should be addressed as civilly as possible. Cooperation will then be forthcoming, allowing you to draw up a new schedule of chores. Getting upsets off your mind is favored, preventing small irritations from festering into larger resentments. Later in the day the social vibe intensifies. You're sure to enjoy an evening of fun and good times, offering heightened personal pleasure.

9. FRIDAY. Dynamic. The New Moon period is usually a quieter phase of the lunar month, but you might be surprised by what's in store today. Water sign people, including Cancers, will insist on amusement at all costs. Partying might be the call, with you responding with wild enthusiasm. An unstoppable rush of energy could sweep you up, up, up and away. Whether it's a spontaneous cross-country flight, an impromptu performance, or an impulsive romance, it's sure to be exhilarating. Liberated spirits who take flight may want to never come down. The only real danger is overdoing physically or relying on false promises.

10. SATURDAY. Restful. Pursuing your own private pleasures would be a fine use of this quiet day. Your spirits remain high, but this is a recovery period after the rush of yesterday's energy. Cancer parents can enjoy a relaxing time playing with the kids and taking it easy around the house. Hobbies and crafts benefit from solo time, letting you brush up your skills and gather supplies for new projects. Giving yourself what you need might come in the form of a massage or other delightful and therapeutic pampering. Catch up on beauty sleep this evening in preference to a big night out on the town, unless it's a formal invitation and you're already committed. Your sleepy mood puts a damper on socializing.

11. SUNDAY. Disenchanting. Being restrained by ordinary routines and household chores may make today seem drab, when you probably want it ablaze with excitement. Rather than being impatient to make it all happen, slow down and focus on what must be done. Deal with all those small, insignificant, but annoying jobs that have been piling up and getting in the way of interesting possibilities. Issues regarding time management and self-discipline could surface. Whatever you genuinely dislike about your lifestyle can prompt a determination to do a complete turnaround. This may include so-called friends who have been taking you for granted, or a bad habit like smoking.

12. MONDAY. Tricky. You have a huge store of energy to help you accomplish today's tasks. However, expect a few unexpected mishaps that cause you to stumble or trip. Keep your wits about you on the way to work and when undertaking even routine activities. The mistakes made by other people could affect you like a pileup on the freeway. Such hurdles are only fleeting however, and before you know it you'll be captivated by the next big activity. The vision and motivation of your partner and fellow workers will help you tune in and get with the program. The biggest mistake would be to super-size a situation, projecting problems out of proportion and biting off more than you will ultimately want to chew.

13. TUESDAY. Helpful. Look forward to a cooperative day. Able assistance couldn't come at a better time. Busy Cancers need to delegate some authority and responsibility to people who are capable and competent. Don't be afraid of being upstaged or challenged. You're likely to receive respect rather than rivalry, and you need the help so cultivate it. Older people with experience and knowledge have much to teach and offer you. It's never too late to learn. The support of a reliable neighbor could also prove invaluable. You can call them to temporarily help out at home if you need to work late. Just don't get to the point where you take helpful folk for granted.

14. WEDNESDAY. Intense. Try to stay loose and flexible even when life gets heated or confrontational. Differences that emerge can be resolved if you view the bigger picture. In some circumstances you're either all right or all wrong, and that should be the end of the matter. Whatever happens, you're certain to learn from the exchange. If a love relationship reaches the snapping point, suggest that you plan a trip together. Getting away from it all could cause a real shift in how you view each other. Appointments with officials should be surprisingly smooth, particularly matters involved with transportation, immigration, travel, or education.

15. THURSDAY. Variable. First thing this morning may find you lingering in the company of your mate or partner. Early exercise will provide a great mood for the rest of the day. This could be a relatively aimless time for Cancers who are in need of structure and direction. Stick with the existing plan and maintain a steady course. Just because life becomes quiet doesn't mean nothing's going on. Remain alert if it's your watch, and keep other people involved as well. A social mood descends this evening, favoring being with friends and enjoying intimate exchanges. However, remain in familiar territory rather than roaming far from your home base.

16. FRIDAY. Emotional. Family relations are featured today. A female relative may be coming to visit, possibly someone you haven't seen in a long time. Use precious time with those you rarely see to heal and resolve any hurt between you. Love will then flow freely and bestow gracious blessings. Just be aware that you may clash heads before mutual acceptance can be established. An argument with your mate or partner needs to be patched up before going ahead with your day. Negotiations regarding the lease or purchase of a new home are likely to be settled in your favor. Your premises can be transformed into a beautiful home with a little creative thought. Let your heart rule your head when it comes to a private affair.

17. SATURDAY. Upsetting. A reminder of some previous disappointment could be upsetting. If you feel you were ripped off or let down by a person you once trusted, an intense reaction may now surface. Or you may need to support someone close in a time of crisis or loss. Your mate or partner could be relying on you to be there for them while they go through a tough time with career earnings or social relations. News regarding a respected older person may bring everyone to a crossroads of sadness and reminiscing, but later normal routine regains its momentum. If you have a big deal on the boil you can see the ingredients start to take shape, hopefully according to your projections and plans.

18. SUNDAY. Active. If you've been missing out on the action lately, there should be plenty available today. In fact, you might be so popular that it's impossible to fulfill every invitation. The end of a personal era has arrived, making this look as good a time as any to celebrate. Even while you're seeing out the old, the new could be making its presence felt. It is said that when one door closes another one opens, but just don't get caught in a round of revolving doors. Once a direction is set, stay with it. By continually changing you'll never arrive where you want to be. Saying farewell to a friend or neighbor can be touchingly poignant, while introducing personally significant new contacts for your future.

19. MONDAY. Vulnerable. Enthusiasm and a positive approach can be overdone. Once the initial buzz has passed, it's possible that not much substance remains. Overexaggerations won't do much to improve business. There's no point in arousing interest if you can't deliver the goods. Learned opinions and slick marketing may conflict with operational realities. It would be wise to follow a feeling of wanting to stop the world in order to get off, at least temporarily. Neglecting work for greener but unfamiliar pastures might spirit weaker Cancers away from profitable and rewarding duties. This is not the time to swap what you already have for what is unknown and unknowing.

20. TUESDAY. Dynamic. There's a strong imperative to be out there representing your business with as much passionate determination as you can muster. Use all the cunning at your disposal if you lack the necessary stamina to successfully complete a test of physical endurance. Personal fortitude and courage are called for. Theories and clever concepts will soon be tested in the crucible of a competitive marketplace. You may be exhilarated with the anticipation of doing combat in the real world, the tension feeding your hunger to succeed. You are on the verge of creating history, at least in your own circle where your reputation matters most.

21. WEDNESDAY. Bumpy. If you have been stepping on people's toes lately, you now have a lot of apologizing and peacemaking to do. Cancers are sometimes viewed as somewhat clumsy by other people, who might be right about that today. If you feel you have two left feet which often wind up in your mouth, maybe it's time to stay mum for a while and stop trying to do so much. Other talented individuals will then have their chance to shine and show what they can do. Not being recklessly aggressive and selfishly competitive, you value and esteem the fine contributions made by your fellow workers. What's good for one can be good for all, despite your misgivings about a certain person.

22. THURSDAY. Mixed. The entry of the Sun into Sagittarius signals a productive month ahead for Cancer people. This is also an appropriate time to hire employees and contractors for assistance where you need it. Keep in mind that the type and quality of personnel you require, or the work you want done, may not be available at the drop of a hat. No matter who you know or what strings you try to pull, certain avenues and experiences are blocked for now. Anyone who demonstrates disregard and disdain toward you or your company is showing true colors. You're likely to neither forgive nor forget bad treatment at the hands of another person.

23. FRIDAY. Troublesome. Doubts about the integrity and honesty of a friend could play on your mind, causing you to question motives. This person may be close with another member of your family or household, which could make matters even more upsetting and confusing. Rather than lingering in uncertainty about this matter, sit down together and talk things out. You might discover, to everyone's delight and relief, that the whole episode was a misunderstanding in the first place. Trust within a group could be at a low ebb, with gossip being spread about various members. Try to organize a team-building experience before the upset becomes too deep.

24. SATURDAY. Uneasy. Social events and public gatherings are prominent in your personal calendar. It's the Full Moon today, which often coincides with people getting together anyway. However, you are not apt to want to attend or play a part in the proceedings. A retiring, antisocial mood may set in, and when that happens you'll prefer to stay behind the scene and out of sight. Be sure to make any necessary excuses early. In that way hopefully no one will be inconvenienced by your absence, although they're sure to be somewhat disappointed. If your presence is deemed essential, attempt to persuade someone to take your place.

25. SUNDAY. Uplifting. The anticipation of spending time alone with that special person in your life could have your heart pinging with sheer delight. Romance and pleasure infuse the atmosphere, as if Cupid himself had chosen to give you a treat. Any doubt or insecurity that may exist between you and your mate can be erased in a profound heartfelt exchange that goes beyond words, both of you trusting what you feel. Although some undermining anxiety may taint the scene, pure magic can be tasted and shared. Creative and artistic Cancers can uncover wonderful inspiration and heightened imaginative possibilities, particularly if left to your own devices for long enough.

26. MONDAY. Confident. As if to make up for lost time, you could be looking for opportunities to socialize. This is a fine day to catch up with relatives and friends from your former neighborhood. You will have little enthusiasm for household chores. If you can afford it, consider hiring someone to help with such work. Or just let it pile up for another day. Being introduced to a topic that grabs your interest might prompt further investigation. It may warrant serious study, leading you to enroll in a course to earn a formal degree. If you are called on to plan and lead a trip, take along reliable maps just to be on the safe side.

27. TUESDAY. Fair. Clashing styles and differing tastes are what define people as individuals. Make an effort to be flexibly tolerant, while learning to genuinely appreciate a loved one's uniqueness. Don't allow minor annoyances or insignificant differences to spoil what's essentially a good relationship. It's human nature that once you're in a situation where everything appears just right, some dissatisfaction quickly sets in. The grass always appears greener in distant pastures, but if you go there you'll only take any discontent along with you. Staying at home would be claustrophobic today, so get out and at least avoid that irritation.

28. WEDNESDAY. Guarded. Make up for lost time by getting down to business first thing this morning. Playmates and fair-weather friends should be avoided so that you can focus your best efforts on your duties and survival. You'll feel much better throwing yourself headlong into activities that pay. If household groceries are running low, head out to the store and purchase what's needed. Cancers who have been seduced into an extravagant lifestyle might want to reconsider their circumstances. Appreciate that a simpler way of living can provide all your real needs. As an unexpected bonus, you'll save money and stress at the same time. It's important to know when enough is too much.

29. THURSDAY. Cautious. Lucrative and imaginative possibilities open up for Cancers who are seeking creative products and services. Just be wary of going into debt while chasing some wild-eyed idea of the next big thing. Cancer salespeople can succeed in clinching a handsome deal with plenty of profit margin to bolster earnings. On the other hand, more gullible types could easily be seduced into making an unnecessary purchase based on a seemingly irresistible offer. Don't take a sales presentation at face value since guarantees may not be what they seem. Unfortunately, everyone is not as trustworthy or transparent as you are. If you must have some precious item, be sure that you can return it if you change your mind.

30. FRIDAY. Rewarding. A powerhouse of productive and profitable work gets this day off to a great start. Business prospers through your unstoppable effort and impressive confidence in your unique abilities and talents. Unbeatable quality of products and services is a perennial key to success. Later in the day, a reunion with friends from your old neighborhood or former pals from student days might come together as if by accident. Among familiar faces, there will be some you love and some you dislike. Meeting up with them all provides an insight into your personal history. Whatever happens, everyone will be content to keep it brief and leave the past behind where it belongs.

DECEMBER

1. SATURDAY. Upsetting. Do not be surprised by this morning's serious mood. Slightly depressing events in your area, or negative communications with neighbors, don't have to affect you negatively if you remain strong. Someone may have an ax to grind, yet you can still come out on top. Soothing people in regard to sudden transportation glitches brings out your Cancer nurturing instinct. Working hard can provide satisfying results if you brace for loneliness. Putting beauty into the picture should cheer everyone up. A passionate, energetic ray from Mars ensures you've got the backbone to take on a romantic challenge and overcome frustrations. Take time to do your own thing as you recover from mental battles.

2. SUNDAY. Mixed. Entertaining overseas visitors and learning something about their home base energizes you with other languages and customs. A mood to break free of the Virgo Moon's earnestness encourages embracing all of the good things in life with a sense of humor. When plumping out the day with enriching family activities, guard against blowing your budget. A wallet has ability to pour cash out like water, making you wonder where it all went. Be conscious of cost. Take a rest from weekday projects. A missing part of the equation needs to be found regarding joint finances. Or you may need to sort though a peculiarity or illusion. Clarity will return in a couple of days.

3. MONDAY. Constructive. Although you may want some solo time, creative projects at home call loudest. A sales party demonstrating quality items or artistic redecorating gets a go-ahead. If refinancing, make considered decisions without blowing your budget. Abundance is there for those who are both grateful and productive. Your good ability to juggle emotions and feelings produces rapport with colleagues and family members. Use constructive energy to get as much done as possible while the mood lasts. Children's activities may take up a lot of the day. You are likely to get a pat on the back for work well done or gain a positive accolade. Be proud of your well-deserved recognition.

4. TUESDAY. Uplifting. Coping with a surprise obligation from an institution or an upset to your travel plans should be today's only worry. Working from home promises to be deeply fulfilling, allowing you to earn money doing what you love. Cancers who are looking for a job should consider what provides happiness. You may apt for a job where you can stay in contact with home and hearth. Generating beauty from home base or cooking delicious treats can bring joy and abundance. The Libra principle of sharing encourages you to reach out to other people. Invite someone fascinating to a fun dinner party, or share stories around the family dining table. The effort you put in will give you enriching rewards.

5. WEDNESDAY. Romantic. Put aside petty concerns and create a romantic mood to refresh the spirit for romance and creativity. The Scorpio energy brings an urge to dive into deep emotional waters. Finding a kindred lover might be surprisingly easy for the unattached. Cancer couples can renew the bonds of affection. Acknowledging important needs that are currently not being met or lived brings an escape urge tinged with pain. Try negotiating for what you desire. Use substances wisely and avoid overdoing. A primal brush with birth or death is possible. Writing down your goals could be crucial in letting the Cancer soul find the peace it needs.

6. THURSDAY. Manageable. Concentrating on the job at hand gives you a feeling of being settled. An urge to do the right thing and fulfill responsibilities puts a hardworking conservative seal on the day. Taking a calculated risk removes an obstacle that has been standing in the way of progress. A small financial tangle may restrain you, but positive headway can still be made. A credit situation needs immediate resolution. Voluntary cutting back to a more frugal attitude will give you extra money in the bank. This afternoon the possibility of limited thinking must be overcome. A work situation may force you to try to give more than is easy for you.

7. FRIDAY. Bright. Factor in a need to be your quirky individual self. Take a break from rigid structures you have been living under. Expressing a bit of zany humor at work is a good way to lighten tension. Just don't joke at someone else's expense. The thought of oncoming weekend freedom may have you prematurely ready to party. If you're going to go overboard in some way, consider safety factors before letting your hair down. There's a bit of craziness in the air as you break out from being under someone's thumb. Some good music or a comedy act can be just what you need to relax this evening.

8. SATURDAY. Helpful. Focusing on tough jobs, even on a usual day off, could have you dealing with a few annoying tasks. Try to get on top of things so you can relax later in the day. Start with the hardest tasks first, such as renewing your driver's license or insurance. Expect to stand in a long line, but cultivate a patient attitude. This will help you learn patience. People who have been holding you back due to their slowness will probably catch up. Giving inspiration you've gained to those who need a gentle helping hand asks you to sacrifice personal goals. Put energy into staying fit, even if it's emotionally and physically taxing. You can raise your core strength with a good workout.

9. SUNDAY. Purposeful. The Moon in adventurous Sagittarius can have Crab people throwing on a backpack and heading off to adventure. Just be wary of trying too hard or pushing yourself too much. Your drive to win is strong. You may experience a peak moment on the playing field or achieve a new personal best. Being prepared for offbeat or bizarre twists gives you needed emotional leverage to deal with unexpected changes. Being ready for anything means you won't scurry back to the nest if things don't go according to plan. A definite sense of purpose charges the day. Once you achieve a goal, pop the champagne cork in celebration. Nothing great was ever achieved without enthusiasm, so go for it wholeheartedly.

10. MONDAY. Fulfilling. Everything may seem bigger and better somewhere else. Choose whether to get into a theatrical drama or to channel your larger-than-life energy in a personal mission. Other people might not share your point of view or may find you too over the top. You have an evangelical quality. Work can feel mythical. Just be sure you're not overestimating your role or ability. Keep in mind that pride goes before a fall. Leaving a job you dislike is possible. So is jumping feet first into a new situation with gung-ho enthusiasm. Take time to make an important decision. Check out the conservative, conventional route before opting for anything too off the tried-and-true path.

11. TUESDAY. Emotional. A mood of not wanting to compromise, courtesy of fiery Mars, gets the boxing gloves out for Crab people, with claws being exposed. Stick up for yourself, but avoid becoming overly aggressive. Aim for a win-win situation if you can, or at least fight fair. Extra tact is required so that you don't step on toes. Close partnerships have a stable quality that gives the security you need to make reasonable demands. Cancer lovers are sure to ramp up their creativity. A passionate tryst is foreseen. Prioritizing areas of your life which need nurturing makes this a feeling day rather than one governed by dry reason. Love is the number one priority.

12. WEDNESDAY. Dedicated. Aim at balancing rigid organizational duties with the demands stemming from the rest of your life. Legacies, inheritances, or personal finances should be examined in greater depth. Coping with the legal system forces you to take a determined practical approach. Becoming overly emotional is unlikely to get you anywhere in what might be perceived as a man's world. Center yourself, then deal with responsibilities in a calm and efficient way. Promise yourself a treat later to celebrate your good results. Romance with your soul mate, and a small flutter, could be the cheer coming at the end of this long day.

13. THURSDAY. Demanding. Obligations involving loans or joint finances can be demanding. Feeling the pinch demands that you tune in to realities which nurture the spirit and organize you in a happier way. Local financial institutions might seem uncaring toward your position. A father figure can be very frugal when you seek a loan. Arguments with a loved one might lead to tension rising unless you cultivate a creative attitude of abundance. Nurturing faith, despite limited outward circumstances, is important to bring the best future results. Later in the evening soothing music or a movie has the make-believe dreamworld giving you rest from the rigors of the day.

14. FRIDAY. Variable. Exposing or dealing with a secret hidden side of your life unveils a mystery yet to be explored. Trying to get facts about joint finances, an inheritance, or a financial institution can produce mainly misinformation. Leaving definite decisions until after the weekend would be wise. Going dancing or otherwise enjoying yourself might be the best use of a day where it's hard to pin down anything definite. Writing or communicating comes easier as the planet Mercury helps you share your thoughts. You will feel linked to greater humanity rather than only your nuclear family. Romance stems from contact with a group.

15. SATURDAY. Expansive. Coming to terms with a fear, or gaining new insight into a problem, sheds light on a dark corner of the soul. Having a quiet, intimate time suits this morning. If you're feeling crazy, you're not alone. There are serious issues you could freak out about, yet there's hope. Dealing with someone's dark side could be necessary. Fortunately you're more emotionally equipped than you realize. Early this evening the mood expands to encompass a distant journey. Hopping on a plane or expanding your mind through study will serve to broaden your horizons. Planning a vacation or going away for a long weekend can fill you with enthusiasm for a faraway place that has something to teach you.

16. SUNDAY. Adventurous. Plan on getting away from home and going on a faraway trip. Let the wind blow in your hair and reenergize your romance. Take time to unclutter your mind and expand. Leaving room for the unexpected and spontaneous could lead to an adventure with a few hair-raising moments. Yet the potential is also there for fun and for seeing the world in a new way. Daydreaming and opening up to the Pisces Moon's artistic influence lets your softer emotional side come out for a while. This may link you to many other people who are feeling the same way about life at the moment. Cancer students can have an exciting revelation about a study path. Authors could decide to self-publish in tune with a trend.

17. MONDAY. Difficult. It could be hard to come back to earth after the freedom and originality of the weekend. It can be tough fitting in with rigid ways of thinking and the demands of work or office politics. Recklessly overestimating your position can lead to your undoing. Keep certain opinions and feelings to yourself until you find a kindred spirit. The original projects you're working on are positive, although they may be too leading edge for some. Toe the line this morning while getting yourself together. The afternoon pushes the Moon into confrontational Aries. Gathering a fighting spirit and asserting your position becomes more likely tonight, but don't give up or be dominated unnecessarily.

18. TUESDAY. Pressured. While working hard on a career project involving the public, be aware of detractors. Other people can be overly cautious about your ambition and effort to succeed publicly. Yet progress can be made if you concentrate more on doing a good job and less on what others think of you. Hard work will win out over criticism in your neighborhood. Conflict with an authority is foreseen if you are not pulling your own weight or rebelling needlessly. A romantic liaison may have to be put on the back burner due to work being a higher priority. Later in the evening, however, the fairy-tale parts of your Cancer nature will find time to take over.

19. WEDNESDAY. Constructive. The flow of your career or profession harmonizes, with good results possible. Public attention is likely to be positive, enhancing your ambition. In-depth research can unveil a vital clue or solve a mystery regarding sales or the vision statement at work. Getting to the bottom of a health issue could be a relief for you. A team or group association involving your partner should progress well, with a lucky break available. Push your own agenda forward tonight within a group or team. Your personal aims are in direct alignment with a community or group association. You have everything to gain by assertively devoting your energy to a common goal.

20. THURSDAY. Opportune. Concentrate on maintaining your down-to-earth attitude and you will achieve realistic results with your team or group association. A hardworking morning following correct logical procedure sees you achieving a lot in an organized, practical way. The afternoon is perfect for exploring business options or advising other people. Seize the initiative, but guard against being reckless or overestimating how much you can do. A positive teacher or mentor could emerge. Make optimistic plans, yet be realistic about expected results. Brace for early evening passion by letting go of work that has been inhibiting growth. Important new beginnings are happening now.

21. FRIDAY. Challenging. Confusing or deceptive influences abound regarding a group or team effort. Conscious procedures are needed to avoid slipping into an overly emotional lack of direction. Power plays are possible today, and there's a challenge to work efficiently. Taking a morning break or a long lunch, and waiting for things to calm down, might be a realistic option. Expect to be tired from hard work and stress. The Gemini Moon is preparing to activate your sector that rules behind-the-scenes deals. Getting a clear answer from anyone, even a partner, will be tricky. Arrange to work in seclusion if possible. You need to investigate developments in the background, watching out for vague or unreliable people. Get plenty of rest.

22. SATURDAY. Sensitive. Try not to sacrifice yourself for someone who is not prepared to pull their own weight. Feeling blocked by those in your immediate environment, or by a sibling, can be a lonely start to the morning. Private time can be healing and refreshing after a busy workweek. Perhaps breakfast in bed and some extra sleep can restore normalcy to your world. During the early afternoon your peace may be interrupted by a challenging partner whose emotions compete with logic. An argument about who should do what could heat up, demanding fairness on both sides. Later take off on your own for a short while. Working things out through humor and logic can mend any dispute.

23. SUNDAY. Emotional. The arrival of the Cancer Moon propels you to focus on personal plans and projects of special meaning to you. Indulging the affectionate side of your nature brings you back to areas of life you're strongly sentimental about. Follow personal dreams, yet be aware that your mate or partner might not want to accompany you. Let them do their own thing and avoid possessiveness. You need extra freedom yourself. This evening is ripe for an argument unless great care is taken to be tactful. Taking an insult to heart or fighting about something close to home can arouse heated feelings. Use the sparring energy to fight a greater fight, and challenge yourself to overcome obstacles in the coming week.

24. MONDAY. Reassuring. A Full Moon in your sign overnight brings emotions regarding family, home, and country to a peak. Protecting your nest and loved ones will be uppermost in your mind. Act on a sense of neighborhood tradition. A tussle between your mate or partner's sense of duty and responsibility may be at odds with your urge to gather the family happily around the fireplace. Cultivating an open, progressive attitude to foreign influences and teachings is vital for emotional health and happiness. Enriching moments involving unusual, eccentric characters can lead to hidden gifts, unlikely to be appreciated by the snobbish. A stranger could have an angelic side.

25. TUESDAY. Merry Christmas! Romantic and creative atmospheres are present for the emotionally receptive. Welcome the chance to create an ideal environment for your celebration. Taking the focus off work is vital to make the most of this day. Organizing comes easily, with attention to detail and a trustworthy conscientious attitude demonstrated by your mate or partner. Take advantage of the quiet, dignified path being offered to you. An older person listened to with respect will offer a special gift. Tonight do not blow the budget via financial extravagance. However, the Leo Moon calls for a colorful, larger-than-life party. Celebrate in style and have a wonderful time right in your own backyard.

26. WEDNESDAY. Bright. The logical you is ready to go on a shopping spree to soothe your emotions with retail therapy. Rebelling against your better judgment is likely. A partner may try to stop you, with a firm authoritarian attitude. Plan on spending only a certain amount of money. Do not buy just because a sale seems so good. The heart arguing with the head looks set to be in disagreement for most of the day. Make sure your inner child has something fun to play with, but don't blow the budget. You've been good until now, so keep it up. Rebelling in a positive way could give you the freedom to be original and imaginative with shared resources.

27. THURSDAY. Deceptive. The urge to splurge to keep up appearances still demands that you be careful with credit or resources. Signing on the dotted line for an impulse purchase can cause you to overlook the fine print. A deceptive air involving finances challenges honesty from yourself or when speaking with clever salespeople. Avoid extending credit or taking out an extra loan. Someone you love may challenge your materialistic standpoint, and ask you to delve deeper into issues that are coming between you. Later tonight more insights are likely regarding extra work that can transform financial woes through willpower and determination. Keeping to the straight and narrow will help you make decisions in general.

28. FRIDAY. Constructive. Work in a thorough, organized manner. There's little to stand in your way this morning. Being dutifully conscientious about details pays off in writing projects, or for communicating creative endeavors as well as community affairs. Early this afternoon the brakes might be put on, requiring an extra burst of energy to forge through obstacles and achieve results. Education, study, or catching up on a backlog of correspondence could take more time than you have. You need to cultivate patience and take breaks when necessary if you're tiring easily. Pace yourself and you'll achieve lasting gain.

29. SATURDAY. Guarded. Enlarging your social circle of acquaintances, or even considering marriage, could bring a positive yes to your life. The afternoon holds eccentric patterns of behavior locally, or a disruption to travel plans. Thoroughly double-check transportation details. Leave more time to drive anywhere if you have an appointment. A rebellious mood could result in a game too exciting for your own good. Be aware of safety in local neighborhood play. Watching the professionals live, or from the comfort of home, holds less risk. A change of scenery, pursuing fresh activities, or visiting new places would do everyone a world of good. You need space to roam and to blow away the cobwebs of your mind.

30. SUNDAY. Careful. Mix with those who really enjoy your company and genuinely like you. Romance is foreseen with someone who cares for you deeply. Single Cancers could make a lasting commitment. A relationship which begins today has a real chance of going the distance. Persuading or winning over people at home might not be worth the trouble. Balancing your own desires with family demands will require some juggling. See if you can reach goals which everyone will be happy with at different times of the day. A more convivial mood arises later when Venus, the relating planet, embraces Sagittarius energy. A good-humored, relaxed approach works wonders, relieving and lifting the oppression of earlier strain.

31. MONDAY. Mixed. The last day of the year starts out tense yet ends on a high note. Coping with interruptions to family ritual, or setting a sudden extra place at lunch, might leave you frantic. Unexpected happenings are the order of the day, so cultivate a sense of humor to get you through. Your mate or partner might have rigid expectations of a New Year celebration, or be in an uncaring mood. Good feelings return late in the evening, when peace and restored harmony float everyone away to dreams of a better world with a sustainable future. Dancing to favorite midnight music, or making the effort to attend a spiritual event, has the potential for you to begin next year in sublime rapture.

CANCER
NOVEMBER–DECEMBER 2006

November 2006

1. WEDNESDAY. Buoyant. Seven planets in water signs, including your ruler the Moon in Pisces, is significant for you watery Cancer people. The element of water is all about feeling and emoting. Your sensitivity level is high, your intuition right on target today. Risk takers and gamblers are well placed to make profitable judgments. Kids can be full of fun and games. Yet it's possible to become so swept away in captivating interests and events that dear ones might express a sense of being neglected or misunderstood. Pleasurable anticipation is fulfilled, as you singles and players get very lucky in love.

2. THURSDAY. Challenging. Those bright, big ideas formulated from yesterday's reading, discussions, or visionary dreams might now be asking to see the light of day. Most of what seemed like wonderful plans and schemes just hours ago will be left by the wayside as impractical, unrealistic, or beyond reach. But perseverance combined with purposeful and sustained creativity will get you where you want to go. An experienced colleague or a training course could give you an edge in achieving a goal that has been set. Career demands may not mix happily today with recreational attractions, which would best be put on hold until the job is done.

3. FRIDAY. Spirited. A robust sense of fun pervades the atmosphere, probably making it hard to concentrate on work and public duties. You may be lucky enough to find a generous fellow worker who will cover your responsibilities for the day. Or you could simply turn your back on the job, not going to the workplace and launching out in more playful directions. Concerns over hereditary health conditions might encourage parents to have youngsters tested appropriately. Kids will likely enjoy the fuss and attention. Cancers in the arts, public relations, education and training, and travel and tourism can entice customers with alluring advertising.

4. SATURDAY. Happy. Pleasures abound this weekend. Only obsessive workaholics and grumpy killjoys could miss such a grand opportunity for treats and delights. A little bit of what you fancy does you good. A series of social pleasures could already be lined up. The wise and efficient Crab will attend to as many of the daily tasks as possible very early, leaving the rest of the day free for fun. There might be so much going on that it is hard to choose among the various options. It could be a simple matter of what's affordable, especially when paying for children, pals, or a lover you want to impress.

5. SUNDAY. Carefree. With a Full Moon on the rise, it could be another day of joyous abandonment. It might be time for the last of water-based activities and the start of winter sports. Social definitions are apt to get turned around when adults and children swap the roles of caretaker and mischief-maker. The distinction between friends and lovers can blur, while previous outsiders now become part of the clan or fold. Attending the right party or gathering may introduce a range of desirable love candidates for the unattached, and possibly prove naughtily tempting to those of you committed. Take care!

6. MONDAY. Quiet. You probably reached a saturation point of partying by bedtime last night, feeling a need to end all the socializing. Today a degree of recovery might be in order if it can be arranged. Despite it being a workday, you may simply decide that the job can wait, and you declare time out. For the persistent pleasure seekers among you, secret plans could be hatched to rendezvous with a lover or playmate beyond the prying eyes of anyone familiar. Parents might cultivate a closer bond with youngsters by encouraging their interests, praising their creativity, and wising them up to the facts of life.

7. TUESDAY. Misleading. Speculative opportunities could look too good to be true, and may be risky if fueled with borrowed money. Some degree of luck is up for Moon Children. Nevertheless, follow your own intuition closely for guidance. Other people's hopes and dreams might sound peachy, but they are unlikely to be solid, practical, or realistic. Be especially wary of intentional deception designed to trick or seduce. Right now you only want to hear what's palatable, even when talking to yourself. Rationalizing or playing with facts might satisfy your mind, but your heart wants the truth. A relationship can be hard to pin down, probably because one or both of you want it that way.

8. WEDNESDAY. Deceptive. Just because everyone is trying so hard to be so nice to each other shouldn't mask a fundamental difference that exists. You might observe an emerging conflict as a third party, but there'll be no joy in sticking your oar in today. Let sleeping dogs lie as you go about your own business, hopefully under the radar and without getting caught up in the exuberant game playing of less scrupulous characters. It might seem to some parents and to those working with children that certain kids are subjected to bad influences that would lead them astray. Discreetly observe the situation before acting. And, above all, set a good example.

9. THURSDAY. Revealing. Things seem more comprehensible and out in the open now. What was obscure and twisted can become clear in a blinding flash of intuitive insight. Nevertheless, action and follow-through are called for to seize the moment and save the day. Events of the second week of October are resounding now. Hopefully this lends better understanding, preparing you for acute intervention or appropriate responses in a week or so. A spontaneous immediacy might propel you in strange directions and crazy tangents, mostly all fun and harmless enough. Just don't mistake these detours for the main game!

10. FRIDAY. Expressive. This is one of those sweet days, which shouldn't be wasted on irrelevant or unimportant chores. Early morning loving and affection can be emotionally rich and nurturing. Encourage youngsters in their academic efforts, athletic try-outs, and amateur auditions. Get unavoidable tasks out of the way first thing without lingering on unpleasant details. An enjoyable public event or cultural offering could be on the agenda. Even if it's formal, official, or bureaucratic, it's likely to be fun. A larger-than-life mood may see you giving a fine presentation or making a memorable splash. Take the camera!

11. SATURDAY. Demanding. Cancer shopaholics should resist the buying impulse today. Maybe you really cannot afford luxurious items and generous gratuities. Credit limits and bills should serve as brakes and appropriate boundaries. Loved ones might doubt their worth to you, and seek to be validated by what you spend on them. Genuine care and affection will serve their needs better than material offerings or gifts. Inconveniently, a business associate or customer may want service on this leisure day. Do what you've agreed in order to honor the contract. Watch out for aggression this evening, as it could trigger real trouble.

12. SUNDAY. Worrisome. A buildup of obligations during the last three weeks can come to the crunch now. The piper will demand to be paid, and it's likely to cost plenty. Expectations of easy money and free lunches are almost sure to be dashed. Certain risks just may not pay off. Cut any losses and live to fight another day. This is a wake-up call to organize affairs into some semblance of affordability. The focus should be on saving and earning rather than spending and owing. What is required is a long-term sea change, not an overnight fix. Determine a realistic plan of action, then relax as best you can without burying your head in the sand.

13. MONDAY. Bright. Mentally wipe the slate clean for a fresh start upon rising. No problems are too hard to solve, and nothing is too difficult to understand. The first helpful consideration may concern developing a positive attitude with an upbeat mood. Planning a journey thoroughly is advised rather than making an actual departure now. Writers can tackle complex subject matter, while communicators might address a diverse audience. The learning process of students is accelerated, picking up pace throughout the day. Asking the right questions leads to the right answers. Speed through outstanding correspondence, and surprise yourself by clearing the backlog.

14. TUESDAY. Energetic. A good idea is one thing, but implementing it is quite another. A concept might seem far removed from its realization. It's up to you to get the spark to arc across that gap. Relying on others for action may prove foolish. They either haven't been listening, don't grasp what you're about, or had no real intention of doing anything. Going it alone may be the only worthwhile option now and will at least assure some progress. There might be so much information circulating in your head that physical activity is a must. Refresh vitality and sharpen awareness with a brisk walk or jog. Anticipate receiving a long-awaited call or letter.

15. WEDNESDAY. Mixed. This might seem a fateful day of mixed blessings, as a variety of encounters leaves you scratching your head about human nature. Coworkers can seem testy, a little hot under the collar. Push may come to shove over territory, authority, and who knows best. Selfish drivers and pedestrians can try your patience, stretching polite manners to the limit. Hold your breath and count to whatever it takes rather than losing it in a bad mood or even rage. Payback might take the form of legal action or intervention by officialdom. The evening is vastly more pleasant. The homestead reassures you with the warm company of loved ones.

16. THURSDAY. Comforting. Doing what pleases might be the best call. After all, anything improves your health when you are feeling happy and content rather than stressed and pressured. If money is tight and financial commitments burdensome, you may turn down social invitations and skip cultural happenings. Your own small, private nest is where you want to be today, not out in the wider world. The budget is probably best served by staying close to home and keeping it simple. Old-fashioned entertainment of board games and song fests can appeal over glossy television and video offerings.

17. FRIDAY. Smooth. Private realms still take precedence. Your mind might be everything rather than on the job, but the subtle threats of a superior could help you regather focus until the workday is done. Splitting time in a delicate balance between weekly chores and the needs of a partner for romantic dedication would tie things together nicely. Be sweet in the morning when leaving, and you'll be treated royally upon returning. Intentions for redecorating and transforming your living space can consume your attention. Purchase tools and materials tonight so you can start first thing tomorrow. Plans for a home business might be discussed.

18. SATURDAY. Tricky. Give thanks that it's the weekend because you're unlikely to feel up to anything demanding. Games and sports are sure to be on the agenda. Take extra care to avoid physical strain and injury if participating in robust activity. Children may need helpful cautions for their own good. Cancers accustomed to regular gambling could wind up broke and signing markers. Singles won't make much headway on the dating scene. A falling-out with someone close might require deep and meaningful conversation long into the night. But it will be worth the persevering effort when mutual understanding emerges.

19. SUNDAY. Variable. Clarity reigns in some areas, while confusion rules in others. Mercury has finally gone direct and is slowly accelerating. A persistent and compelling creative concept or idea is screaming to be shared with a broader audience, even a global one. Whether it's just a state-of-the-art gadget or a profound soul communication, make the most of every opportunity to get it out there and make it fly. Sexual experiences are clouded by misunderstanding and apprehension. Dating can excite the mind but disappoint the body. Internet chats might be alluring, but even the gender of that other person could be in doubt.

20. MONDAY. Fortunate. When looking out at the wider world, it might be easy to fall into self-pity if you're feeling comparatively poor and somehow stuck. While you're aware the answer is hard work and commitment to a disciplined budget, things still seem testing at times. This New Moon offers possibly the last good chance this year to try your luck with some prospect of success. Perhaps the best fortune would be to land a fulfilling job with adequate pay. Or it may be conceiving a child, winning a lottery, recovering health, or meeting an exquisite love. Put your hat in the ring and risk rejection or failure. If you're not in it, you can't win it.

21. TUESDAY. Exuberant. A day spent in productive endeavor will leave a satisfied feeling of a job well done. You'll be happiest if given scope to do things with creative flair and flamboyance. No task would seem too big. It's a time for enthusiastically doing what you do best. Customers will love your offerings, and service with a smile is sure to work a treat. Coworkers are probably only too happy to go along with a team effort for a project close to your heart. Unexpected disruptions can distort timetables and expectations later, but this is merely a temporary glitch. Keep things homegrown rather than relying on distant suppliers.

22. WEDNESDAY. Steady. Rather than following the current trends and fashions, pay attention to what you actually do and how you go about getting results. This applies to your occupation, your grooming, and the daily routines of life. Focusing on ends instead of means could be distracting and even costly. Employment is stable and secure, even if promises of promotion seem a little dubious or far-fetched. A fair day's work for a fair day's pay is today's motto, and earnest skillful efforts will surely be rewarded. Creative and artistic Cancers get fine reviews, while those in sports and entertainment deliver benchmark performances.

23. THURSDAY. Strenuous. Building a strong business with long-term potential takes experience and smarts. Given the fine astrological weather for self-employment and commercial ventures, this might be the right juncture to consult advisers. Effectively consider all the angles with them, including legal and tax implications, banking and financing options, and employment regulations. Close relationships can seem to be in limbo, and would benefit from earnest clarification and serious commitment. For singles who have narrowed the search to genuine individuals, finding common ground could be harder than anticipated.

24. FRIDAY. Promising. The tone of the times has changed with last night's entry of Jupiter into Sagittarius. For you Cancer people, this should bring renewed enthusiasm for occupational efforts and more opportunities on the work front. Don't expect an overnight sensation, though. Right now, you'd be wise to cast around for helpers and collaborators who can tackle your biggest projects. If you feel more comfortable in the passenger's seat, hitch a ride to the top. Whichever you choose to be, employer or employee, there'll still be plenty to do. An older individual you are instinctually drawn to is part of an unfolding picture.

25. SATURDAY. Cooperative. It's a morning when the needs of significant others come before anything else. Stick with duties, delivering and doing whatever has been promised. The afternoon sees a refreshing change of mood, which brings greater understanding and humanity to all interactions. Beavering away with your partner on what started out as a tedious chore can turn into a labor of love, as you pleasantly fall into step together. Repairs and projects around the house can be best accomplished with skilled tradespeople rather than amateurish muddling through. Watch carefully to learn the tricks and avoid the traps.

26. SUNDAY. Disconcerting. With tough times looming in the week ahead, you might want to soften the hard edges. Romantic inclinations can soar out of all proportion, as rose-colored glasses color your view of your lover or spouse at the moment. Just don't get ridiculously overcome with idealistic hopes and good intentions. Promises made impulsively in a glamorous moment could come back to haunt at a later date. Integrity is the touchstone, while fantasy will prove empty and disappointing. A cool anger may end up being directed at those who have acted thoughtlessly, disappointed expectations, or dishonestly led you on.

27. MONDAY. Pressured. You'll know where you stand today when bills arrive, probably expected but still onerous. Whether they're business costs or personal expenses, deadlines have either been reached or are fast approaching. If you can't manage to pay, make arrangements for credit or a short-term loan as soon as possible to avoid the inevitable negative repercussions. If you have bitten off more than you can chew or have overestimated your prospects, you might feel foolish and embarrassed. Making certain hard decisions now will save a lot of unnecessary extra work making up for lost ground. A shaky start can end with justifiable hope.

28. TUESDAY. Positive. You've survived a financial crisis and learned from it. The trick is to be more practical and less procrastinating. A distinct mood swing to the upside might be accompanied by positive communications that can broaden your horizons beyond narrowed confines. There's a big world within reach, especially through an intelligent application of appropriate technologies. Enlarge your range of potential markets. Improve productivity wherever possible. Foreign contacts in a global market become increasingly important for success. Long-distance flirting seems harmless enough for now.

29. WEDNESDAY. Tense. Letting off steam with a customer or colleague may seem initially justified, but you could end up stuck in a protracted dispute. It might take lawyers to untangle the issue if it unravels into a real mess. Put feisty energy to better use. Bite your tongue and get the job done. But if you feel abused or manipulated, stand up for your rights. Perhaps checking with superiors and regulatory bodies is the first port of call. A midweek sporting event could turn into a crackerjack contest, both gripping and entertaining. Physical exercise and sexual expression are sure to improve your mood and release tension.

30. THURSDAY. Accomplished. Don't let substandard pay or poor working conditions stop you from giving it your all. Grab the attention of whoever pays you to notice your relaxed and efficient service and delivery. Your no-nonsense mood assures progress and more to come. It may be a lucky day for job seekers. Entrepreneurs and accountants alike might think up all kinds of measures and shortcuts to reduce costs and improve a sagging profit line. Be competitive on quality and service, then offer a bit more to give the consumer value for the price.

December 2006

1. FRIDAY. Disconcerting. Facts that are stranger and bolder than fiction could enthuse some Cancers to heroically take on a massive endeavor, even against the odds. Any endeavor that's impulsively initiated will definitely need sustained follow-through. Nervous excitement shouldn't overwhelm common sense. A potential office affair could boil over for all to see, bringing its own version of chaos. A public display of interest in an attractive person might make your current partner feel rejected, even if it seemed harmless to you. It's easy to flirt with people who are unavailable.

2. SATURDAY. Topsy-turvy. Cancers having to turn up to a job today may be lucky to arrive, let alone get anything done. Being under pressure and having your routine disrupted can make things tedious or difficult. Even if you are not on the roster to work, you could be called in to take the place of someone who is sick, on vacation, or quitting. Housework and other chores may become unmanageably disorganized, making you feel as if you're getting nowhere. Visit friends or join them in a spontaneous outing, thereby getting a change of scene. A pal with career problems might want your ear to unload their anxieties.

3. SUNDAY. Burdensome. When the going gets tough, the tough get going. And that certainly applies today. Sustain yourself through difficult challenges, not just yours but those of others as well, by turning to sources of wisdom, inspiration, and fine example. This is a perfect turning point for beginning to practice whatever you preach. The proof is in the pudding, so look for results beyond mere good intentions. Relationship tensions within your social circle and extended family can be reaching a breaking point. Allow natural and inevitable endings to occur without intervening. Picking up the pieces for dear ones is a burden you don't need.

4. MONDAY. Unsteady. A dam full of change can burst and overflow at this evening's Full Moon. Prior restraints and fears can collapse or become recognized as unnecessary to ongoing welfare. Not only is your luck out for now, but totally unexpected situations can arise that test all your patience and capability. While one can never be fully ready for every eventuality, fate will favor the prepared mind. Stop struggling with what you can't change or influence. Become alert enough to deal with what is staring you in the face at the present time. Shifting your beliefs about how the world works is probably essential.

5. TUESDAY. Strenuous. You'd probably prefer to dive for cover as the day's agenda and workload seem a tad overwhelming. Coach yourself into a more positive frame of mind. Roll up your sleeves to get the job done. Certainly, a bit of quiet time out or a period of calming exercise will give you the stamina and focus to accomplish the essentials. Some Cancers need to make a mighty effort to earn enough money for the extra holiday bills. Other Moon Children will be well paid for work that causes personal inconvenience or stress. Maybe it will simply be a matter of having to do whatever is commanded. Do it now, and expect to be rewarded in time.

6. WEDNESDAY. Beneficial. Stressful happenings and demanding circumstances may have begun to take their toll on your body. The Moon is in your sign today and tomorrow. So now is the time to check in with yourself and determine exactly what sort of shape you're in. Being your own best healer and doctor is sensible self-responsibility. Health professionals can be expensive or off the mark in their diagnosis and prescriptions. Quite possibly the one big change you need to make concerns lifestyle, diet, and health care. Being yourself, while whirling through the daily round, may not suit near ones. But be true to yourself first and foremost.

7. THURSDAY. Opportune. Self-employed Cancers and those of you in business can discover a broad range of contacts for your goods and services. Promoting yourself and your enviable track record of accomplishment is sure to get attention from your targeted audience. But your reputation might spread much farther with the help of the right people and the empowering leverage of communications technologies. Be prepared for a huge response to your offerings. Teaching practical skills to a group as well as training staff and apprentices can be most successful. They will make loyal allies. A brush with fame is a genuine possibility now.

8. FRIDAY. Lucrative. With six planets lined up in Sagittarius, enthusiastically make hay now. Work is likely to be pilling up, orders are on the increase, and your desk may be full to overflowing. That's all good because it will translate into money in the bank before long. Dynamic energy, expressed occupationally and helpfully, will almost certainly bring more wealth and abundance. Perhaps it's this particular season of the year that is so productive for you. Whatever the source of good fortune, reaping the benefits will take effort and labor. Hiring competent help may be essential to cope with any overload in a timely fashion.

9. SATURDAY. Spirited. In the midst of so much to do and so many places to go in this seasonal frenzy, take a breather and feel the real spirit of the holidays. A profound apprehension of their true meaning might dawn. It cannot be measured or valued by how much is spent on gifts and entertaining. But this is not a matter of turning into a miser. Show your deepest appreciation of intimates and loved ones by choosing suitable gifts with deep personal sentiment. Let inspired imagination guide appropriate choices. If you can't extract yourself from the material world, you will be mixing business with special treats for customers.

10. SUNDAY. Empowering. A hardworking employee or colleague may be a worthy candidate for an entrepreneurial partnership. It seems that someone has already proved their mettle through persistent effort and successful accomplishment. Approach them before other headhunters beat you to the punch. Signing or renewing a contract for employment is not simply about the salary. Loving the job and being in tune with the people who go along with it are equally important. Completing the bulk of shopping and holiday preparations can be achieved with enough money and priceless help from a spouse or lover. Even sales assistants could be helpful.

11. MONDAY. Chaotic. Haggling about how best to perform a particular task won't make it happen any sooner or any better. Get over being pedantic, picky, and critical. Let others get on with what they're doing in their own way. Distractions abound in the form of annoying calls, junk mail, spam, and other irrelevant correspondence. Running around to fulfill diverse chores might mean catching cabs, trains, and buses or making short car trips in order to cover the territory. Anticipate hectic traffic, long lines, and the usual seasonal madness. Booking travel and holiday accommodations might seem like entering a lottery!

12. TUESDAY. Pressured. Trying to firm up practical arrangements for festive entertaining with siblings or neighbors can reach the too-hard point. Some Cancers could be tempted to jettison the whole deal and call off the intended gathering. However, that might hurt too many feelings or create an unnecessary burden of guilt. Stop trying to control whatever is going to happen. Surrender to the inevitable. News of the imminent arrival of guests can make preparations even more frantic. Maybe you owe these people in some way, and it will be important to reciprocate impressively. Inconveniently, a certain individual from the deep, dark past might get in touch.

13. WEDNESDAY. Tricky. Keeping everyone happy could be a juggling act at best. Somebody is certain to be displeased no matter what you do. The home front takes priority over workplace demands and business concerns today. Trying to make time for friends as well as family might be pushing things. A lover can become cooler if you give too much attention to parents and relatives. An elderly person who is indisposed or unwell would be cheered by a visit, however brief it might be. Any sincere show of care will go a long way in helping them to recover and regain health. Leasing or purchasing a residential property can hit snags and need further negotiation.

14. THURSDAY. Comforting. Beat the rush and arrange an early holiday party at your place. Decorate appropriately and tastefully. Here is a chance to show off recent home improvements and stylish decor. You better half is sure to lend a willing hand in making this an elegant occasion. Consult a pal with culinary expertise who can advise on an easy, tasty, impressive menu. Some good old home cooking will be a surefire hit. A catered affair might be a better option for Cancer already too busy. If you feel less socially inclined, a quiet night with your lover can be dreamy. Enjoy luxury treats together while whispering sweet nothings.

15. FRIDAY. Easygoing. Determine just how much money you will need to survive the festive season within the comfort zone. Once the weekly figures are totaled, some of you can count on a cash bonus in addition to the normal paycheck. Living arrangements and accommodations for holiday visitors should be worked out before their arrival. Shopping for last-minute gifts and seasonal provisions might be wisely done early today in order to avoid the weekend crowds. A jolly bon voyage dinner in relaxed and comfortable surroundings could be on the cards for any loved ones who are traveling away for the upcoming holidays.

16. SATURDAY. Playful. A mishap or minor accident can happen in the pursuit of pleasure today. The delight of a competitive playmate might drive you to overexertion. The consequences could be a physical sprain or strain that requires attention and treatment. A new lover's sensual desires may be so overwhelming that getting to know each other on an intimate level becomes secondary. Love and vulnerability go hand in hand, something that is very uncomfortable for you Cancer people who value personal security so much. Kids are such endearing company that you join their play. Be young again, just for a day.

17. SUNDAY. Sociable. Despite the pressured temptations of last-minute shopping, postpone going to the stores for another day. The same goes for laboring away at work brought home for the office or pondering business matters. Give full and primary attention to the quality of social connectedness in your life. Most human experiences are more fun in company. Take advantage of this opportunity to receive and dispense the milk of human kindness. Celebrate the beliefs and culture that you share in common with many people in the community. Being alone and cut off now would be hard.

18. MONDAY. Bright. This is an almost impossibly upbeat day. It might have you splitting your sides with laughter, even as you're getting through a power of work. Shovel back the piles of chores that have grown, demolish the to-do list, and love it! You could show a real appetite for both work and food, so watch what you eat as the hours roll by consumed by what you're doing. While it might not be the right time to go on a diet, you could improve your physical condition with passionate forms of exercise including dance and aerobics. Things get a bit wild and reckless later. Seek an invitation to a Sagittarius birthday bash.

19. TUESDAY. Exuberant. Expect a bunch of news to arrive today, most of which should be very interesting to say the least. The information disclosed to you might mean extra work on your behalf. But in the spirit of the season, you're likely to pitch in with everything you've got. The pace in the workplace can be electric, with coordination in all facets of an enterprise. A positive attitude will not only make the time fly, it will also produce the intended results and then some. Generosity could be taken too far. Promises are made that have little physical possibility of happening despite all the good intentions. Exaggeration is everywhere.

20. WEDNESDAY. Refreshing. This morning's New Moon points a dark finger at the truth of certain relationships. One insight could be a need to value yourself enough to maintain a partnership with integrity. Holding different expectations from those of another can lead to harsh judgments. Reflecting on what keeps you apart from near and dear ones might motivate new behaviors in the months ahead. Many interactions coming up can involve financial and even survival issues. Engaging the services of a professional would be money well spent to free your time for personal affairs.

21. THURSDAY. Delightful. This is a day made for loving. Even business transactions and formal routines are stamped with a friendly attitude of genuine human concern. Don't get suspicious when reticent folk suddenly become affectionate. Later today the Sun enters Capricorn, your partner sign, warming even conservative types with its light. The perfect gift for an intimate partner can present itself, but it might cost handsomely unless you shop hard for a deal. Money talks when trying to impress the right person. Travelers and vacationers can find attractive company, as strangers and foreigners seem instantly familiar.

22. FRIDAY. Steady. The overnight solstice weaves its magic at the turning of the seasons, and has much to contribute to the spirit of the day. The soothing presence of a trusted companion is worth more than any amount of ambitious scrambling. A willingness to delegate could be a lesson to learn right now, since you may be forced to leave important personal responsibilities in the hands of others. For Cancer businesspeople, it's at times like these that you appreciate reliable staff and outside contractors who can sustain an enterprise in your temporary absence. Evening brings a generosity of spirit on the social scene.

23. SATURDAY. Evocative. Spending time with teammates you esteem would be a touching way to show appreciation. Gift giving among people who won't see each other on the big day might feature now. Remember, any presents exchanged shouldn't be compared price-wise. But some people just can't help themselves when it comes to what things cost. The conversation of older people might evoke fleeting memories of golden days gone by. Real honesty could emerge in a relationship when both of you tell it like it is. One connection may seem heavy, weighed down by such concerns as taxes, illness, or death.

24. SUNDAY. Nostalgic. Departures and leave-taking flavor this day with a tinge of sadness, as you may be separating from someone you rely on or are close to. Express your Cancer sentimentality openly. Take heart in the deep feelings and profound understandings mutually shared. Any agreement reached today, especially around business and employment, can prove sustainably profitable and enduring. Christmas Eve marks a deadline for gift buying and party preparation. There's no more more putting it off. You know what you're doing, so just do it. But don't drain your credit limit.

25. MONDAY. Merry Christmas! Expectations are sure to be fulfilled when you reach into your Christmas stocking. But some of the gifts might shock, reminding you just how different tastes can be. A deeper meaning or significance could attach to eccentric gestures. Experiences that don't turn out as planned certainly make an occasion even more special and memorable. Moon Children in transit over any distance should have speedy passage. It may feel exhilarating to be en route to a different and distant destination. Entirely unexpected greetings can startle, forcing you to improvise a quick response and reciprocation.

26. TUESDAY. Hectic. Visiting with a diverse range of characters is sure to arouse controversy on whatever subject comes up. Voices could be very loud today, making humor and compassion essential qualities for enjoying a sociable time. Jokers will have their tricks, maybe on a bigger scale than usual. So check what's happening to avoid finding yourself at the center of someone else's idea of fun. You might be asked an embarrassing or revealing question in front of others. Mishaps in transport and communication might be blamed on the stars, as service people have no ready explanation.

27. WEDNESDAY. Energized. It would be a brief break if you are back at work again. Even if you're not, it would be beneficial to get outdoors for aerobic exercise and physical exertion. So when you do have to return to the day job, you'll feel refreshed, all ready to tackle the new year ahead. Ambitious Cancers might try to get a flying start by initiating projects and making critical decisions now. This could be a little premature, and may prove costly or contradict a superior of greater experience. Any minor task that requires strength and motivation can be tackled with a good expectation of success.

28. THURSDAY. Active. Disagreement may arise when it comes time to make a purchase or pay a bill. It shouldn't be hard to resolve the difference with the right information and accurate detailed records. Cancers working with the general public might experience some troublesome customers who are impossible to please. Be vigorous in doing your job, with a reasonable and appropriate amount of assertiveness. It could be hard to leave loved ones to do battle with the world. But get into it with enthusiasm rather than complaint. Despite a fear of criticism, you confidently display creative works of high quality and marked skill.

29. FRIDAY. Fine. A formal social occasion with your partner would be perfect this evening. Even with a focus firmly set on your chosen companion, many other meaningful encounters can also be enjoyed. Worthwhile business contacts can emerge comfortably in naturally relaxed circumstances. Special time with an acquaintance would bring you both closer, whether the connection is private or official. A friendship recognized now might mature into a long-lasting bond. An extended family gathering would be a good opportunity to introduce a recent partner into the clan. Everyone who loves you is sure to approve of your choice.

30. SATURDAY. Varied. Reading too much into a casual flirtation might lead to disappointment. Take your joy in the moment rather than building castles in the air that can't be sustained or paid for. Consideration of a partner's pleasure can become an expensive habit that will drain the bank balance to anxious levels. If the buck stops with you as far as the bills go, then restrict the spending. Memories of loved ones who have passed on can give poignant moments, as their presence continues to be sorely missed. The realization that another year is over might briefly bring a wave of sadness. Endings on the basis of truth are better than lingering in a half-life of illusion.

31. SUNDAY. Surprising. Your mood may be reclusive rather than party-oriented despite traditional expectations of what one must do on this last night of the year. Many Cancers may be in a service role, helping in the background. This might be especially needed if things go strangely wrong and a crisis develops. An urge to take a risk can overcome your common sense. If you're determined to explore underworld territory, take an experienced guide who knows how to handle themselves. Anything goes in the early hours of 2007, which may turn out to shock and startle before adjusting perspective and settling in to a new year.

WHAT DOES YOUR FUTURE HOLD?

DISCOVER IT IN *ASTROANALYSIS*—

**COMPLETELY REVISED THROUGH THE YEAR 2015,
THESE GUIDES INCLUDE COLOR-CODED CHARTS FOR
TOTAL ASTROLOGICAL EVALUATION,
PLANET TABLES AND CUSP CHARTS,
AND STREAMLINED INFORMATION.**

Star of Animal Planet's "Pet Psychic"

SONYA FITZPATRICK THE PET PSYCHIC

She can talk to the animals.
Read their minds.
Diagnose their problems.
Heal their illnesses.
Find them when they're lost.
And offer comfort from
beyond the grave.
This is her story—and the remarkable
success stories of her "clients."

*Includes Sonya's 7 simple steps to
communicating with pets
Plus—practical information on care and
feeding, emergency preparedness, illness, moving,
and introducing new pets into the household.*

0-425-19414-0

Now in paperback from Berkley

Beyond These Four Walls
Diary of a Psychic Medium
by **MaryRose Occhino**

The extraordinary memoir from the "remarkably gifted medium"* who has helped many with their struggles—and faced her own as well.

Born to a family of "intuitive" women, MaryRose Occhino has used her "celestial whispers" to open the minds and hearts of people seeking a connection with those who have passed on. Then, at the age of thirty-nine, she was diagnosed with multiple sclerosis and forced to face her own hard times. Now she tells her fascinating story—of learning to see beyond the walls of this world, while making the most of life in the here and now.

0-425-20021-3

Available wherever books are sold or at penguin.com

Cell Phone Psychics

Horoscopes to Your Cell Phone

Send a text message with your date of birth and get your personalized daily horoscope via text message to your cell phone every day for only $1.99 for a week!

Just Text SUPER and your birthdate to 82020

If your birthdate is Feb. 15 1968
your message should look like this

SUPER02.15.68 and be sent to **82020**

Text YOUR Message to a LIVE PSYCHIC

Send a Text message to one of our LIVE Psychics from your cell phone any time, anywhere Just text the word ISEE to 82020 and get the answer to that important question!

Dating - Just Text DATE to 82020

to find that "Special Someone" right on your cell phone!

Chat - Just Text CHAT to 82020

Make new friends, have fun stay connected!

Live Text services are billed to your cell phone account at a rate of $1.99 per answer message and .99c per request message. Horoscope service is billed at $1.99 for a weekly subscription with daily message delivery

Chat and Dating Svces are billed at .99c per message.

All services do not include your normal messaging or bandwidth fees from your carrier

Compatable with AT&T, Cingular, Sprint, Verizon & Nextel